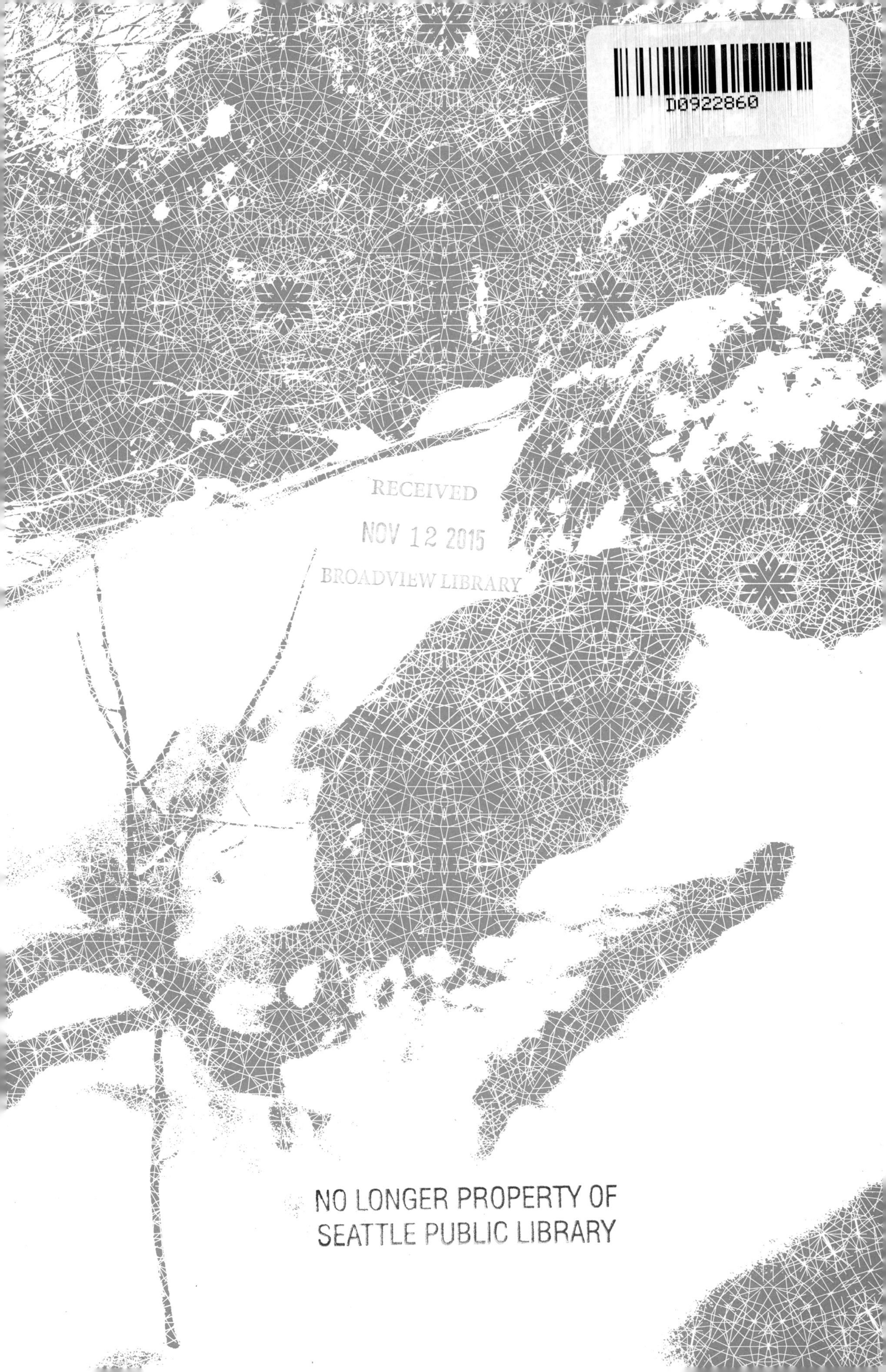

RUSSIAN OLIVE TO RED KING

KATHRYN IMMONEN & STUART IMMONEN

ADHOUSE BOOKS

Published by AdHouse Books.

Thanks to Pam Bustin, Chris Duffy, Ray Fawkes, and Sheldon Inkol.

Printed and bound in Singapore.

Selections from *Ostrov Sakhalin* by Anton Pavlovich Chekhov, 1894, translation © copyright 2015 Immonen Illustrations, Inc. Use is also made of "Buffalo Gals", trad. American, written by John "Cool White" Hodges, 1844 and excerpts from *A Midsummer Night's Dream*, by William Shakespeare.

AdHouse Books, 3905 Brook Road, Richmond, VA 23227

For more books, visit www.adhousebooks.com

ISBN-13: 978-1-935233-34-3

First printing, May 2015.

10 9 8 7 6 5 4 3 2 1

RUSSIAN OLIVE TO RED KING

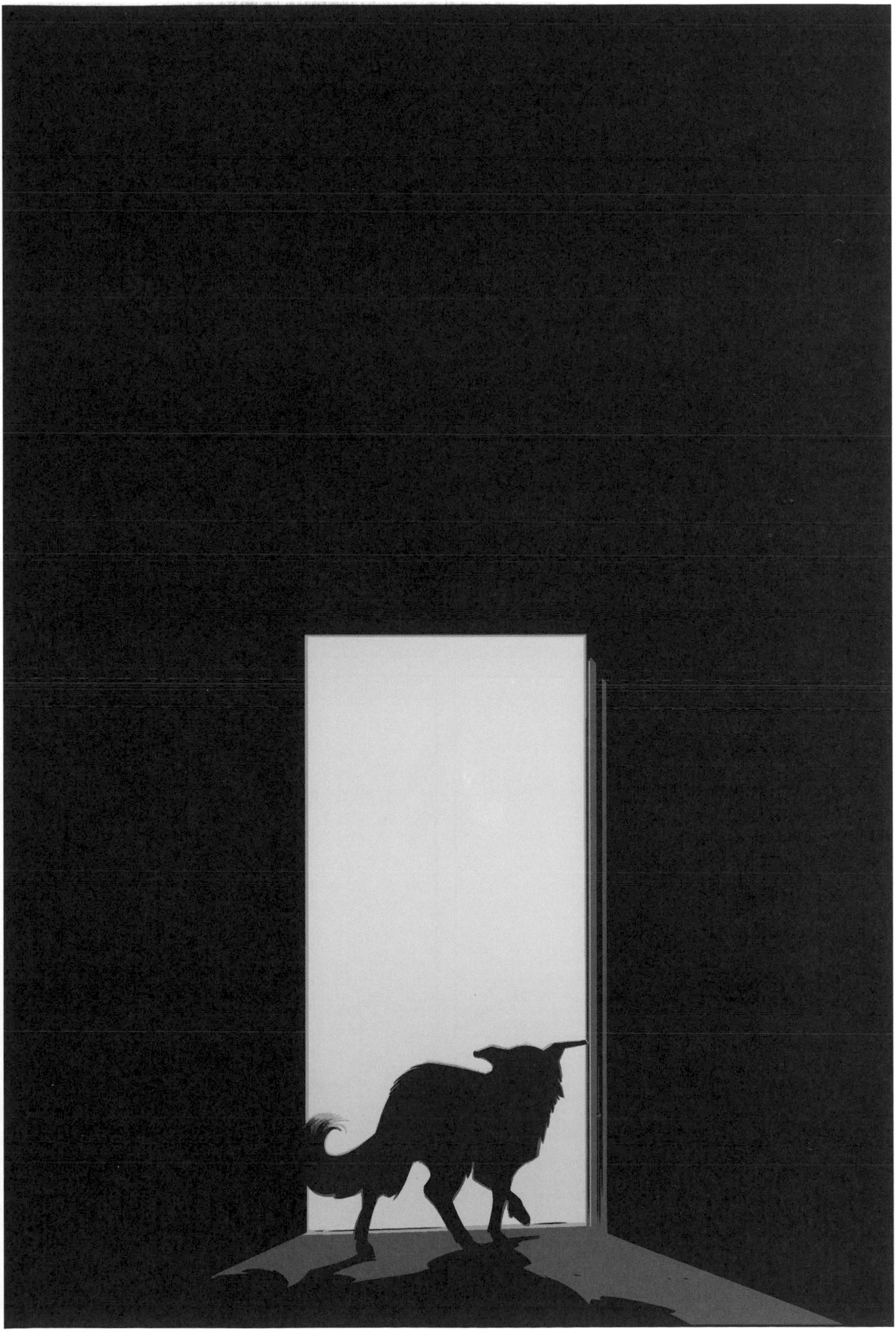

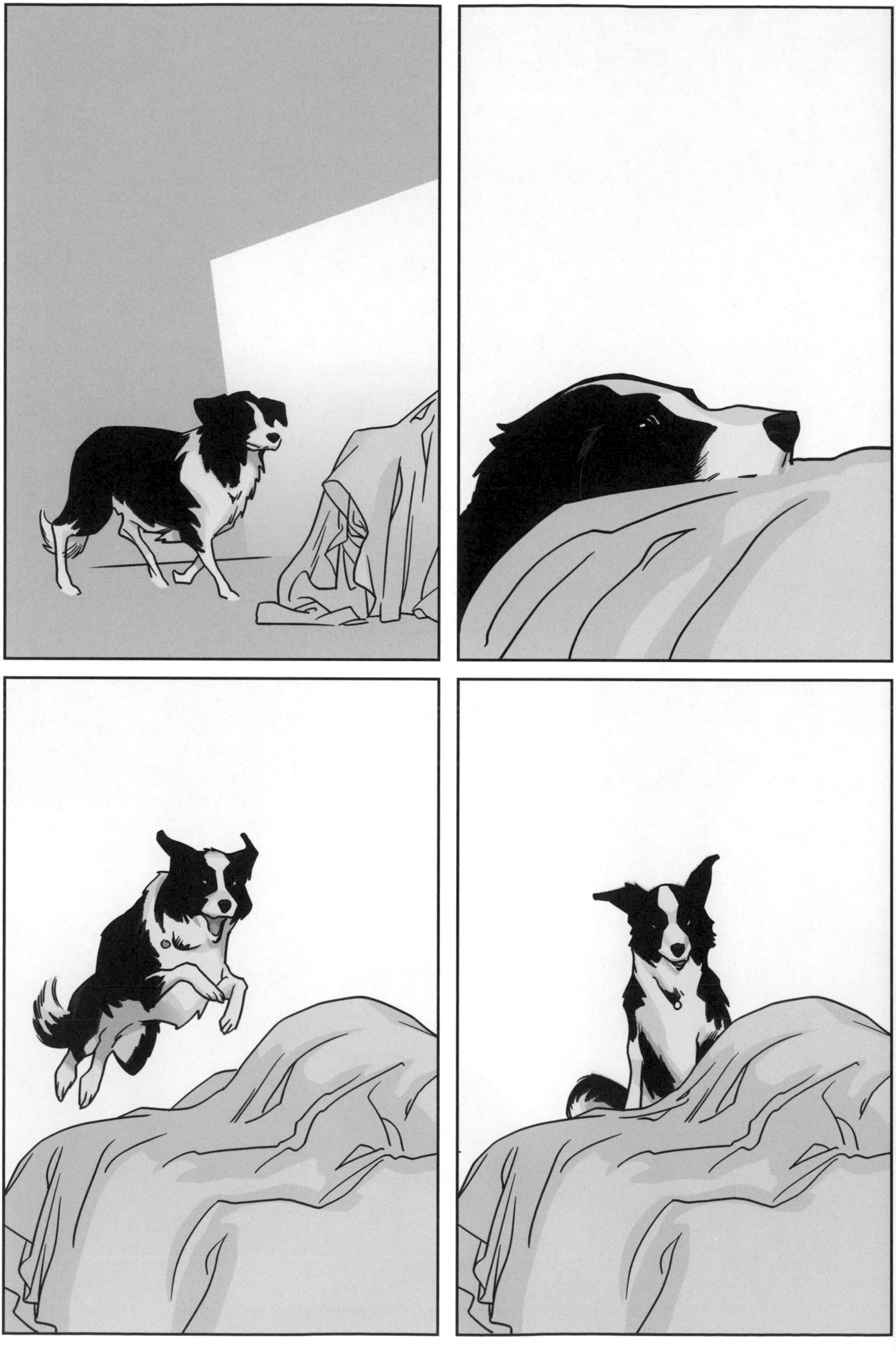

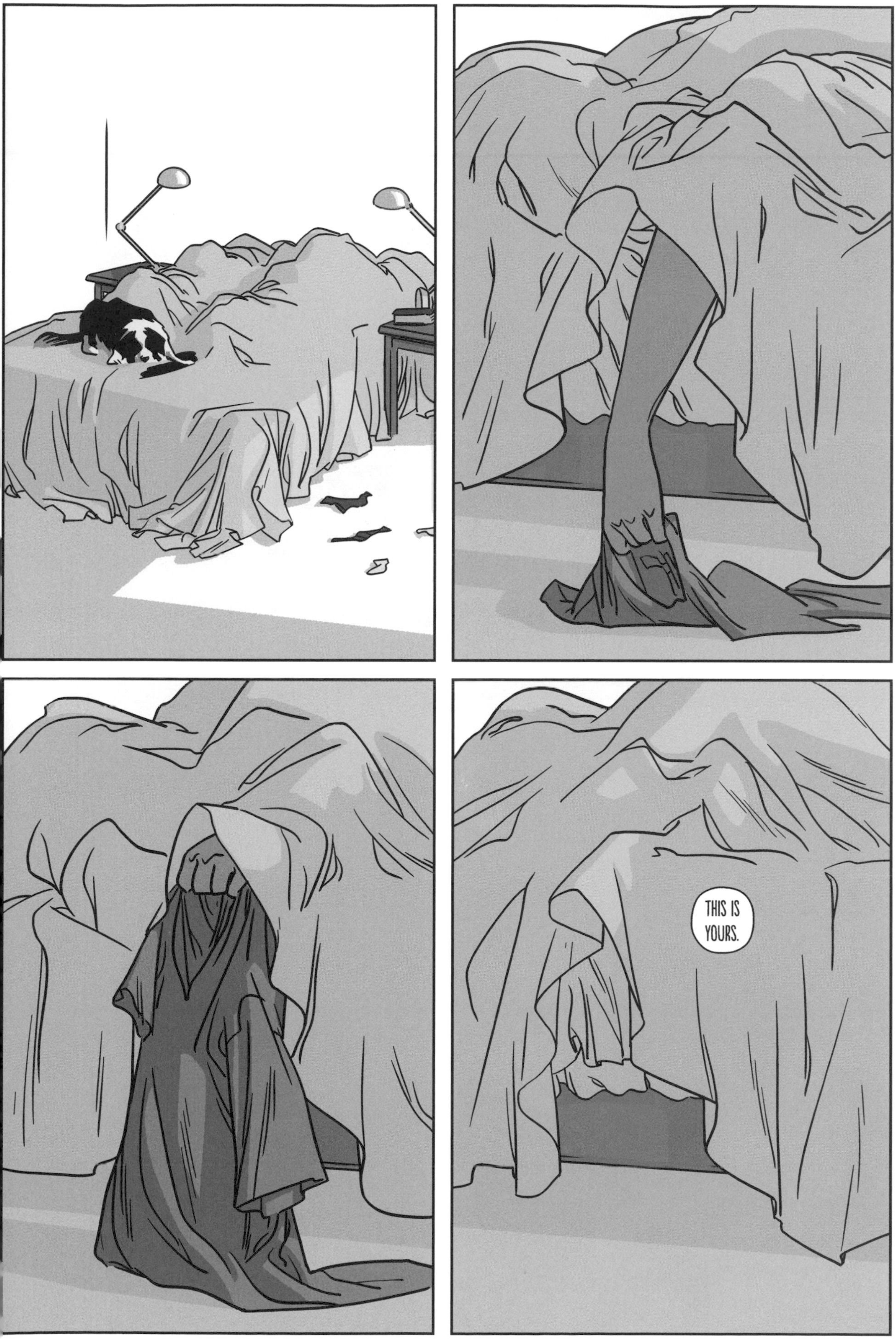
THIS IS YOURS.

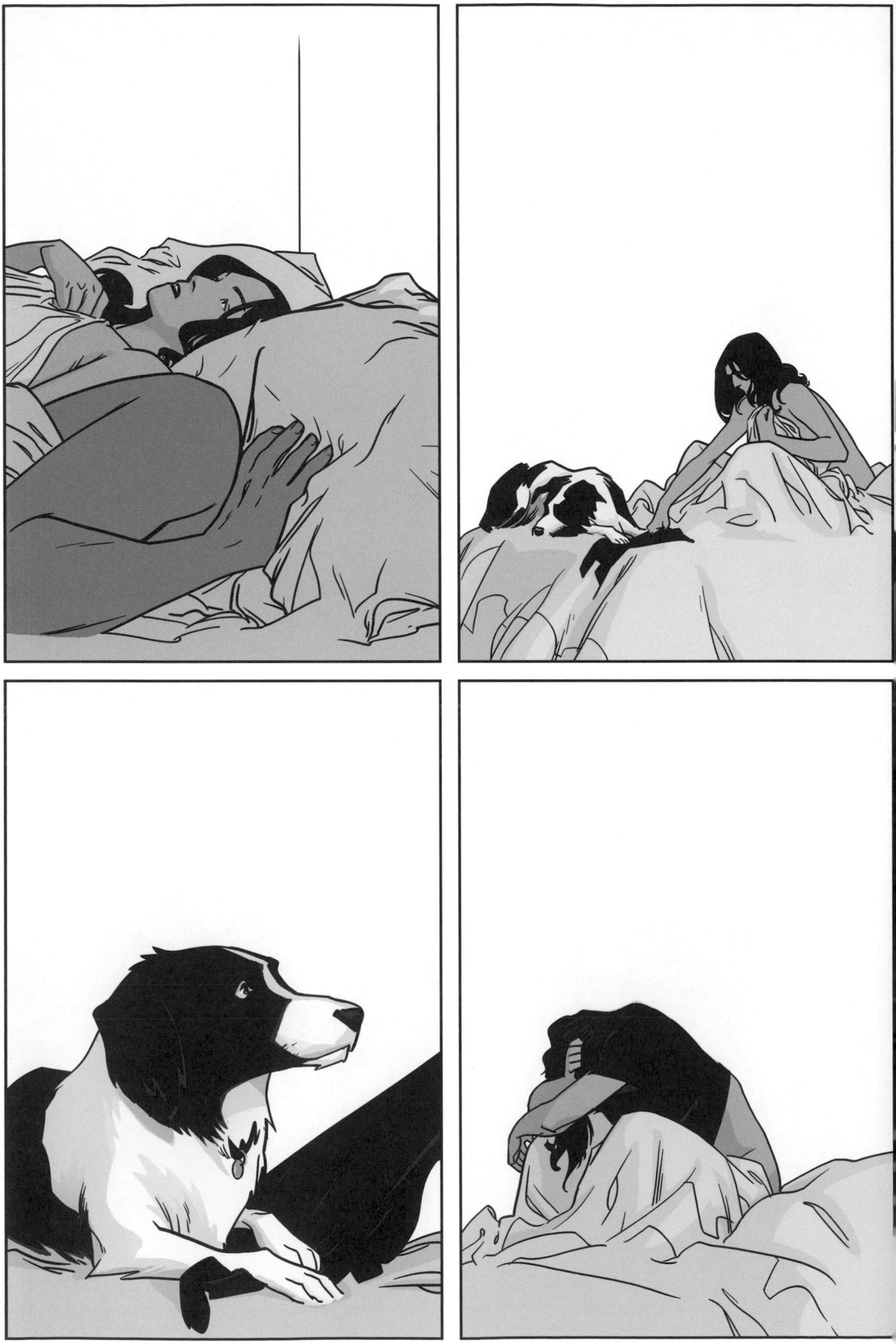

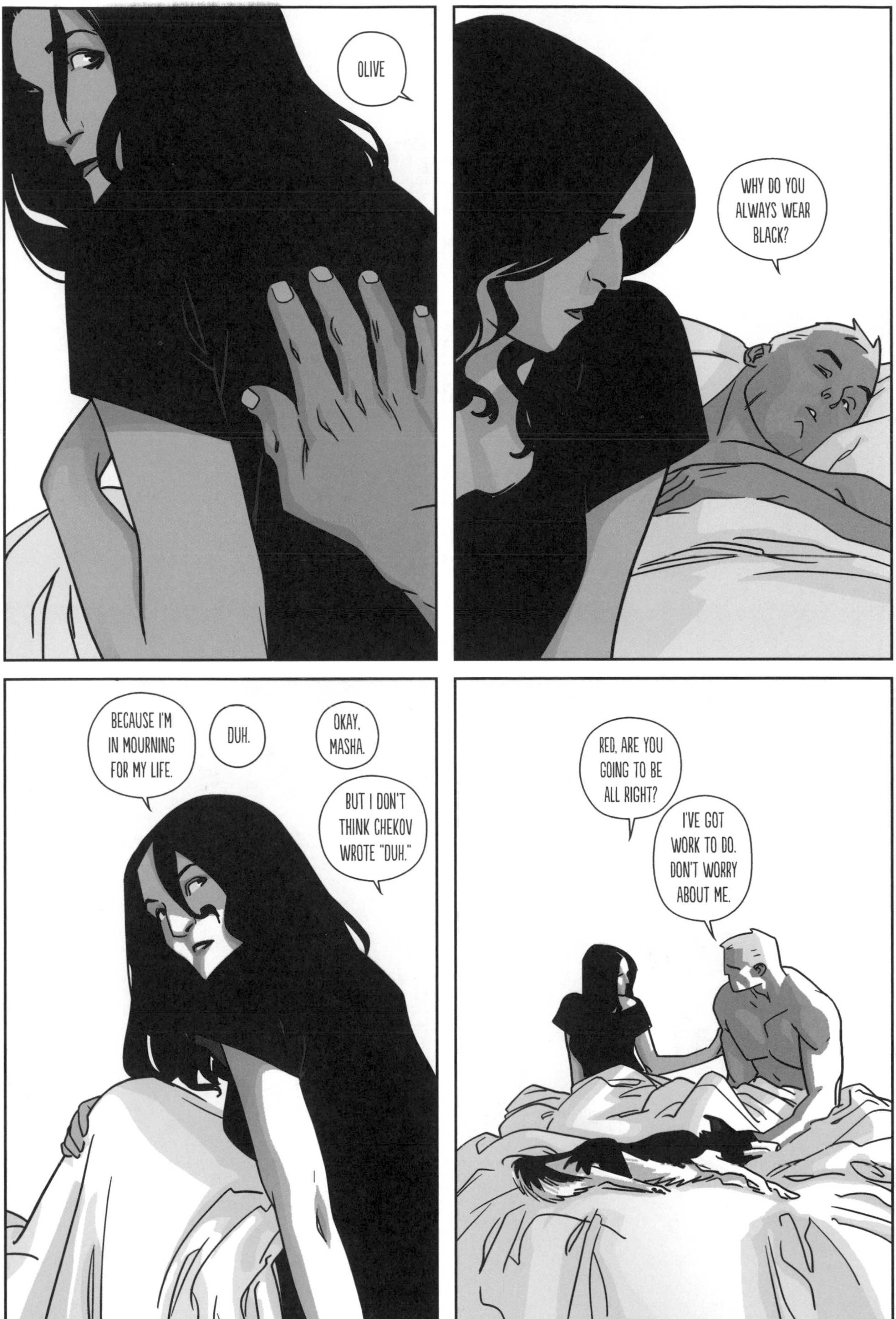
OLIVE
WHY DO YOU ALWAYS WEAR BLACK?
BECAUSE I'M IN MOURNING FOR MY LIFE.
DUH.
OKAY, MASHA.
BUT I DON'T THINK CHEKOV WROTE "DUH."
RED, ARE YOU GOING TO BE ALL RIGHT?
I'VE GOT WORK TO DO. DON'T WORRY ABOUT ME.

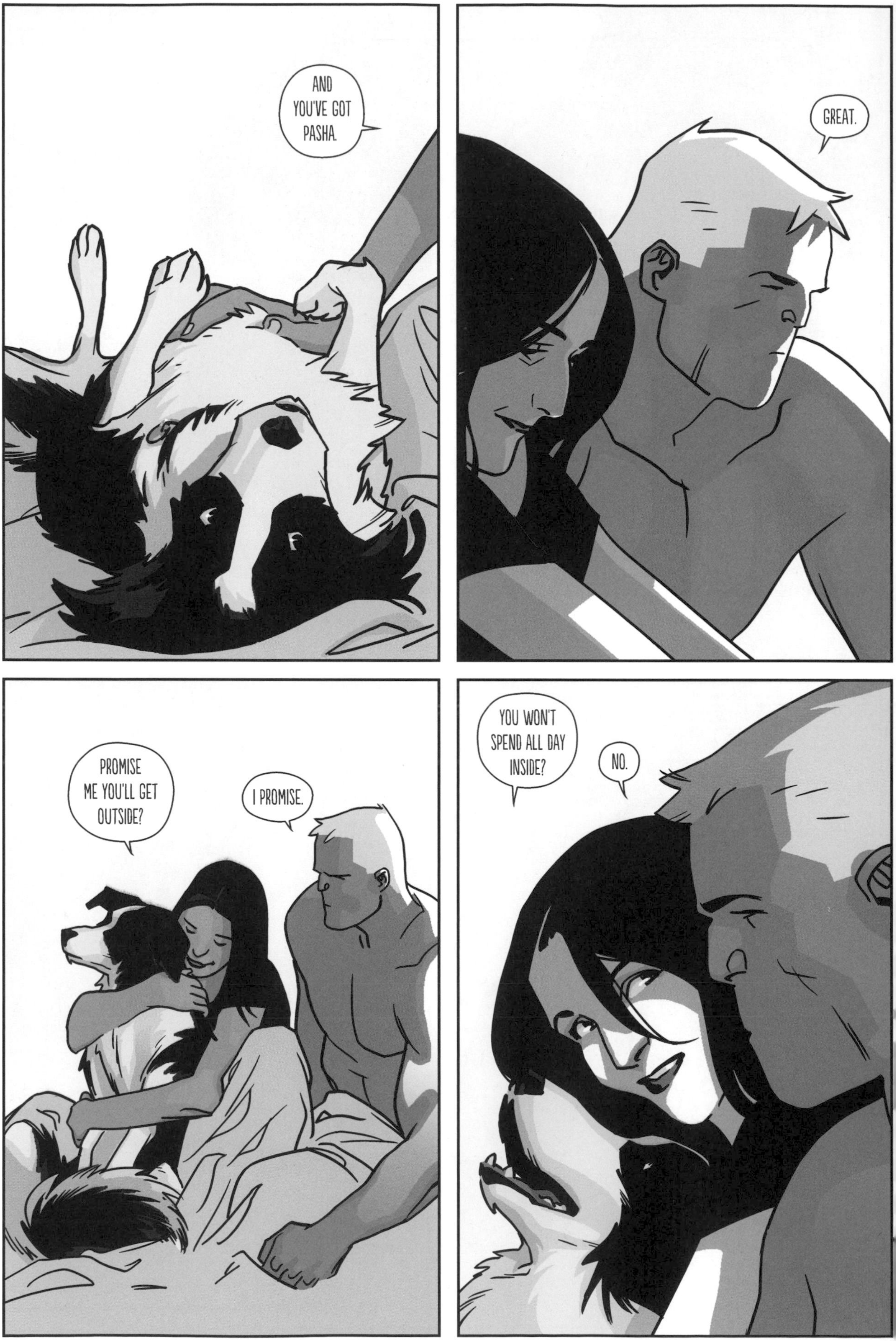
AND YOU'VE GOT PASHA.
GREAT.
PROMISE ME YOU'LL GET OUTSIDE?
I PROMISE.
YOU WON'T SPEND ALL DAY INSIDE?
NO.

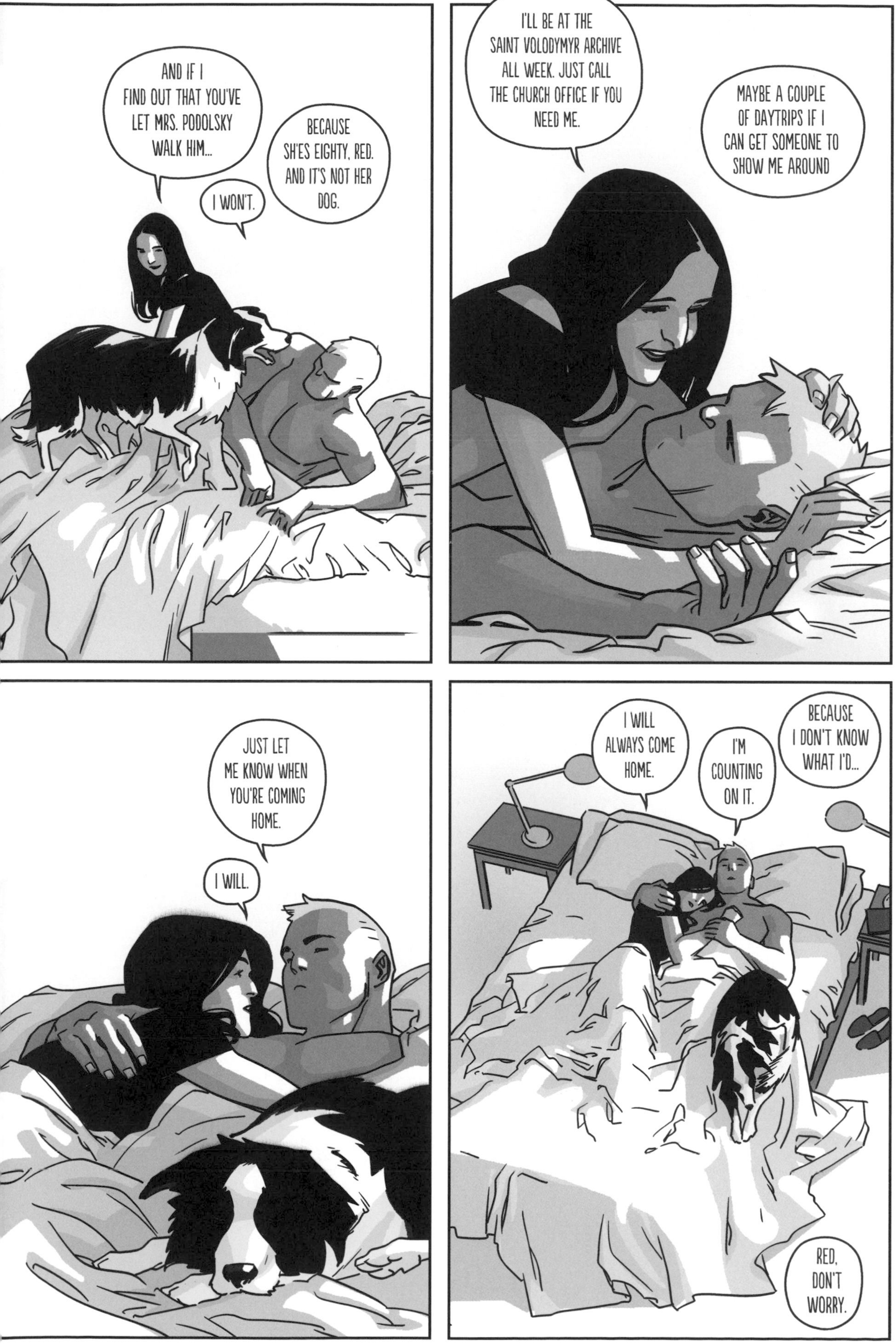
AND IF I FIND OUT THAT YOU'VE LET MRS. PODOLSKY WALK HIM...
I WON'T.
BECAUSE SH'ES EIGHTY, RED. AND IT'S NOT HER DOG.
I'LL BE AT THE SAINT VOLODYMYR ARCHIVE ALL WEEK. JUST CALL THE CHURCH OFFICE IF YOU NEED ME.
MAYBE A COUPLE OF DAYTRIPS IF I CAN GET SOMEONE TO SHOW ME AROUND
JUST LET ME KNOW WHEN YOU'RE COMING HOME.
I WILL.
I WILL ALWAYS COME HOME.
I'M COUNTING ON IT.
BECAUSE I DON'T KNOW WHAT I'D...
RED, DON'T WORRY.

I

"And why do
I come here?"

I ask myself,
and my journey
seems to me
very unwise.

— Chekhov
Ostrov Sakhalin

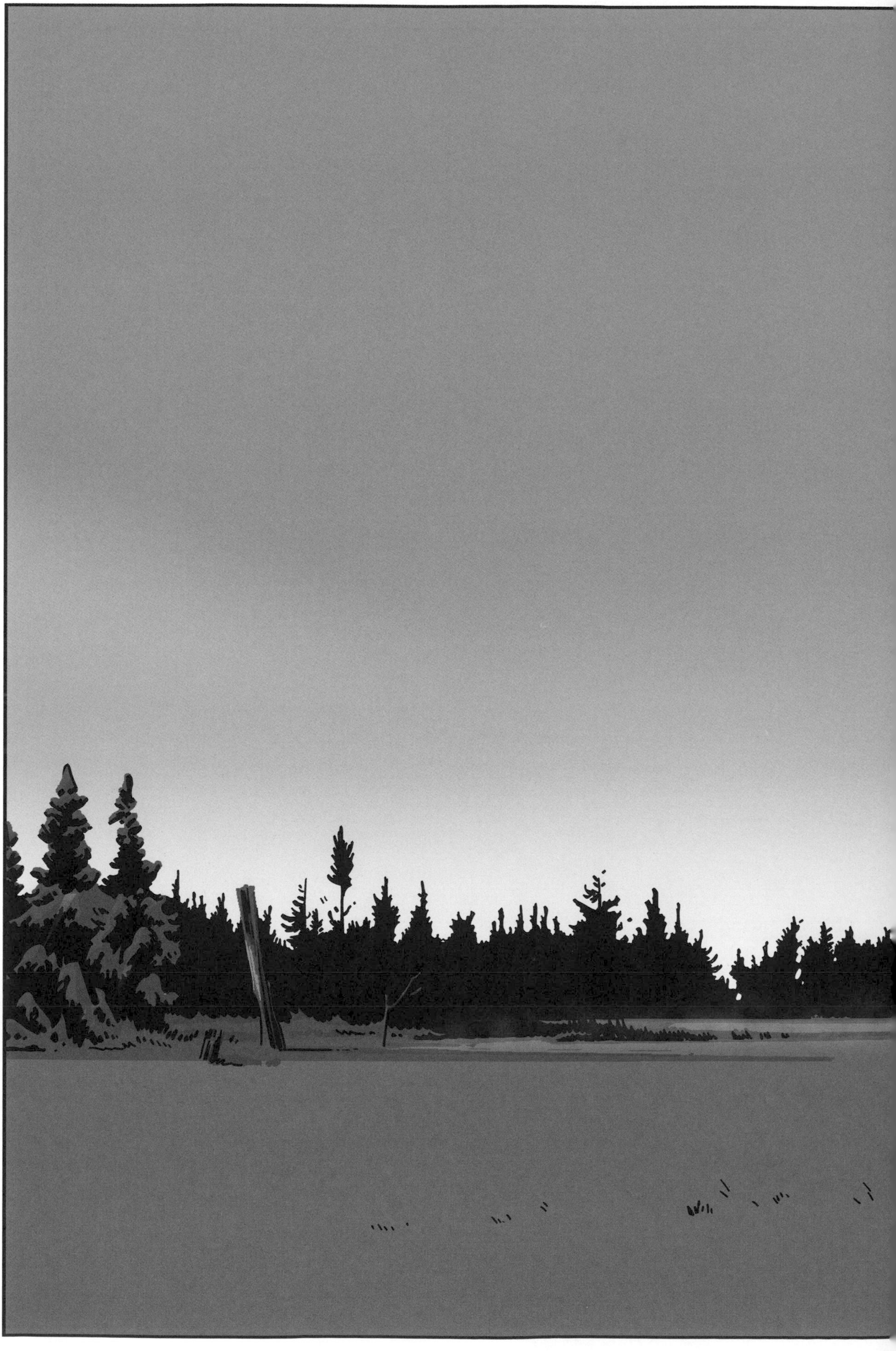

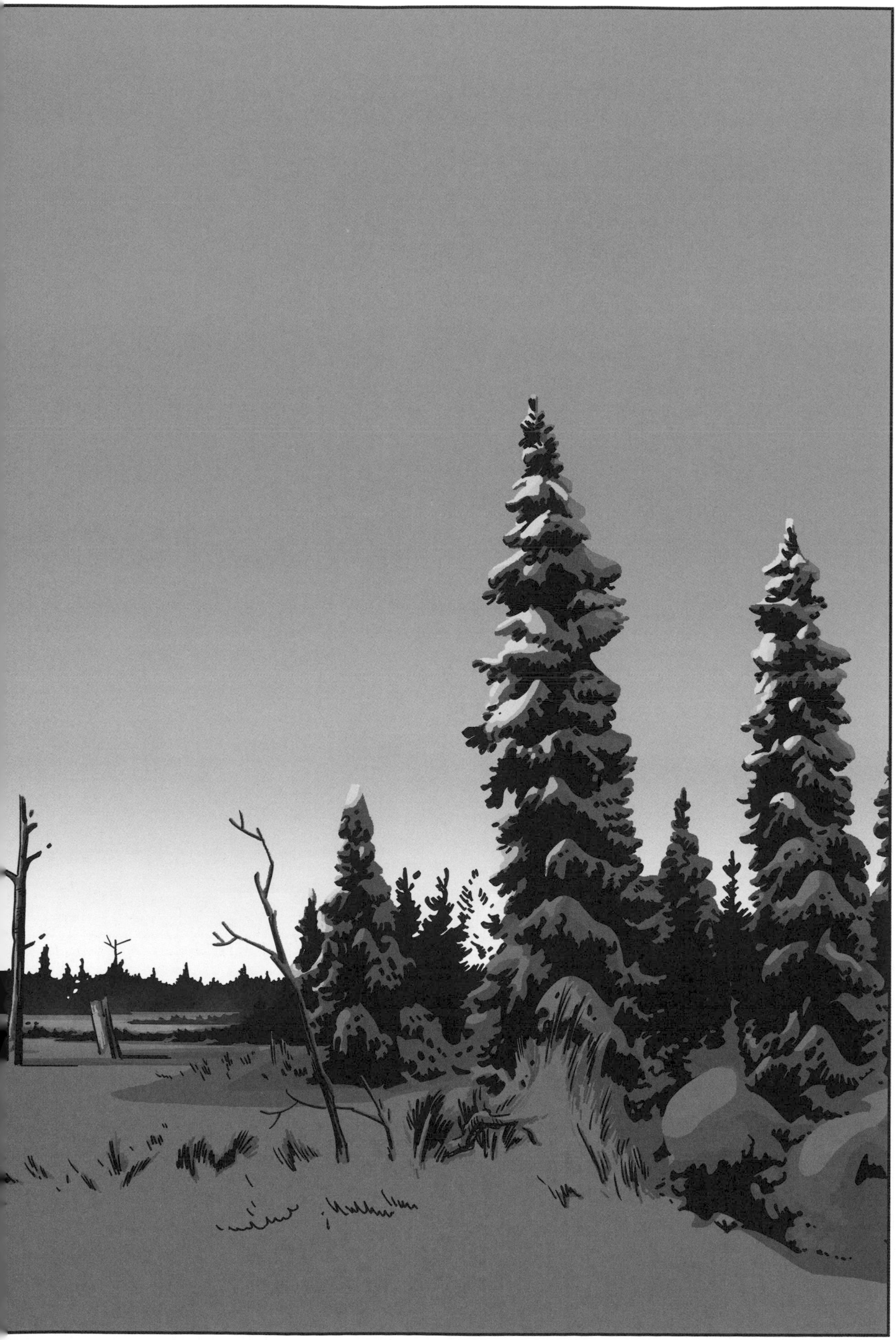

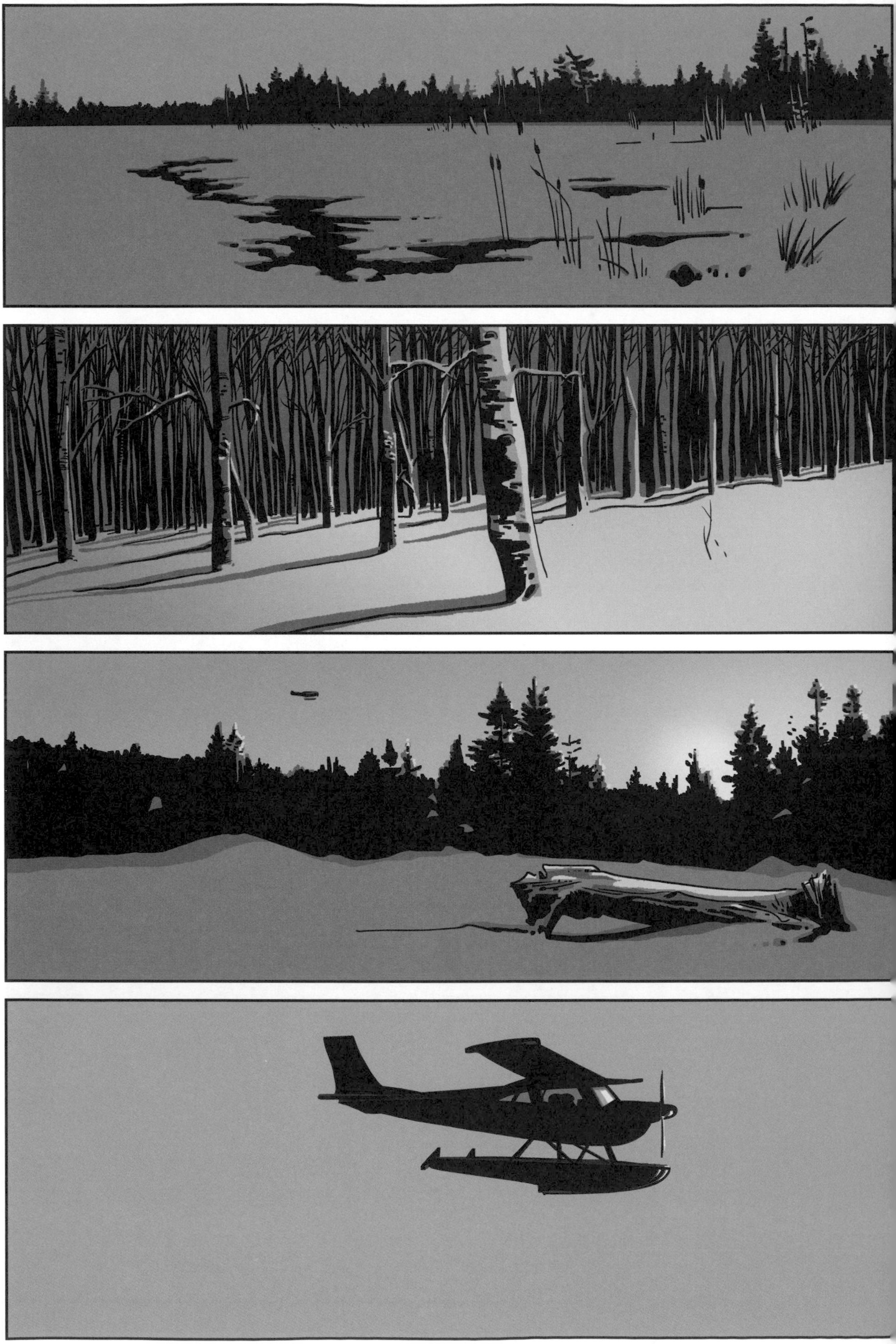

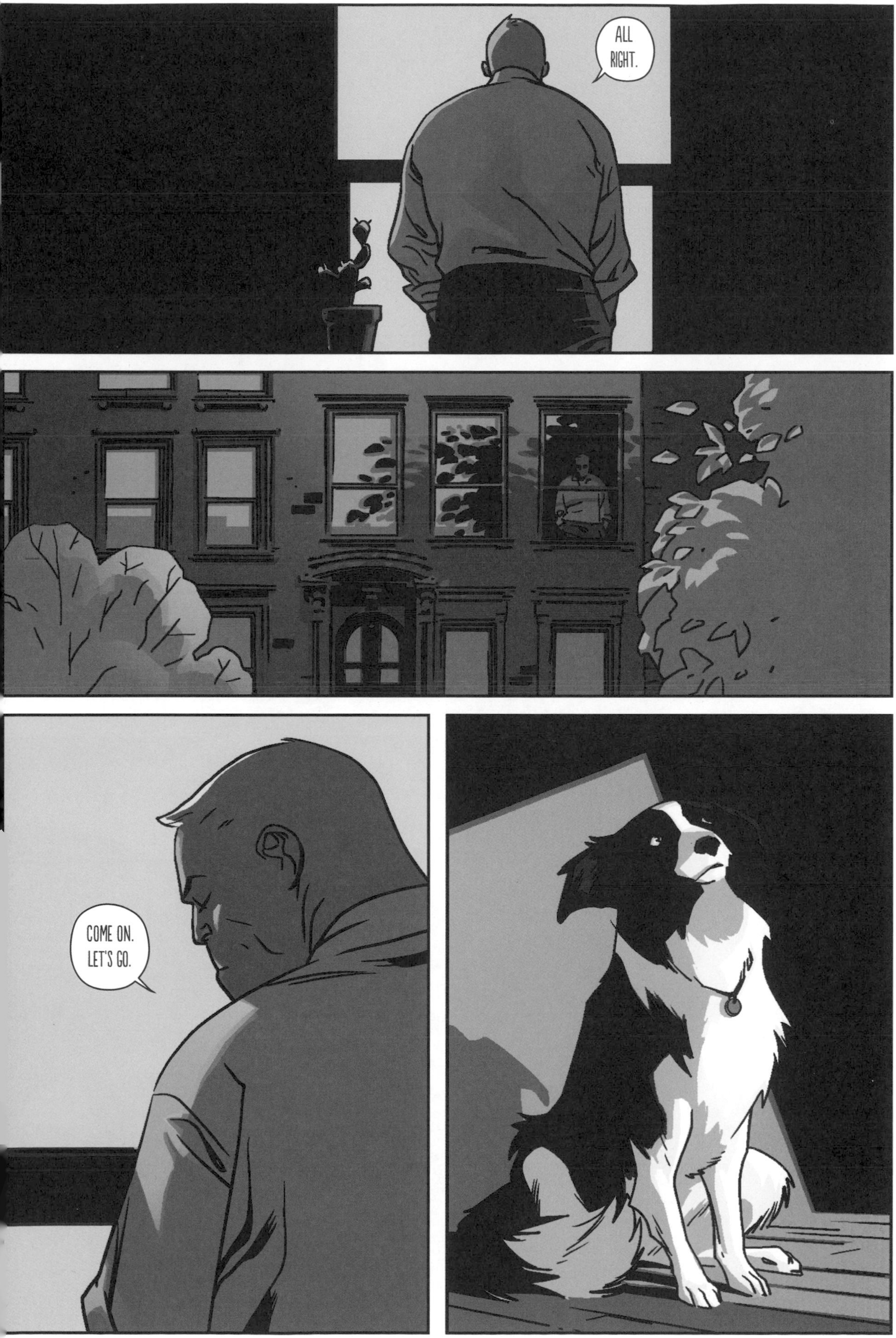
ALL RIGHT.
COME ON. LET'S GO.

THANKS FOR AGREEING TO FLY ME UP HERE, ROSSI.

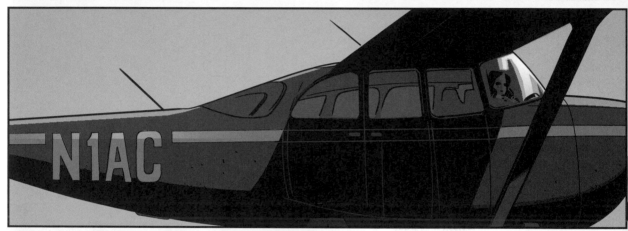

I KNOW YOU WEREN'T PLANNING ON IT.

NOPE.

DIDN'T MUCH FEEL LIKE GETTING OUT OF BED THIS MORNING.

MOST MORNINGS. SIXTY IS MILES AWAY FROM FIFTY-NINE, I TELL YA.

WELL... ANYWAY.

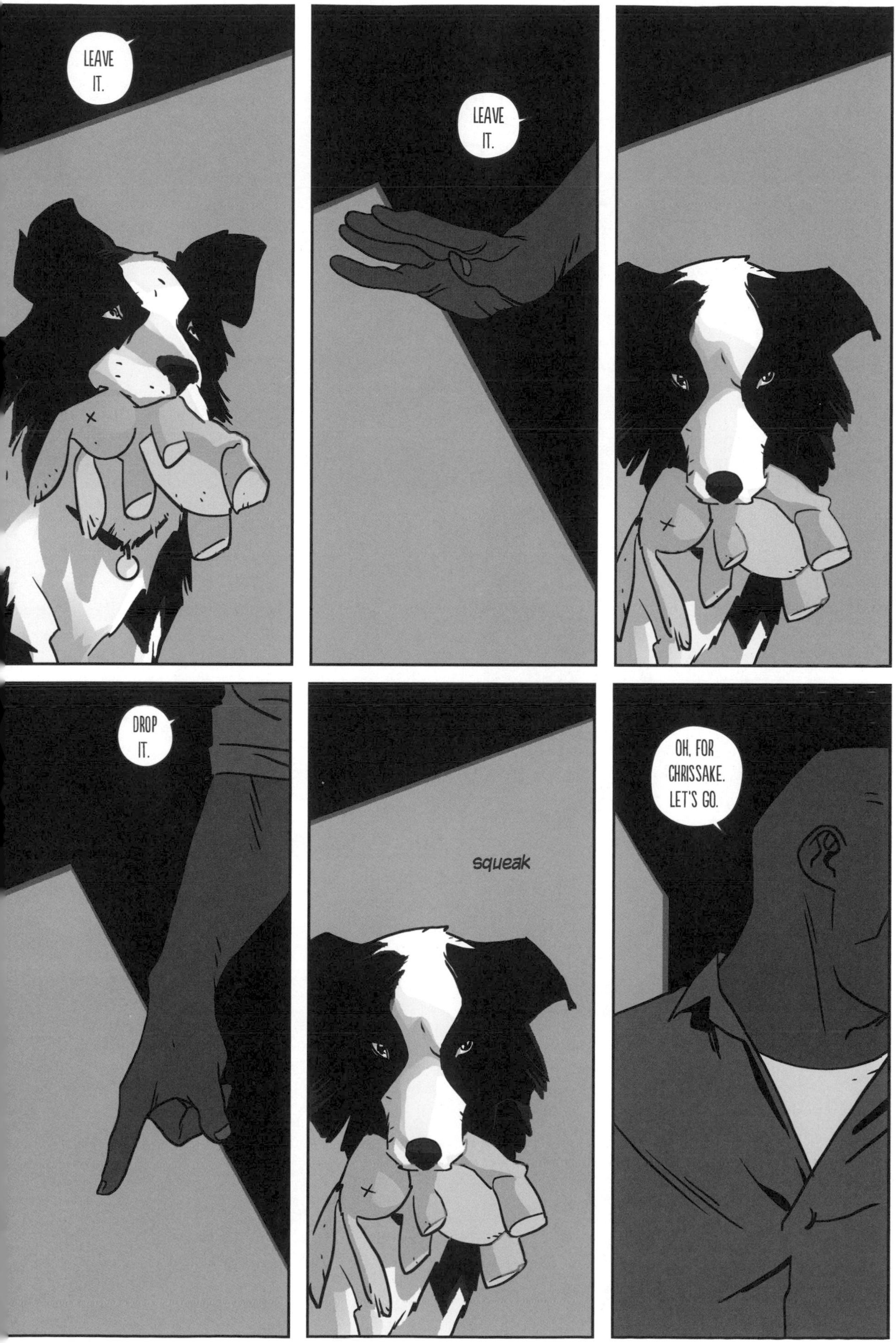
LEAVE IT.
LEAVE IT.
DROP IT.
squeak
OH, FOR CHRISSAKE. LET'S GO.

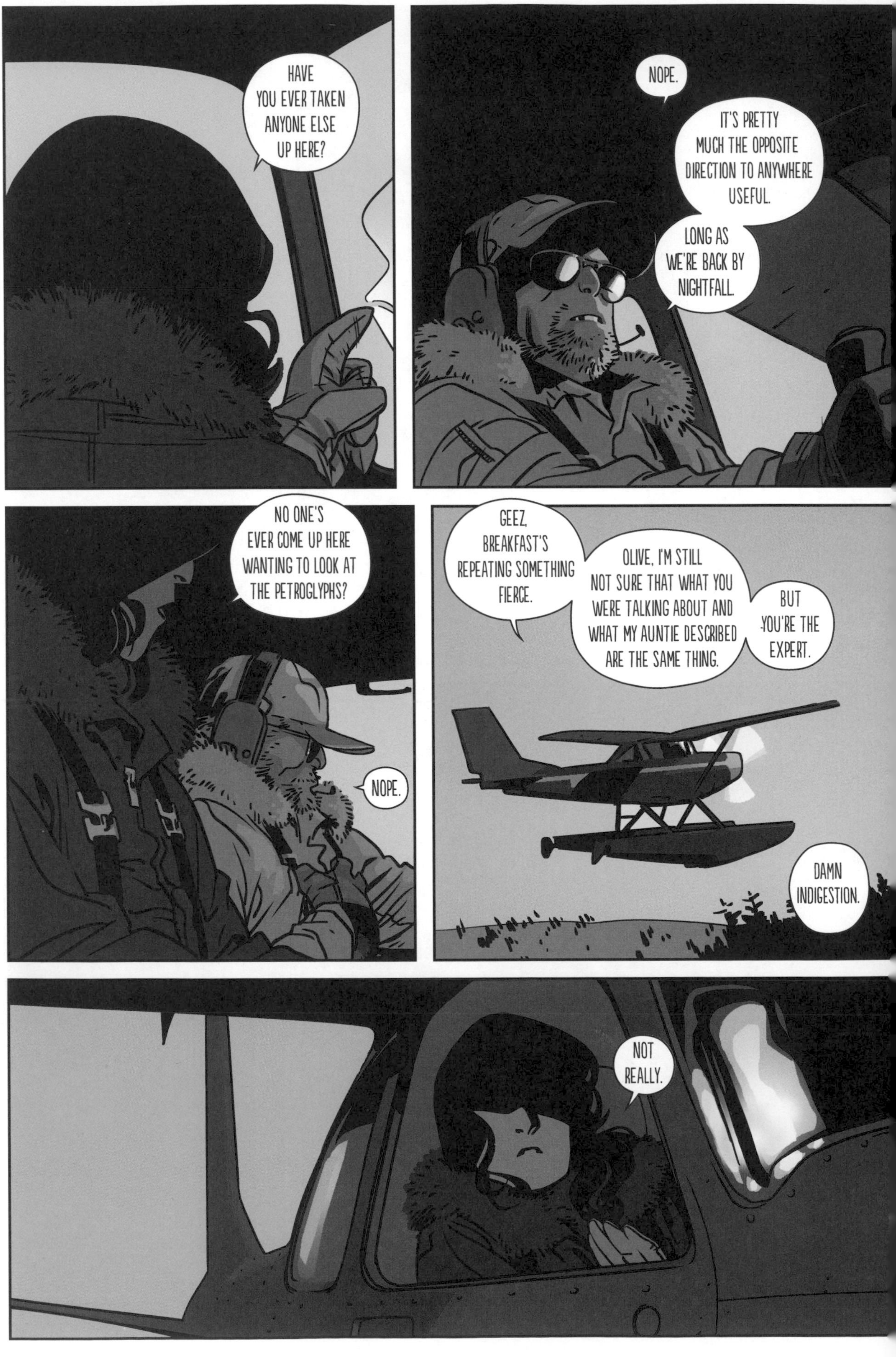
HAVE YOU EVER TAKEN ANYONE ELSE UP HERE?
NOPE.
IT'S PRETTY MUCH THE OPPOSITE DIRECTION TO ANYWHERE USEFUL.
LONG AS WE'RE BACK BY NIGHTFALL.
NO ONE'S EVER COME UP HERE WANTING TO LOOK AT THE PETROGLYPHS?
NOPE.
GEEZ, BREAKFAST'S REPEATING SOMETHING FIERCE.
OLIVE, I'M STILL NOT SURE THAT WHAT YOU WERE TALKING ABOUT AND WHAT MY AUNTIE DESCRIBED ARE THE SAME THING.
BUT YOU'RE THE EXPERT.
DAMN INDIGESTION.
NOT REALLY.

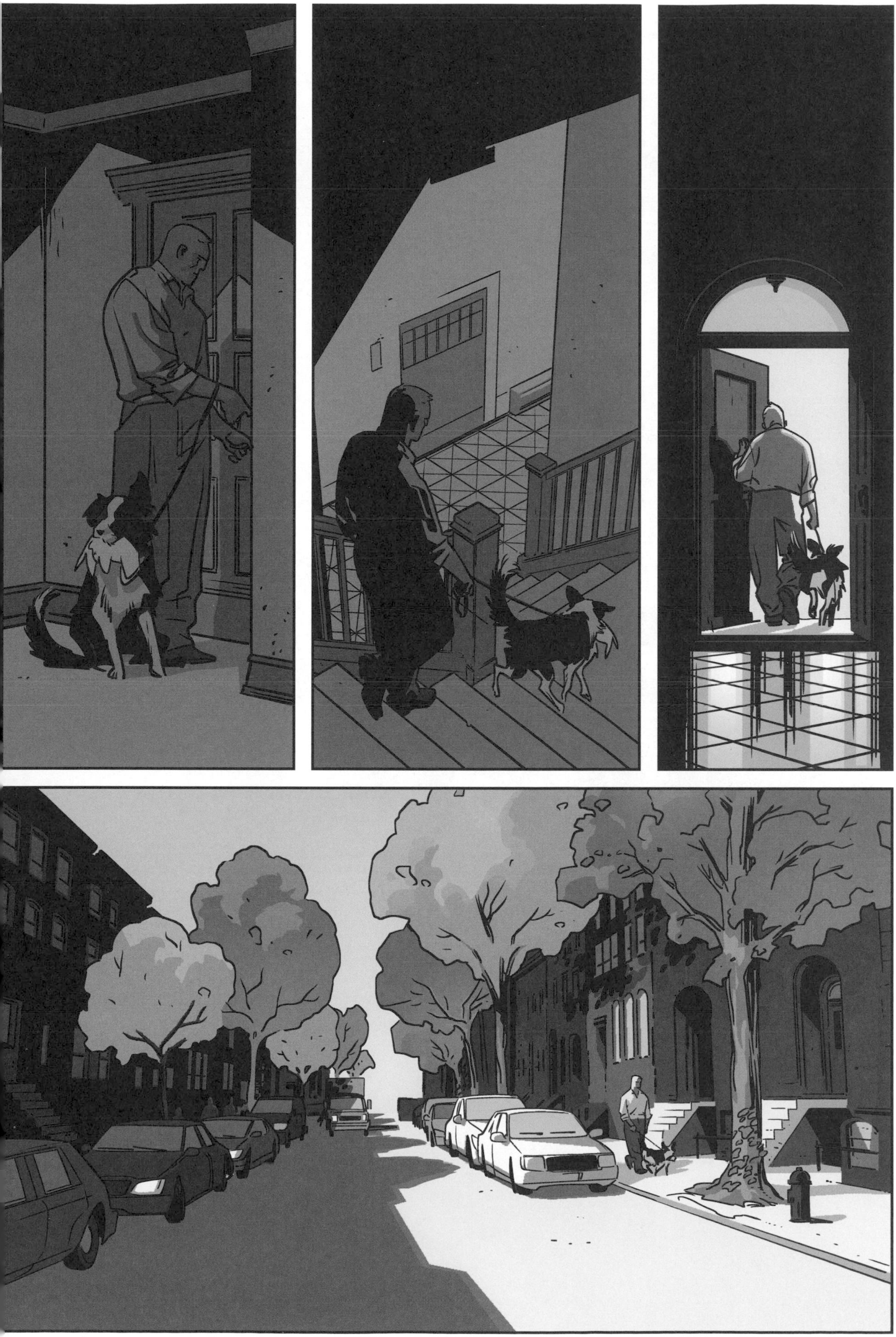

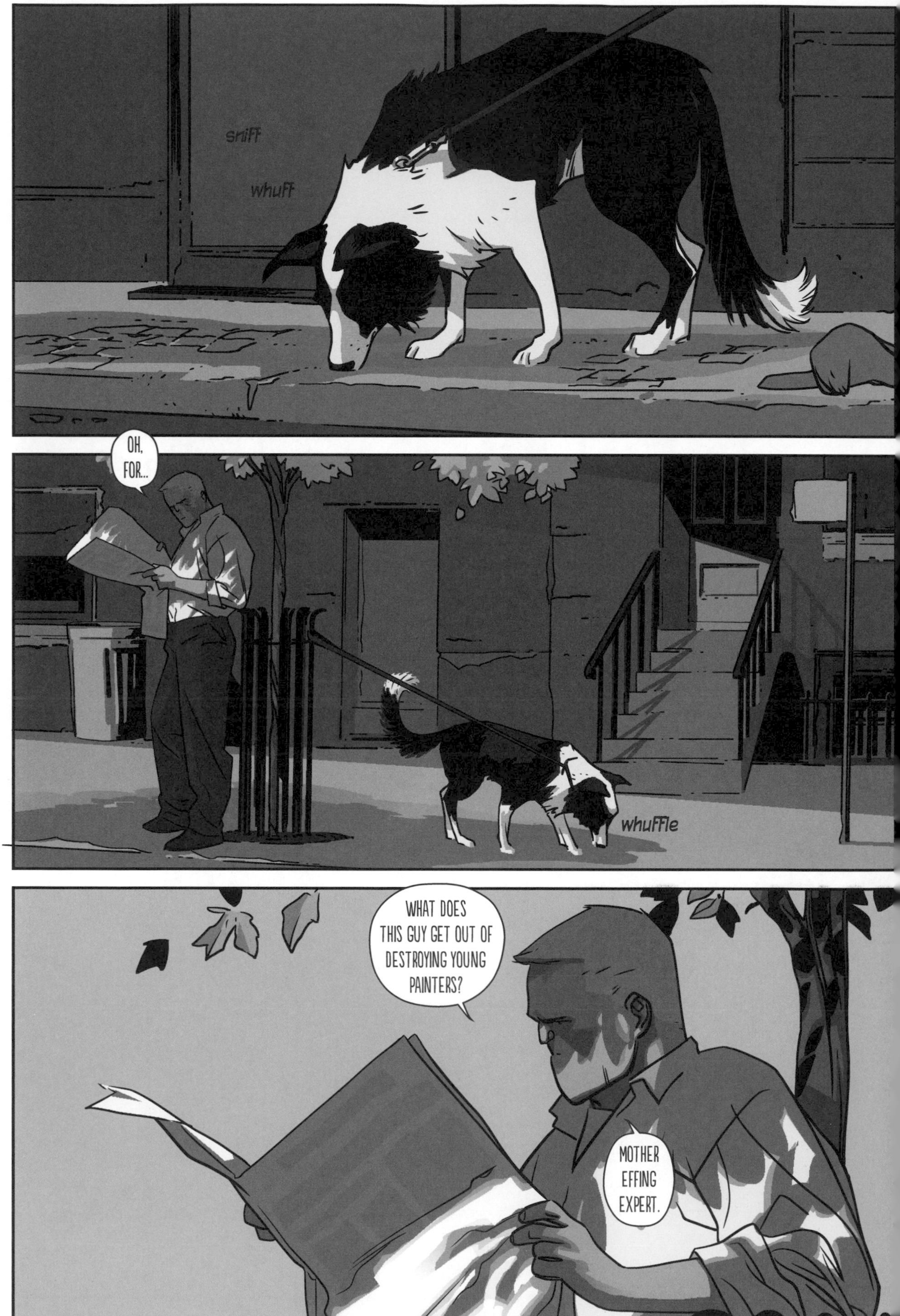
sniff
whuff
OH, FOR...
whuffle
WHAT DOES THIS GUY GET OUT OF DESTROYING YOUNG PAINTERS?
MOTHER EFFING EXPERT.

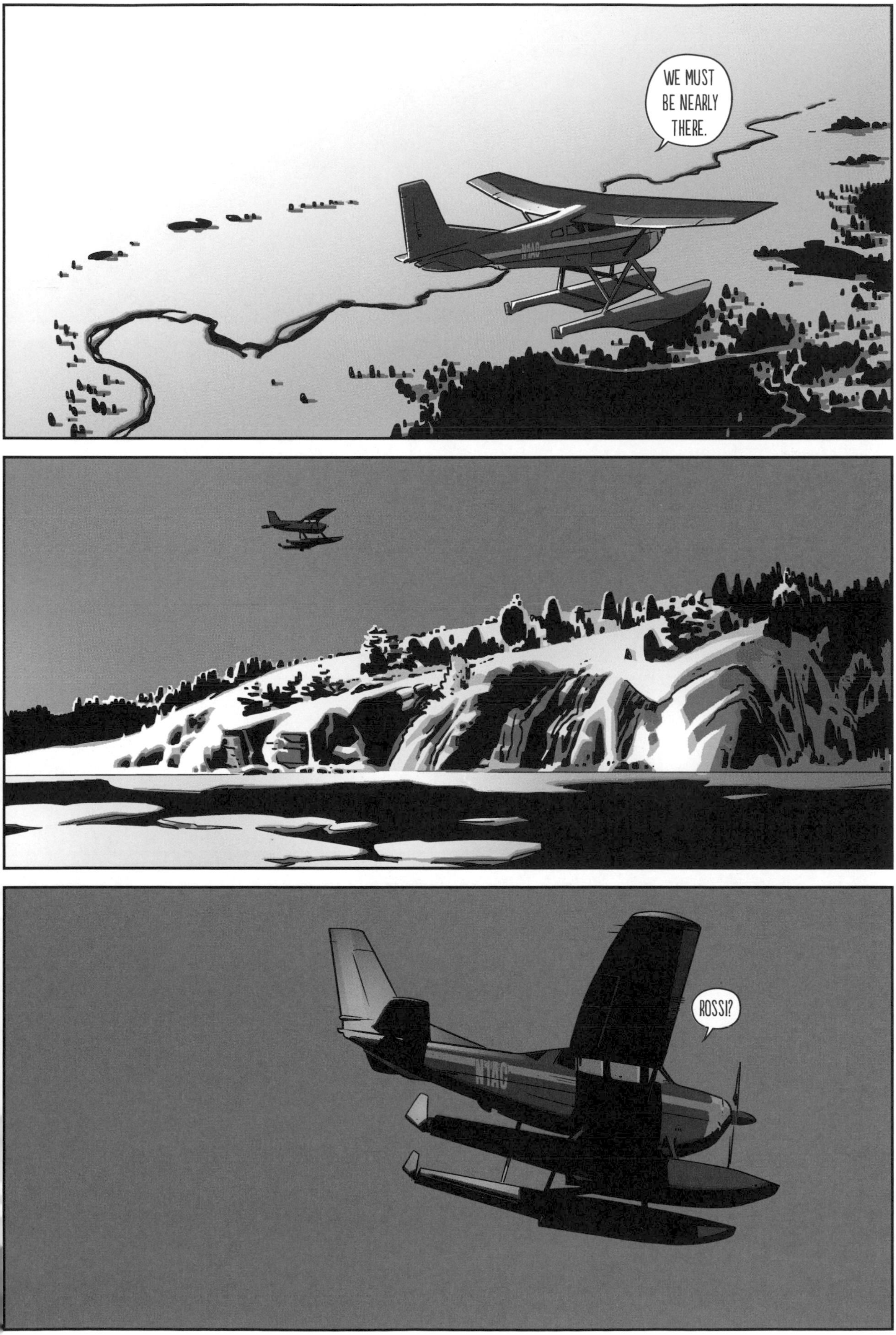
WE MUST BE NEARLY THERE.
ROSSI?

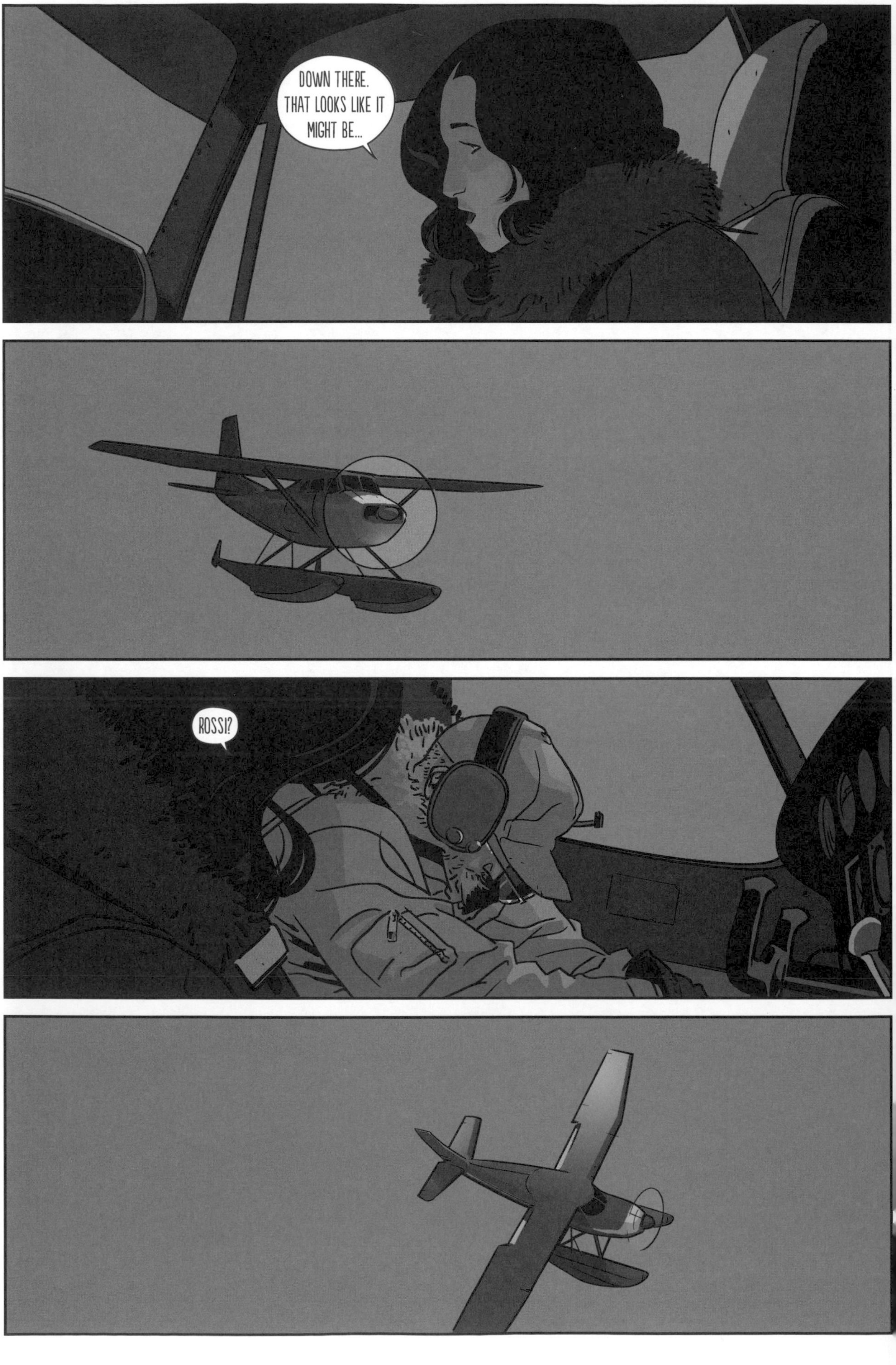
DOWN THERE. THAT LOOKS LIKE IT MIGHT BE...
ROSSI?

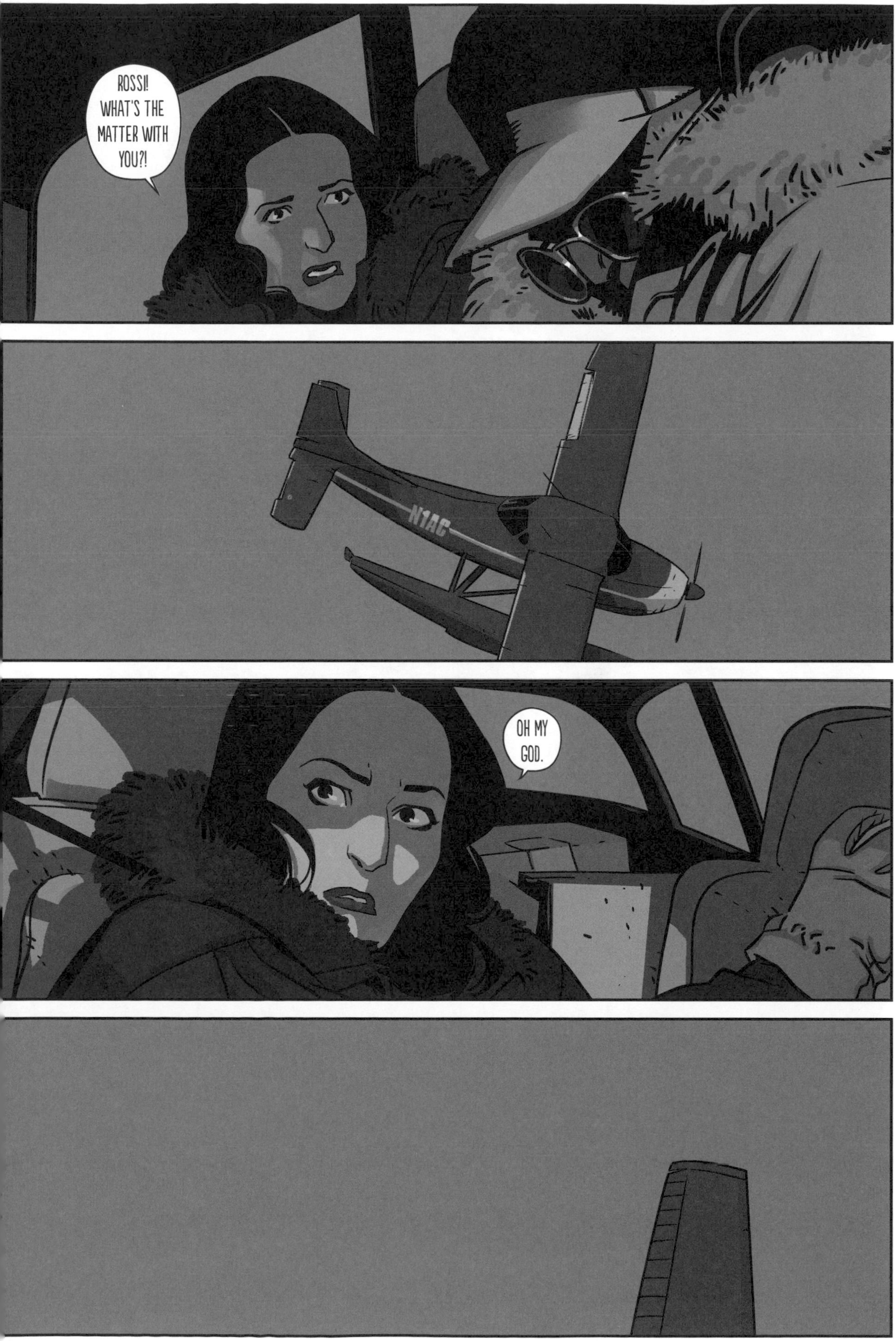
ROSSI! WHAT'S THE MATTER WITH YOU?!
N1AC
OH MY GOD.

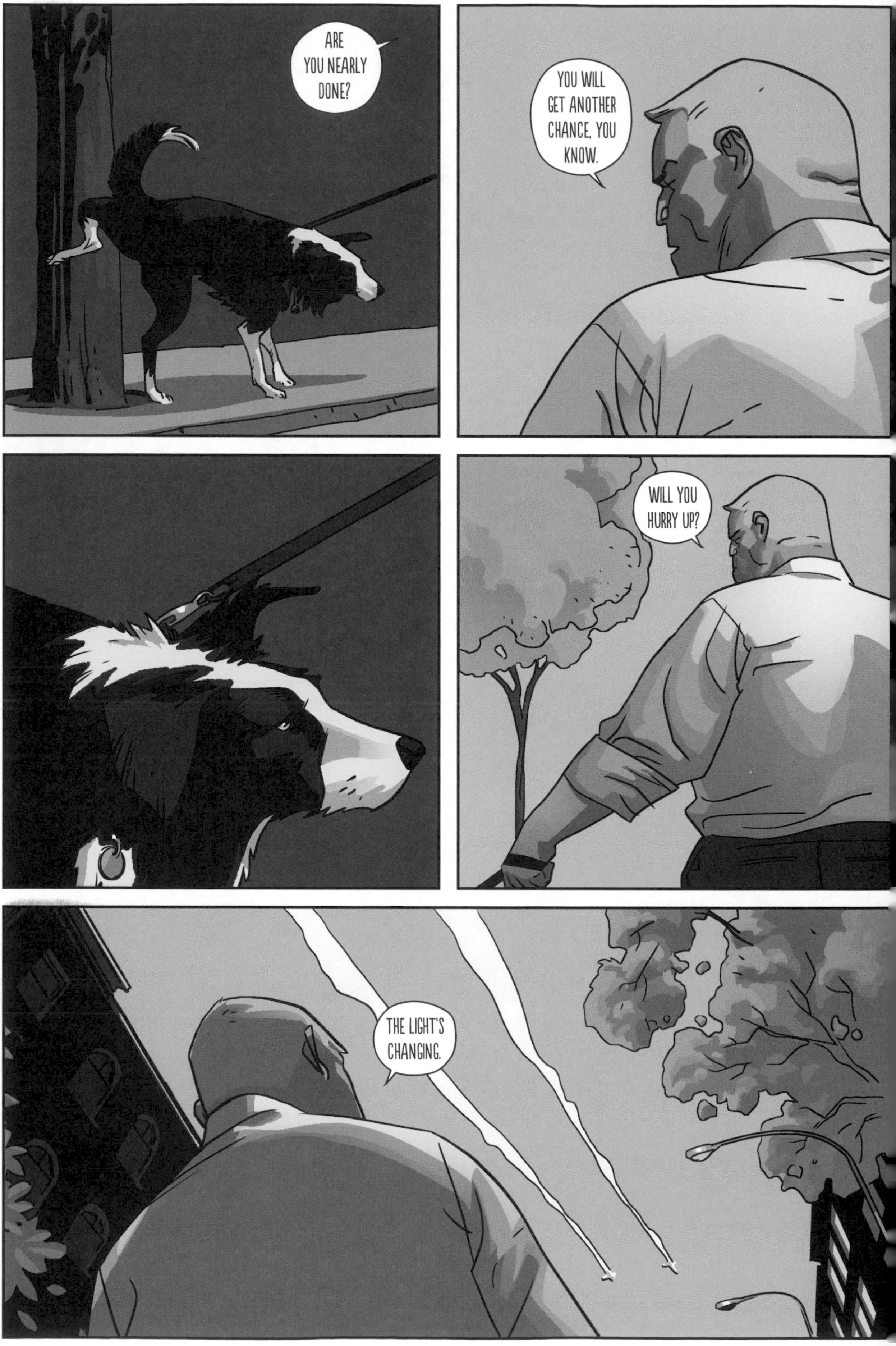
ARE YOU NEARLY DONE?
YOU WILL GET ANOTHER CHANCE, YOU KNOW.
WILL YOU HURRY UP?
THE LIGHT'S CHANGING.

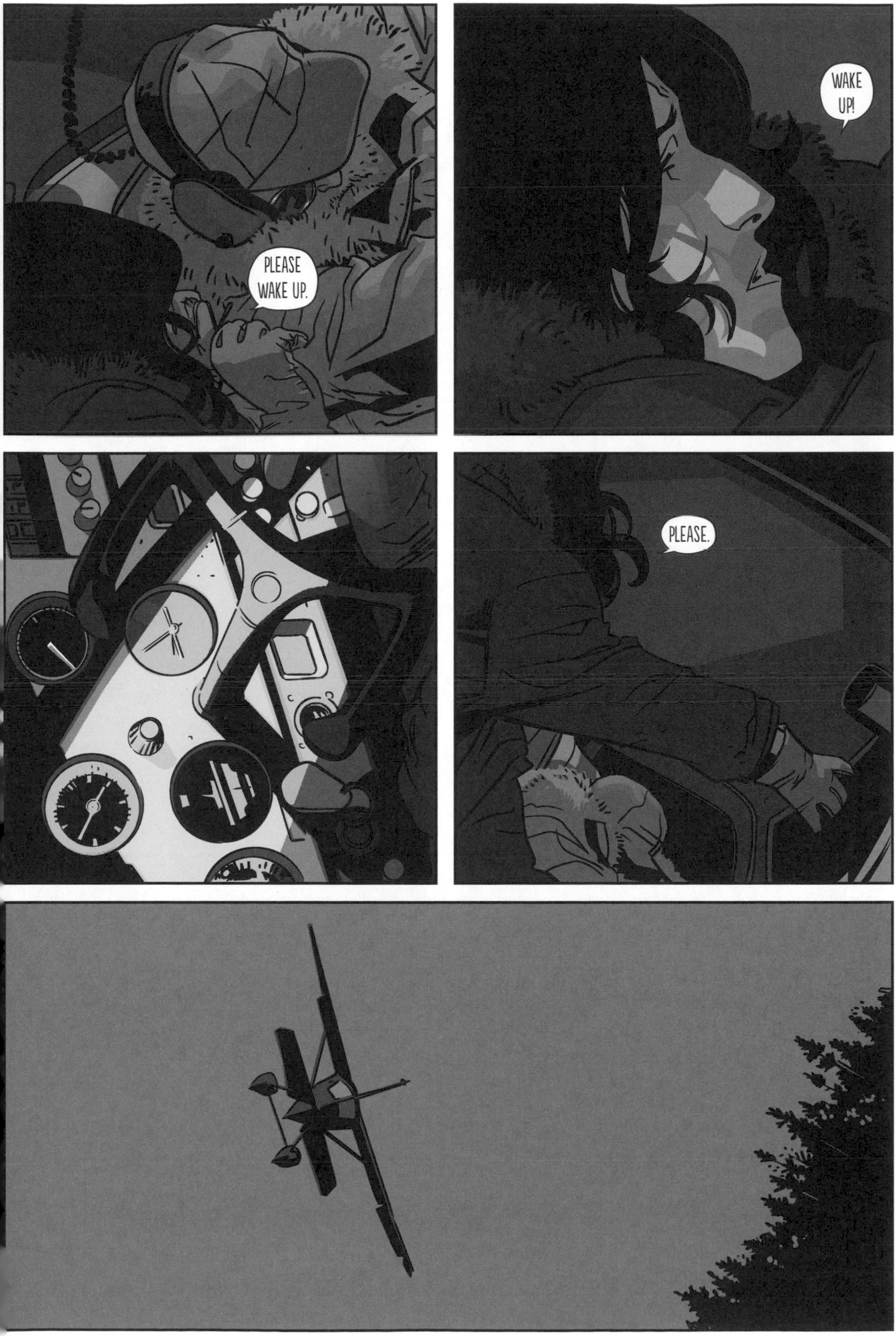
PLEASE WAKE UP.
WAKE UP!
PLEASE.

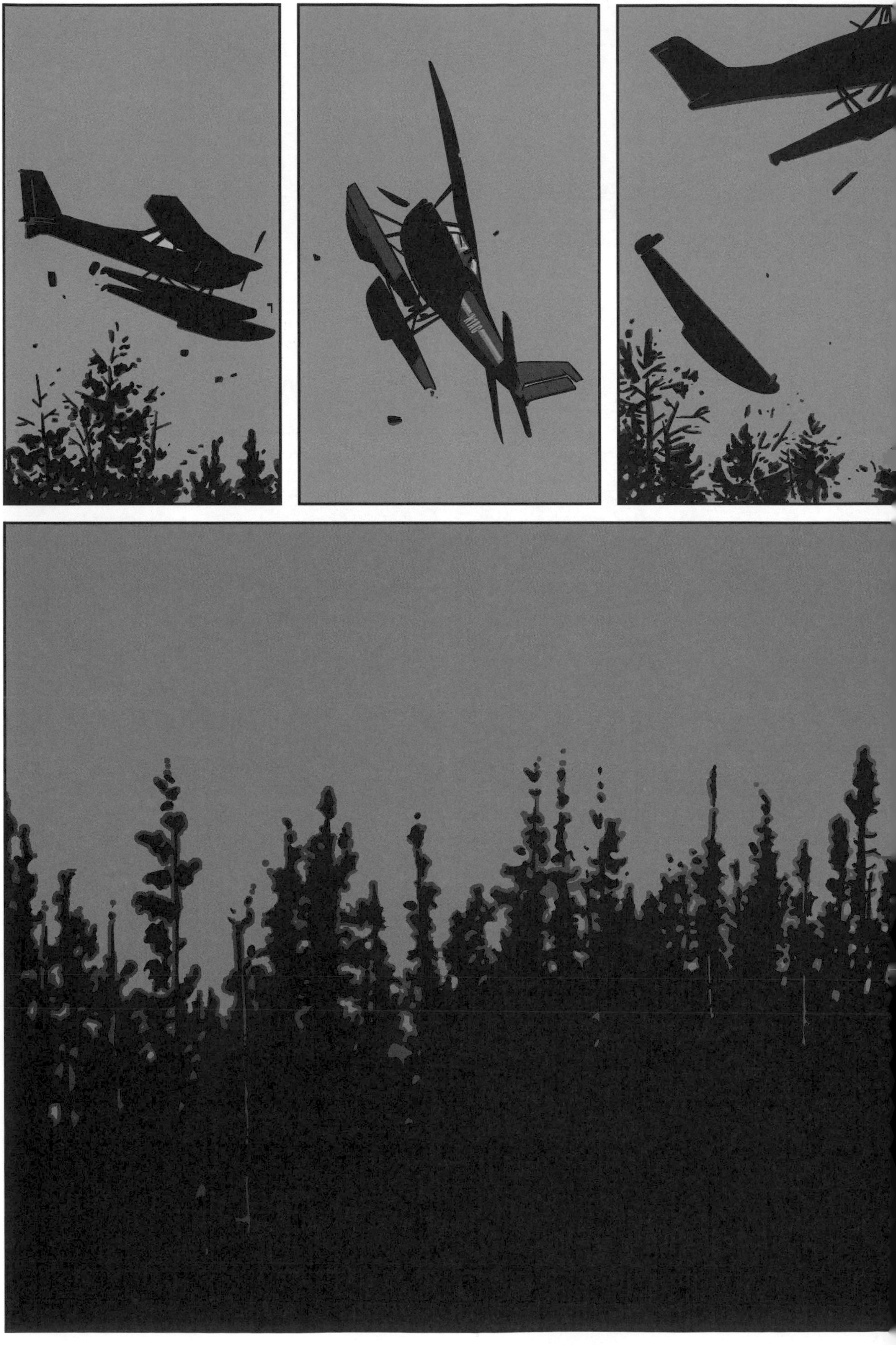

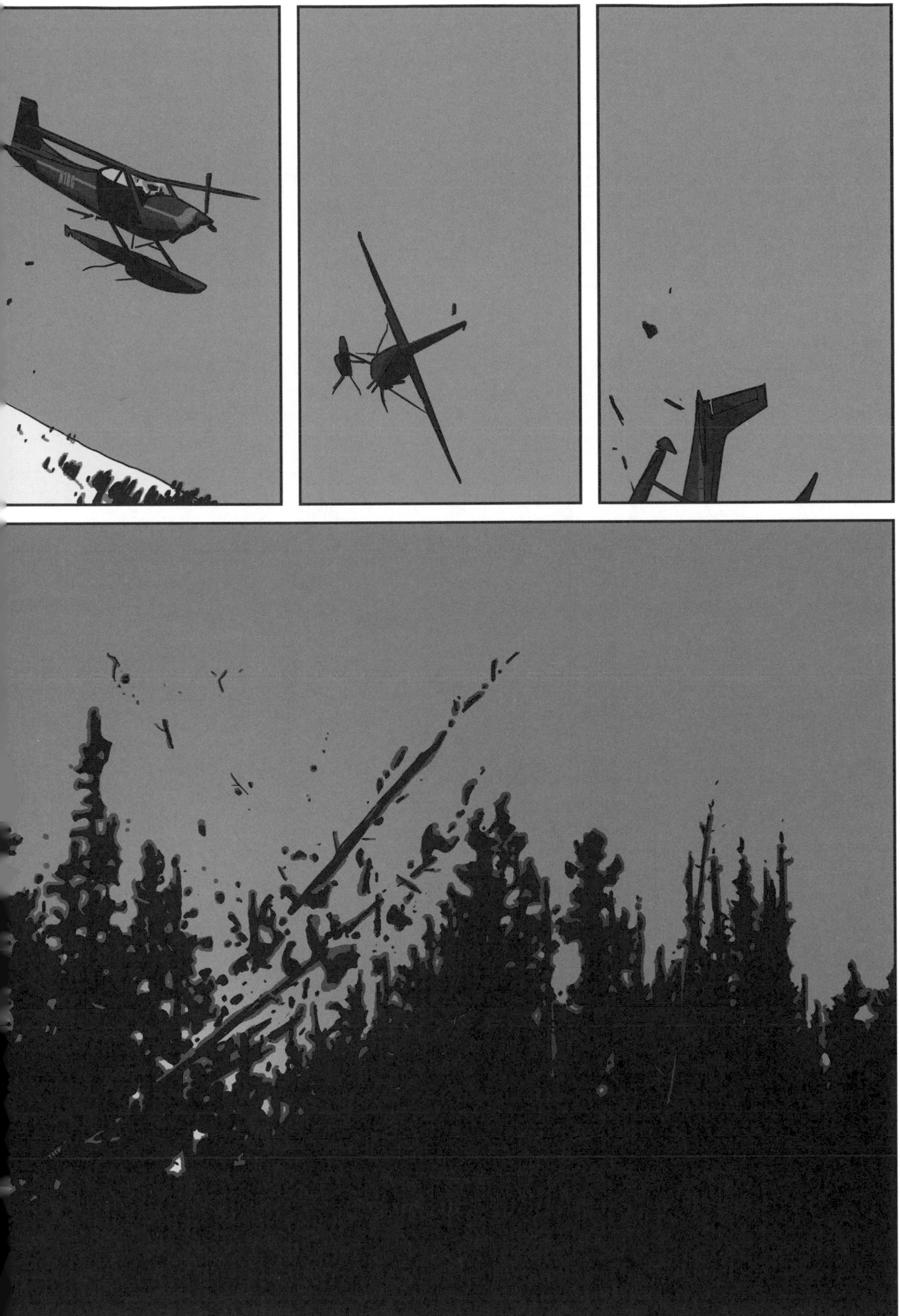

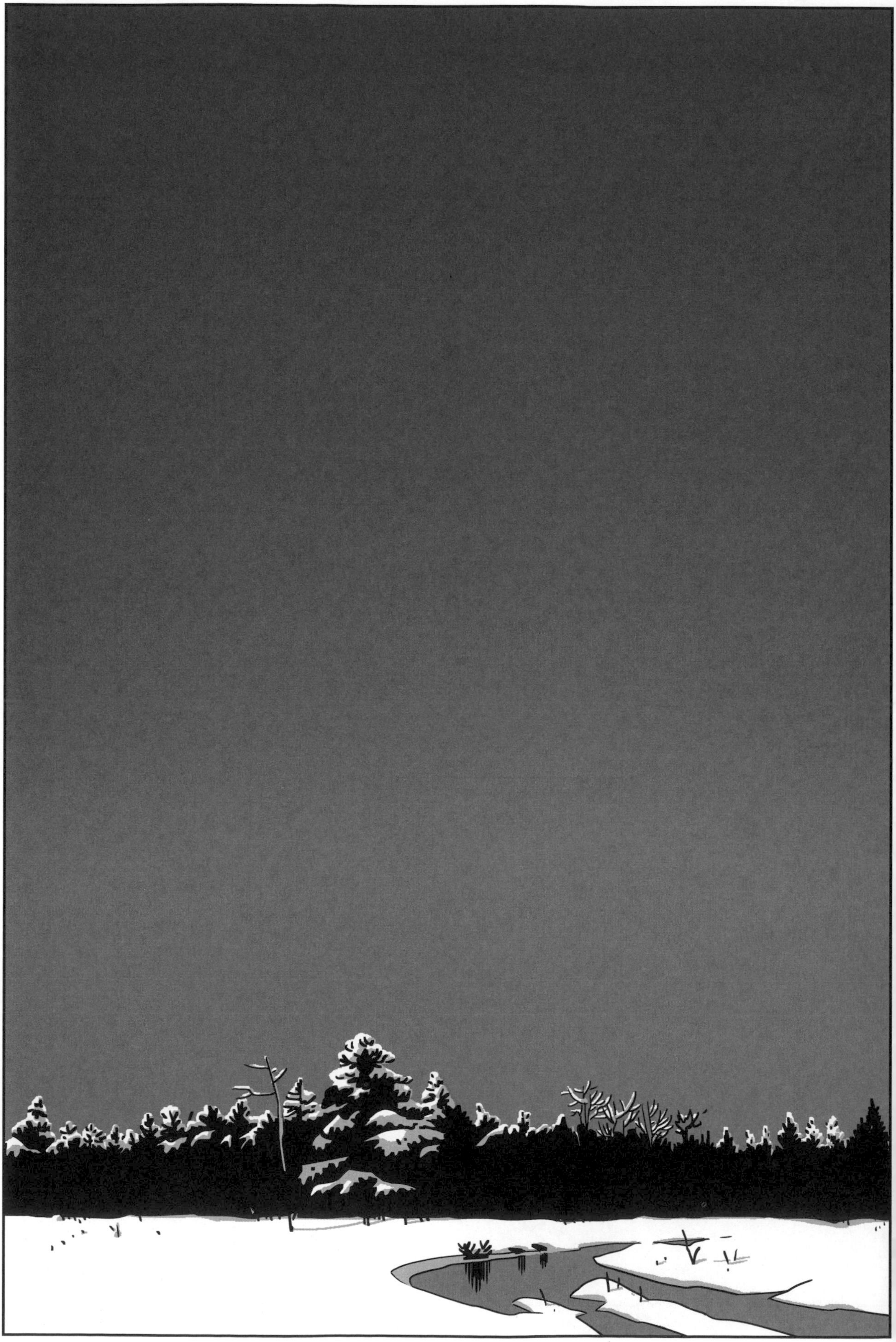

II

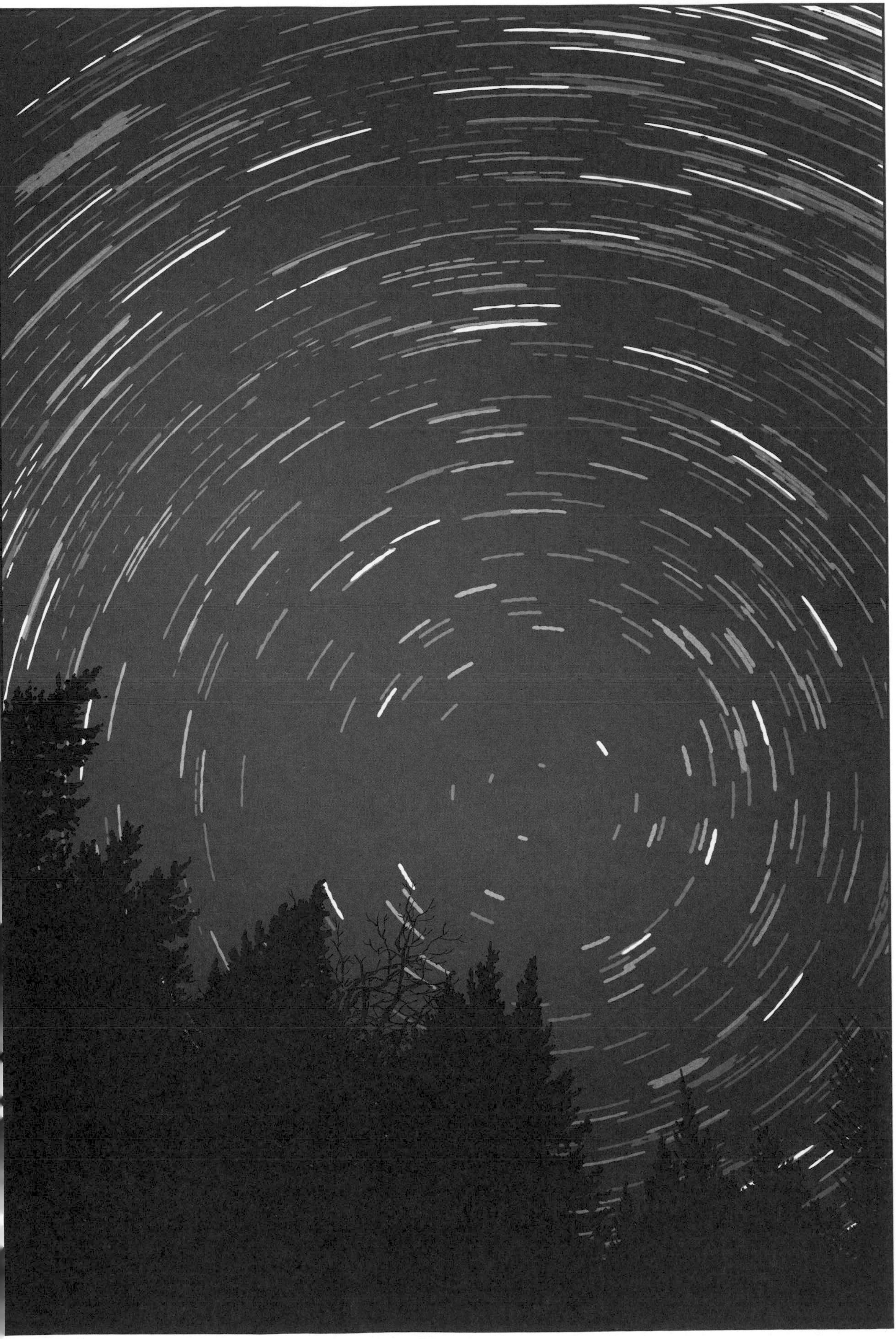

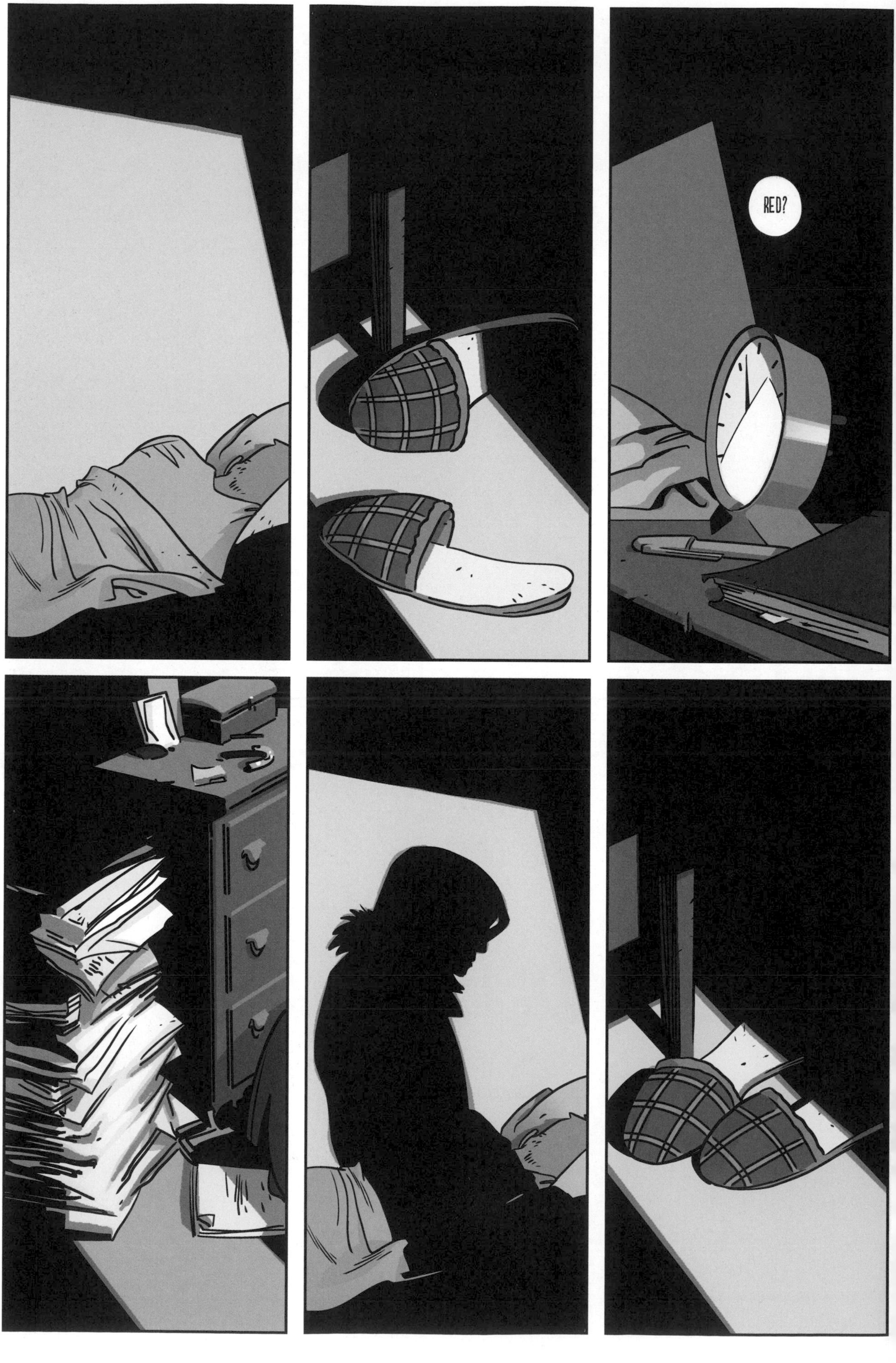
RED?

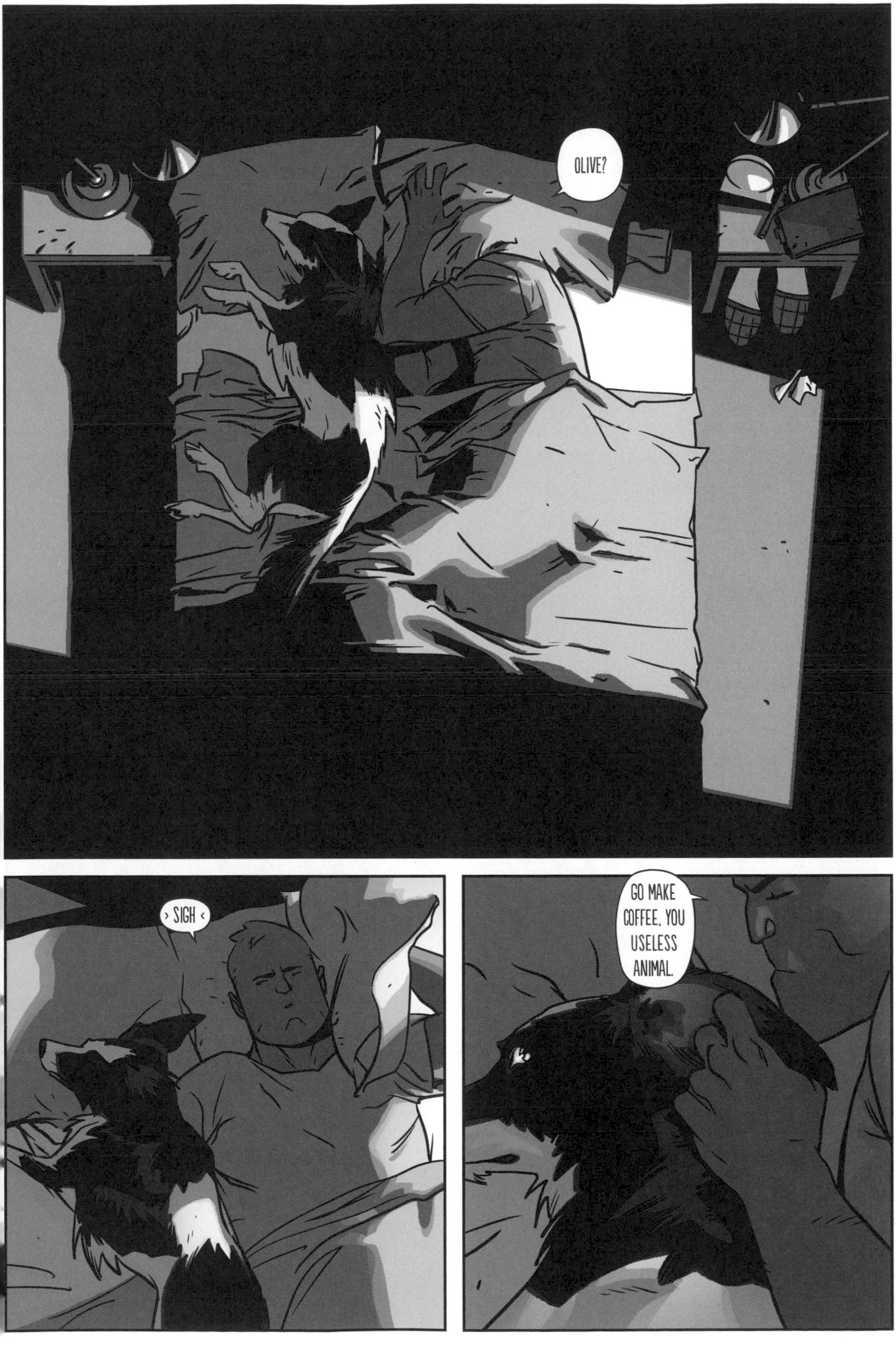
OLIVE?
› SIGH ‹
GO MAKE COFFEE, YOU USELESS ANIMAL.

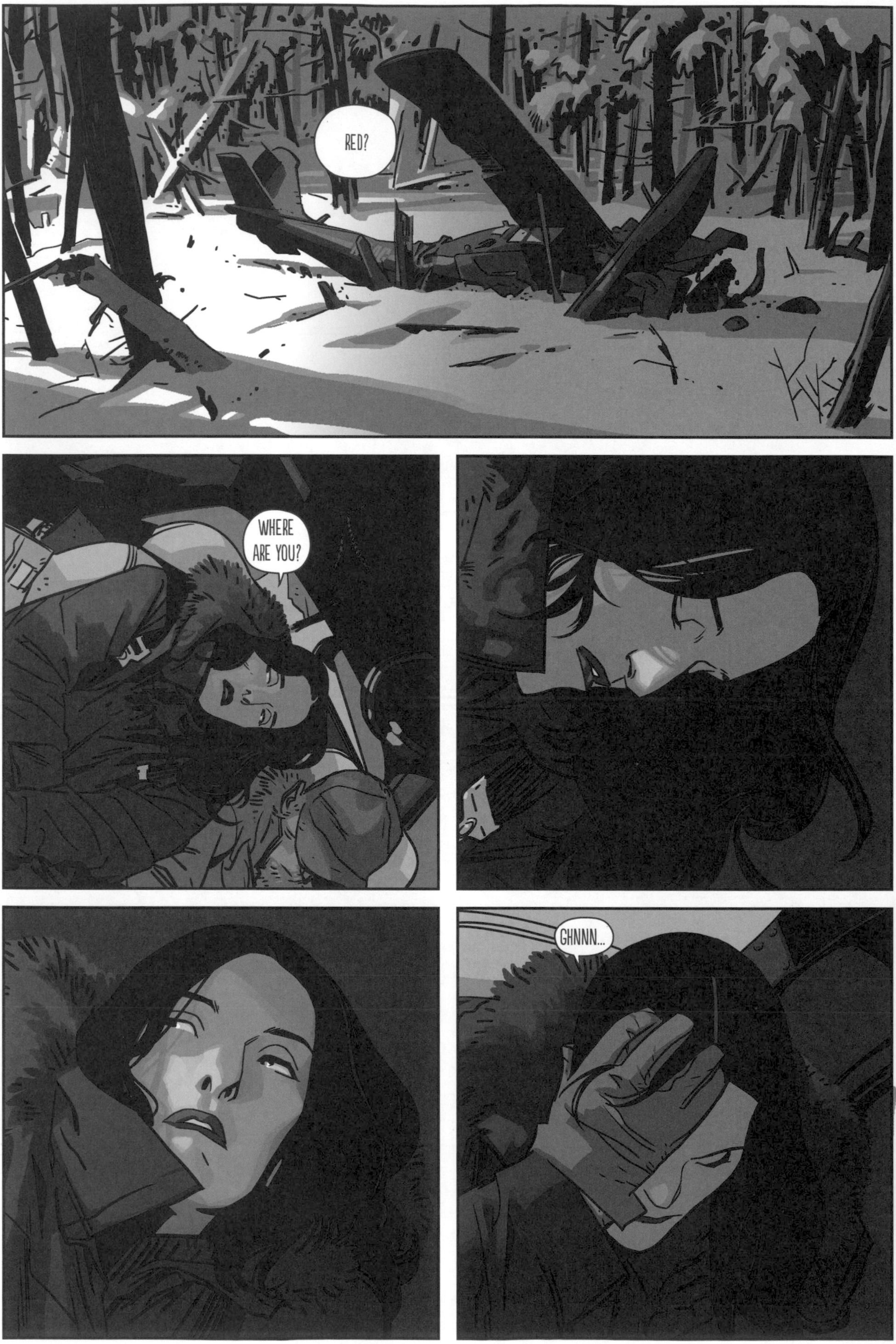
RED?
WHERE ARE YOU?
GHNNN...

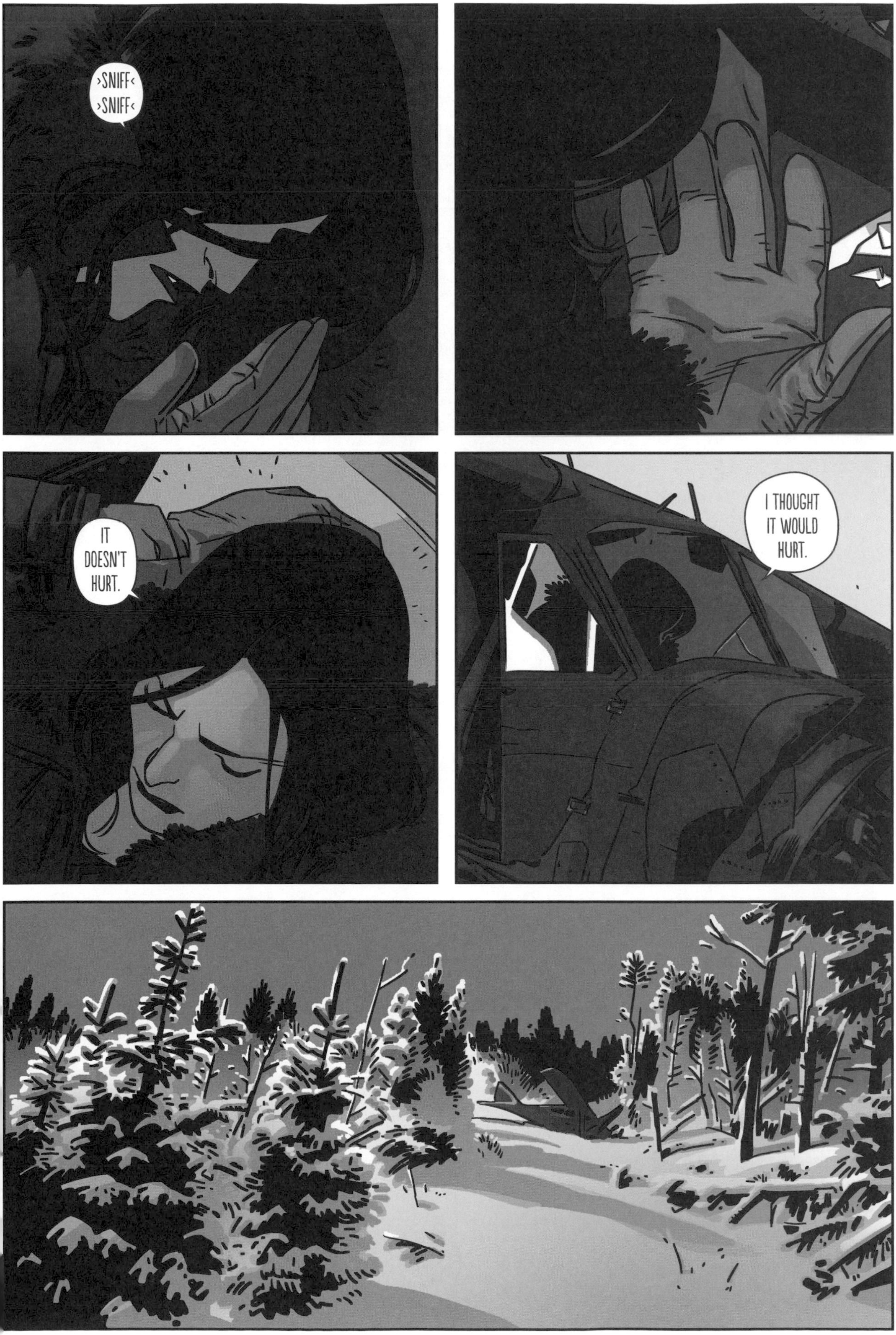
>SNIFF<
>SNIFF<
IT DOESN'T HURT.
I THOUGHT IT WOULD HURT.

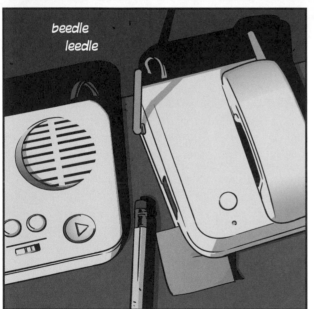

beedle leedle

beedle leedle

YOU HAVE REACHED RED AND OLIVE'S. PLEASE LEAVE A MESSAGE AFTER THE TONE.

beeep

RED. IT'S MARTIN. IT'S TUESDAY.

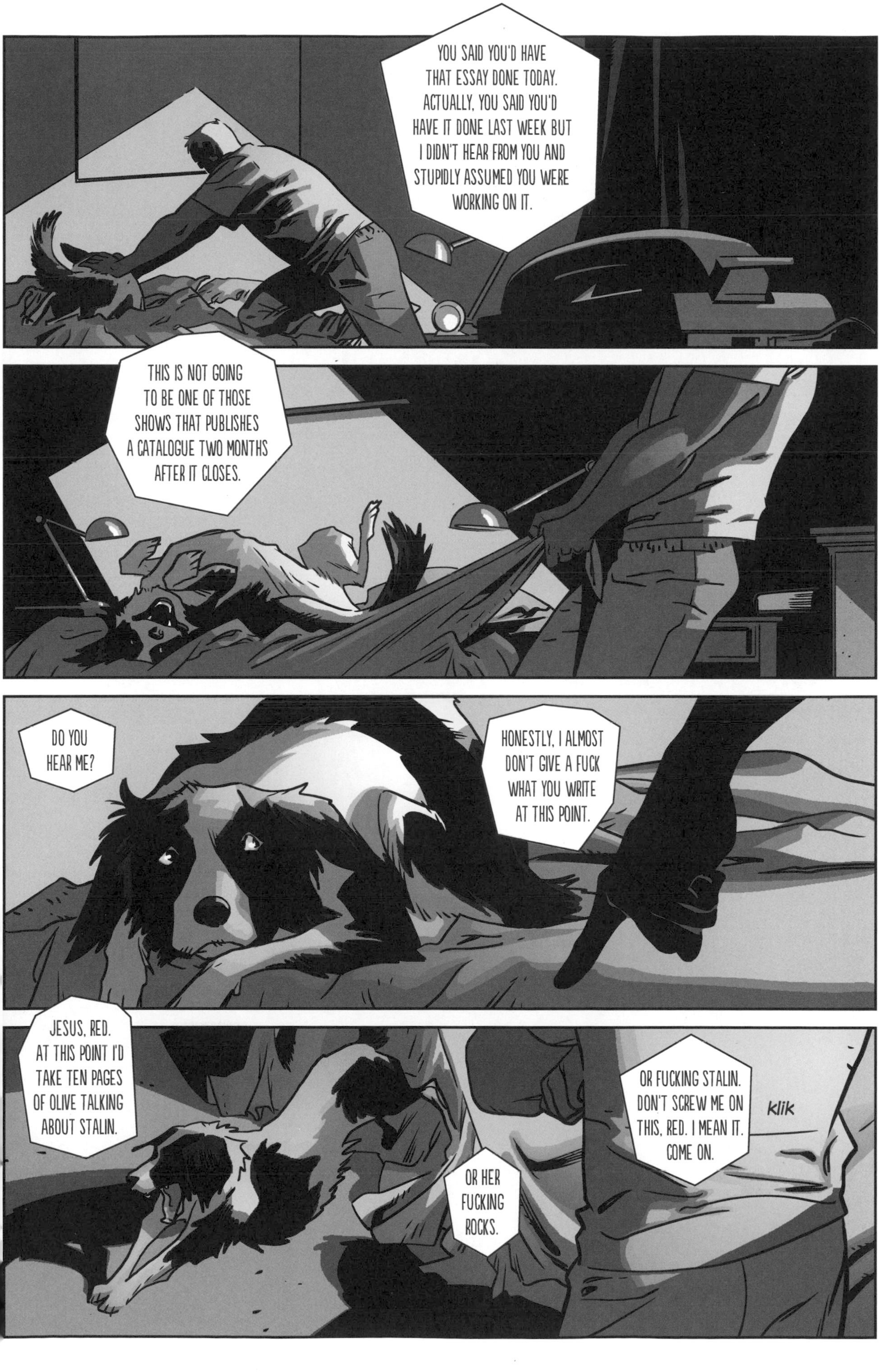
YOU SAID YOU'D HAVE THAT ESSAY DONE TODAY. ACTUALLY, YOU SAID YOU'D HAVE IT DONE LAST WEEK BUT I DIDN'T HEAR FROM YOU AND STUPIDLY ASSUMED YOU WERE WORKING ON IT.
THIS IS NOT GOING TO BE ONE OF THOSE SHOWS THAT PUBLISHES A CATALOGUE TWO MONTHS AFTER IT CLOSES.
DO YOU HEAR ME?
HONESTLY, I ALMOST DON'T GIVE A FUCK WHAT YOU WRITE AT THIS POINT.
JESUS, RED. AT THIS POINT I'D TAKE TEN PAGES OF OLIVE TALKING ABOUT STALIN.
OR HER FUCKING ROCKS.
OR FUCKING STALIN. DON'T SCREW ME ON THIS, RED. I MEAN IT. COME ON.
klik

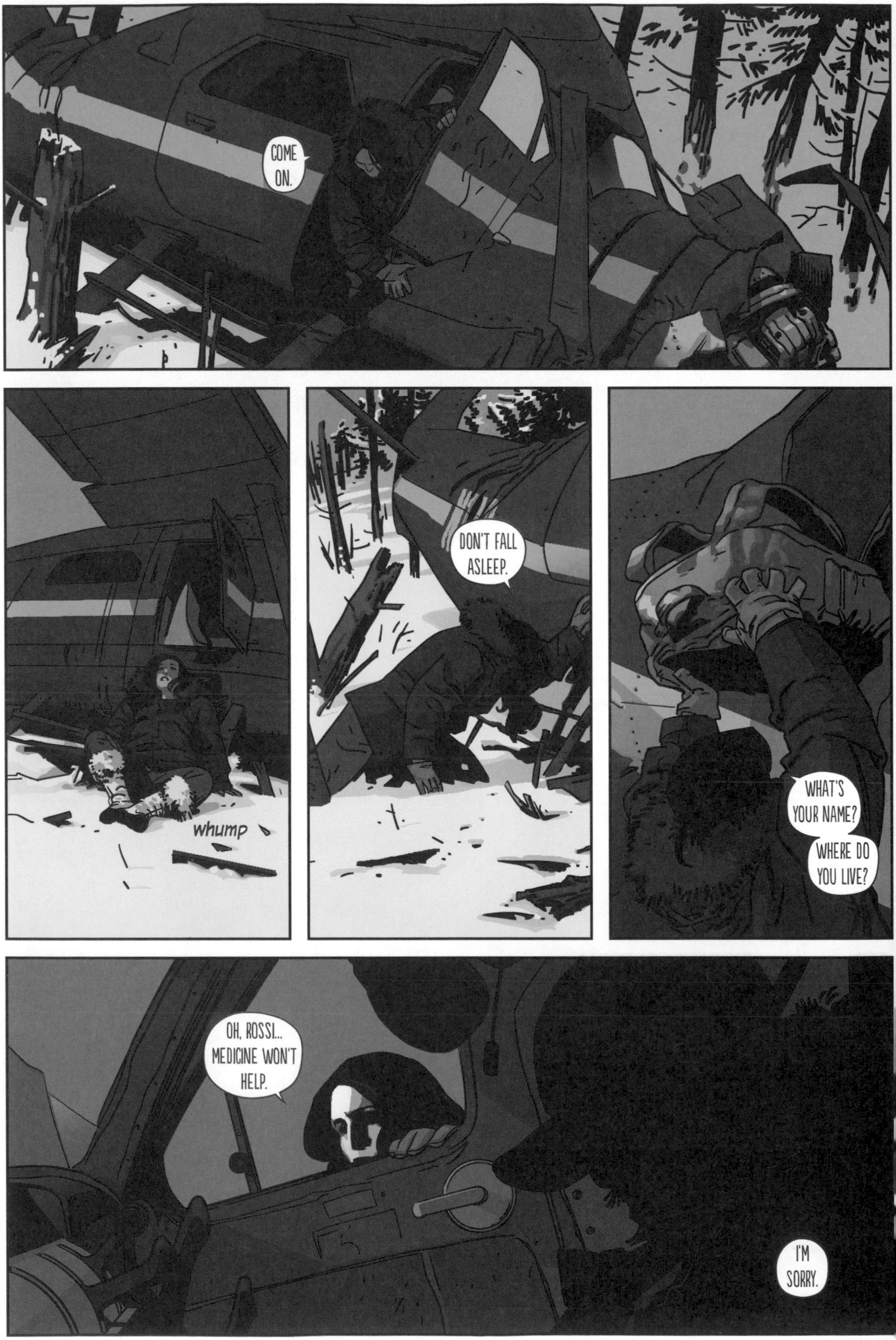
COME ON.
whump
DON'T FALL ASLEEP.
WHAT'S YOUR NAME?
WHERE DO YOU LIVE?
OH, ROSSI... MEDICINE WON'T HELP.
I'M SORRY.

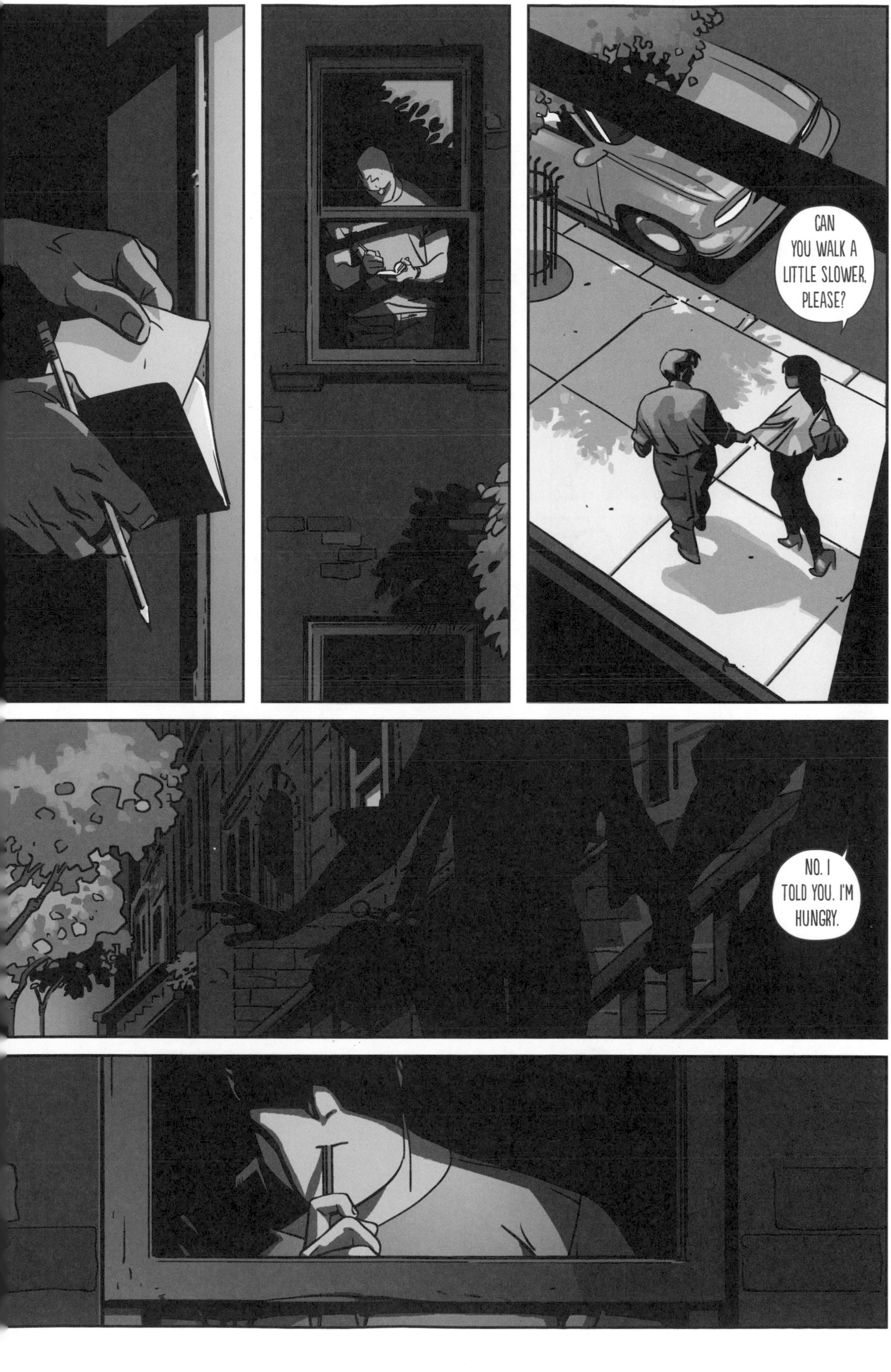
CAN YOU WALK A LITTLE SLOWER, PLEASE?
NO. I TOLD YOU. I'M HUNGRY.

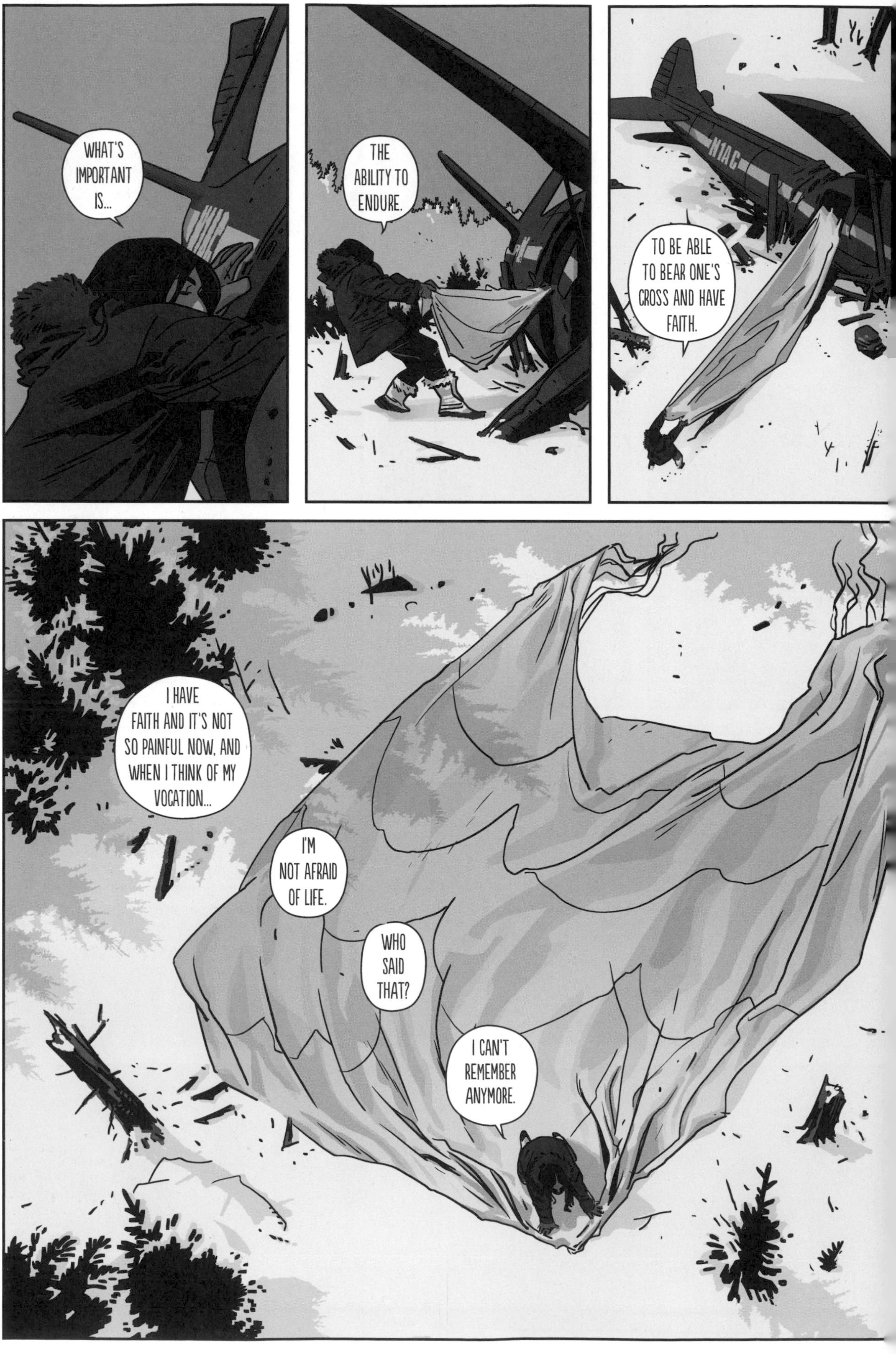
WHAT'S IMPORTANT IS...
THE ABILITY TO ENDURE.
TO BE ABLE TO BEAR ONE'S CROSS AND HAVE FAITH.
I HAVE FAITH AND IT'S NOT SO PAINFUL NOW, AND WHEN I THINK OF MY VOCATION...
I'M NOT AFRAID OF LIFE.
WHO SAID THAT?
I CAN'T REMEMBER ANYMORE.

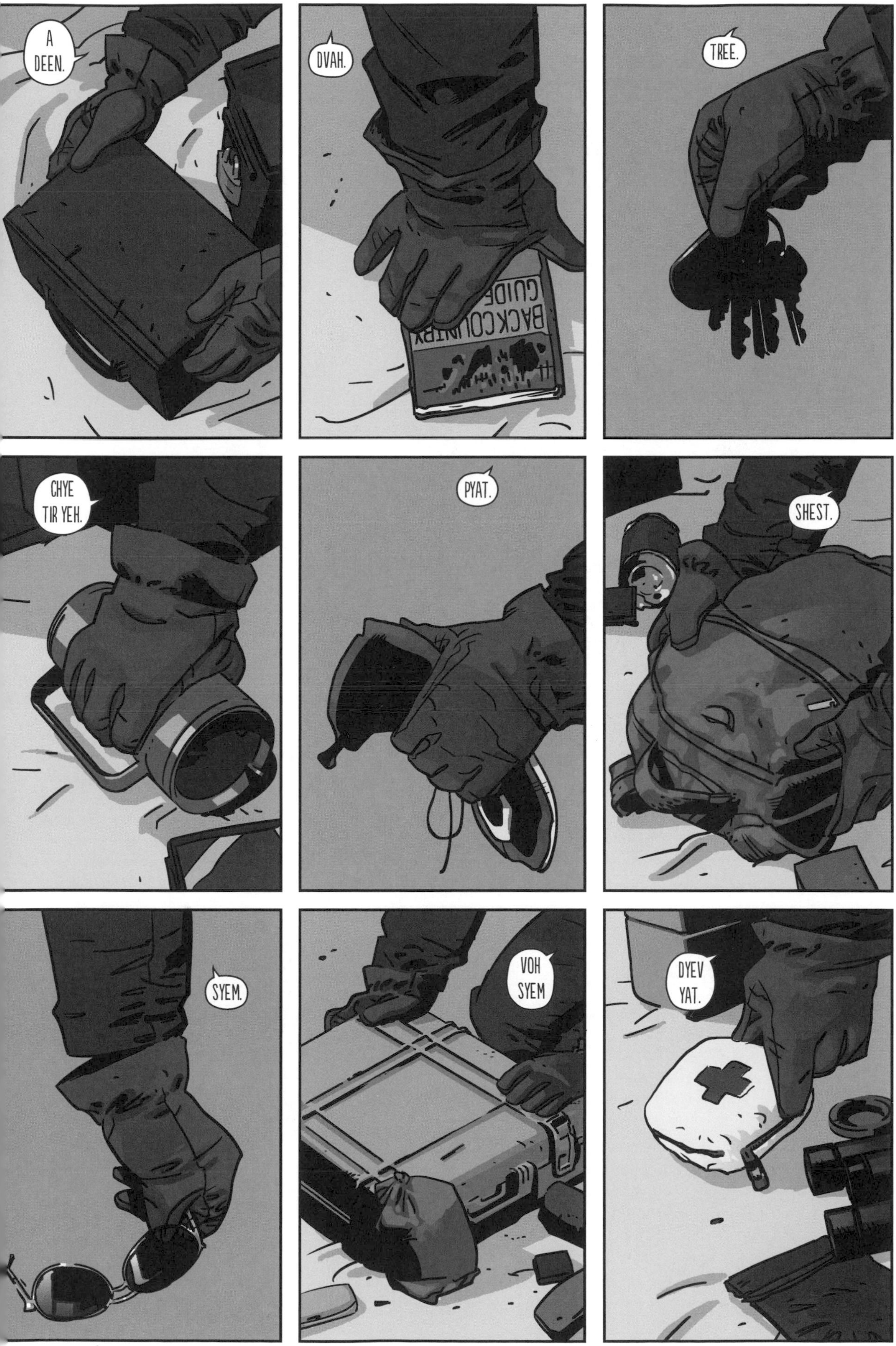
A DEEN.
DVAH.
BACK COUNTRY GUIDE
TREE.
CHYE TIR YEH.
PYAT.
SHEST.
SYEM.
VOH SYEM
DYEV YAT.

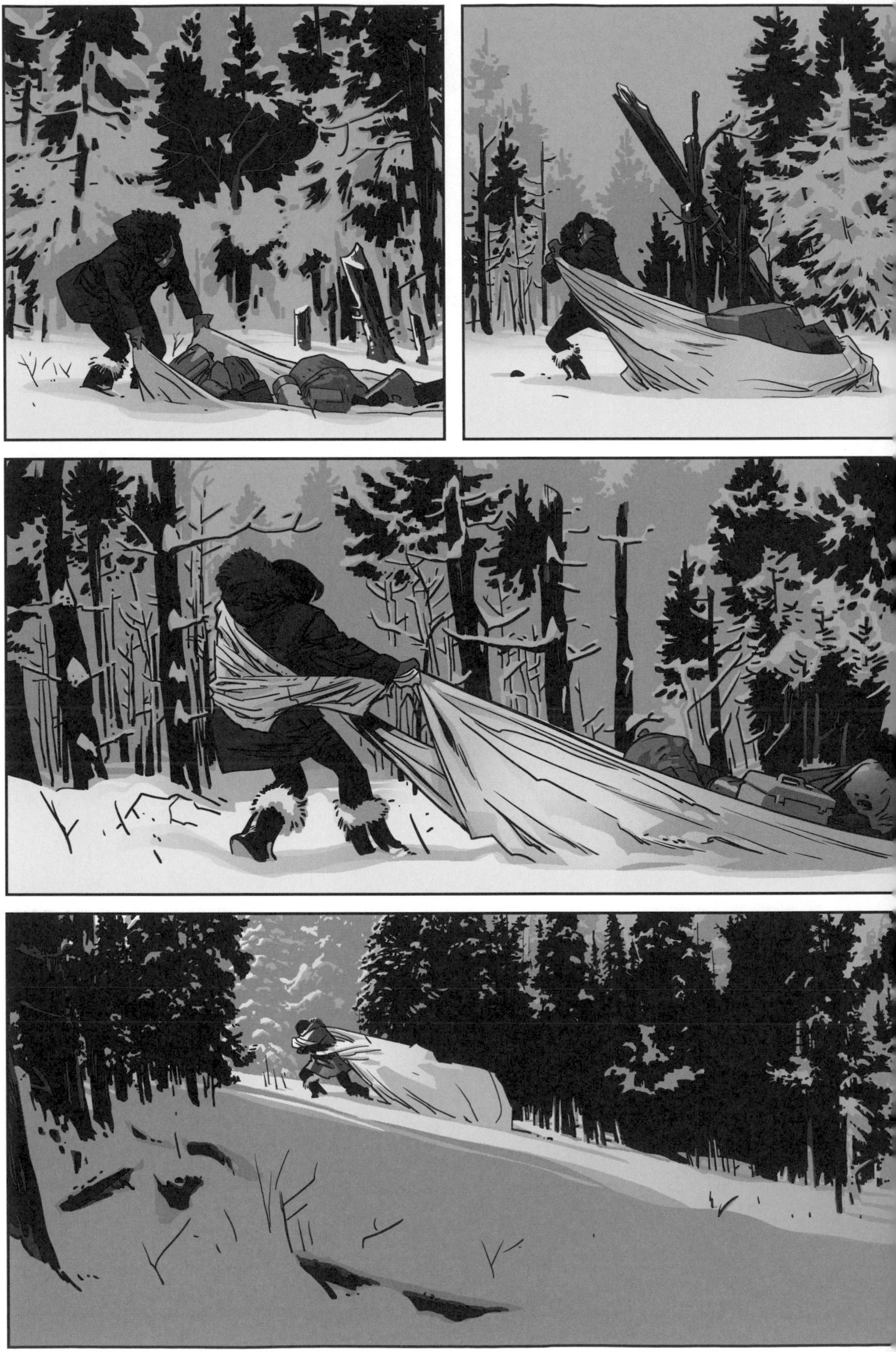

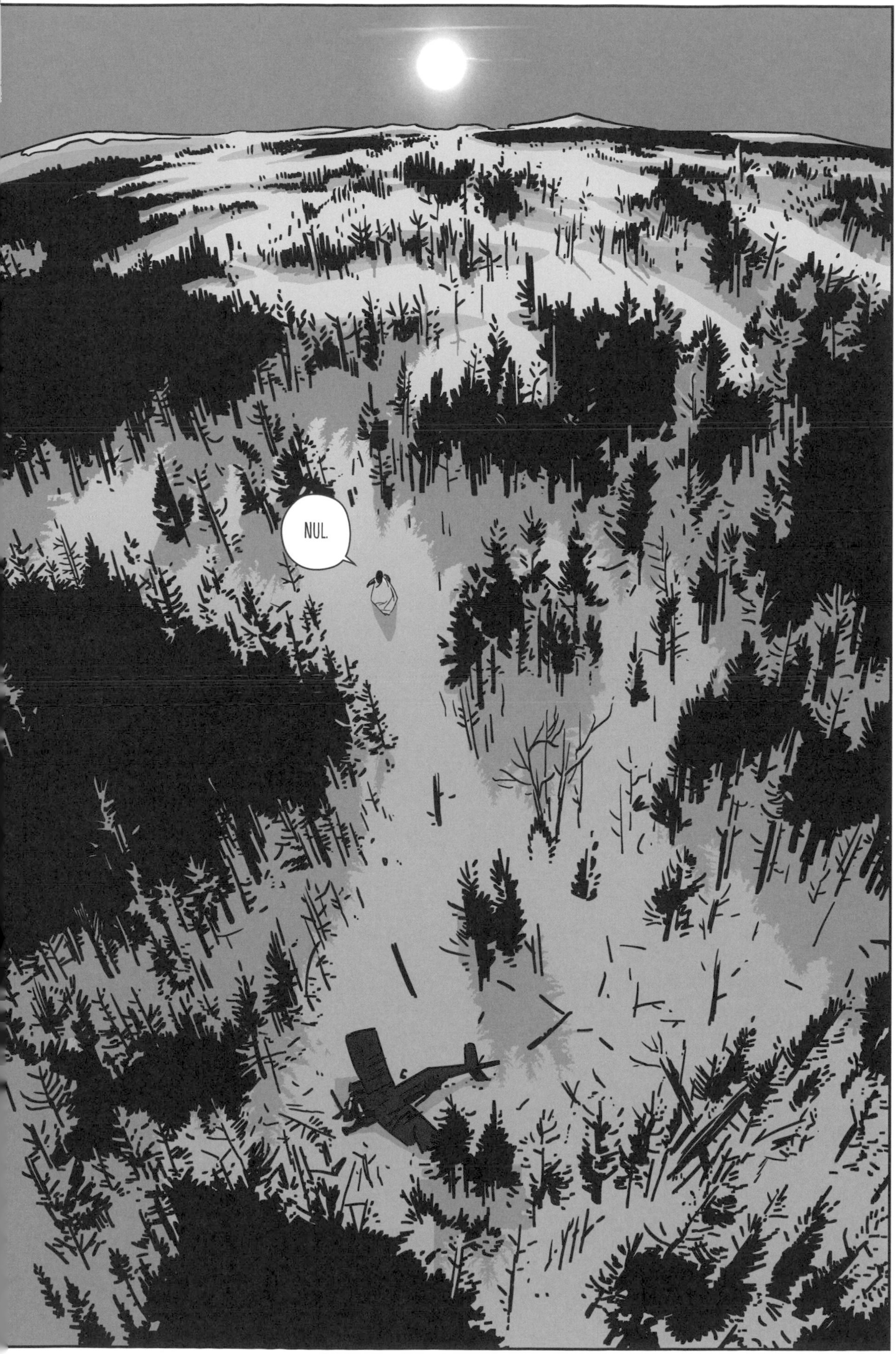
NUL.

III

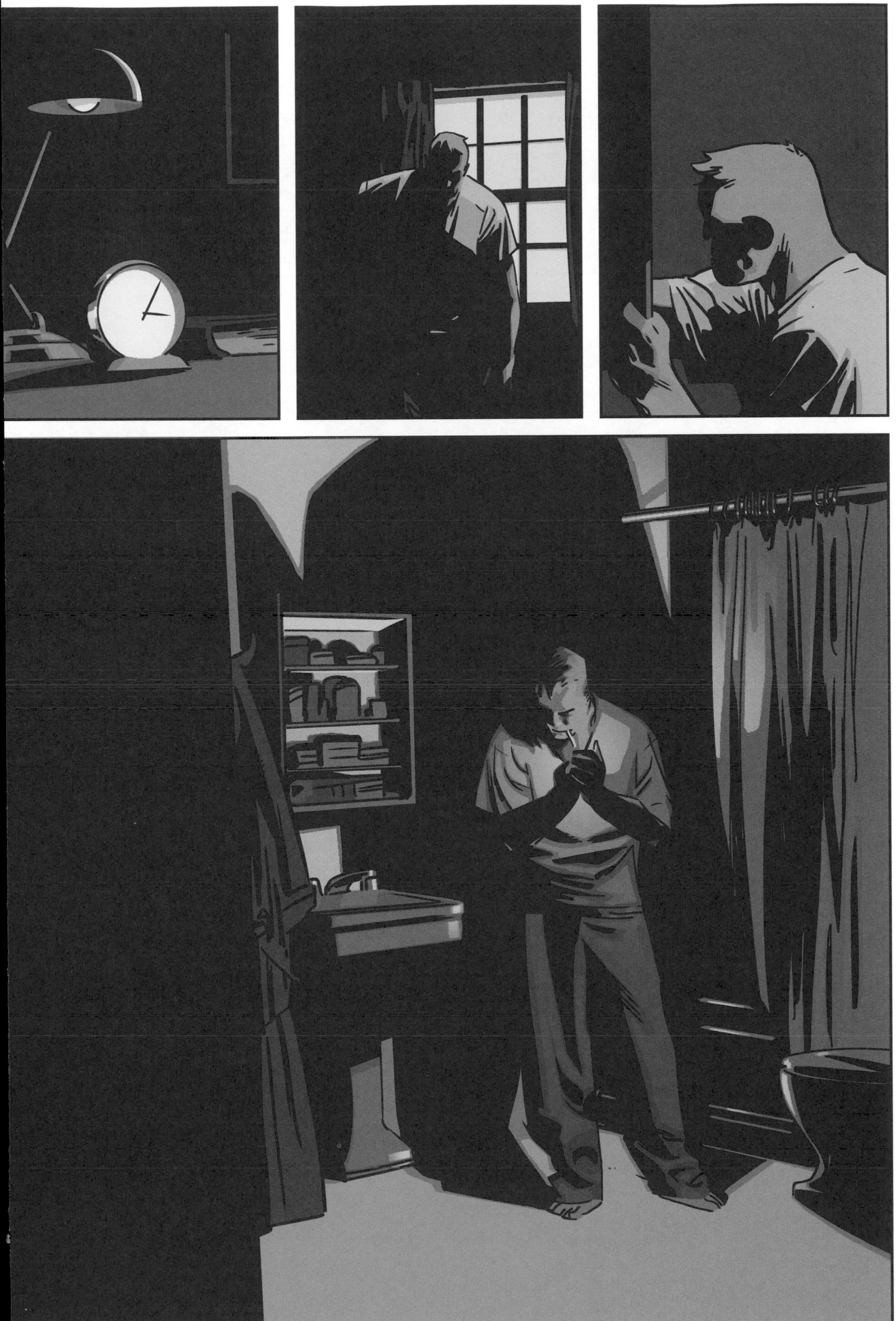

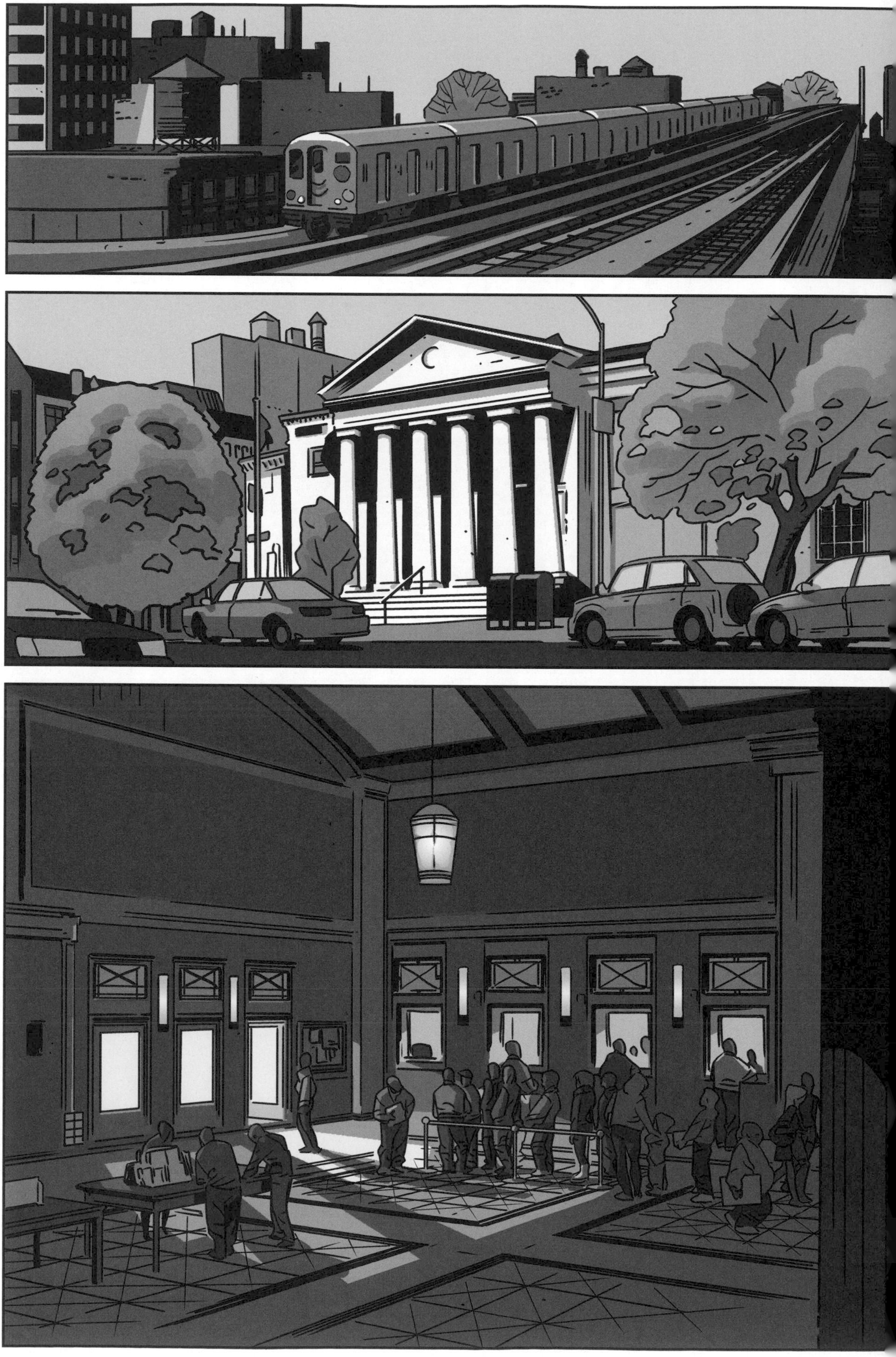

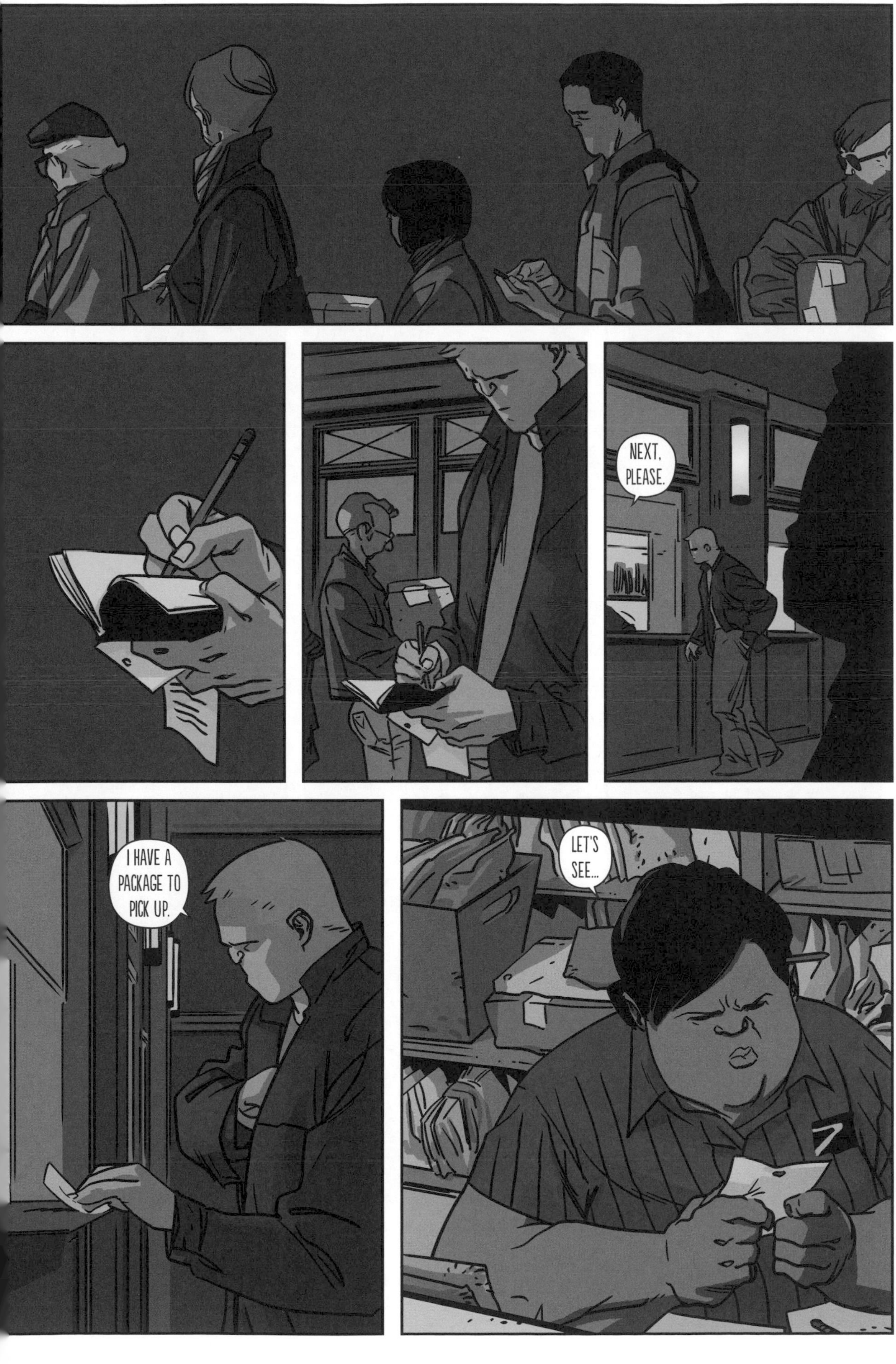
NEXT, PLEASE.
I HAVE A PACKAGE TO PICK UP.
LET'S SEE...

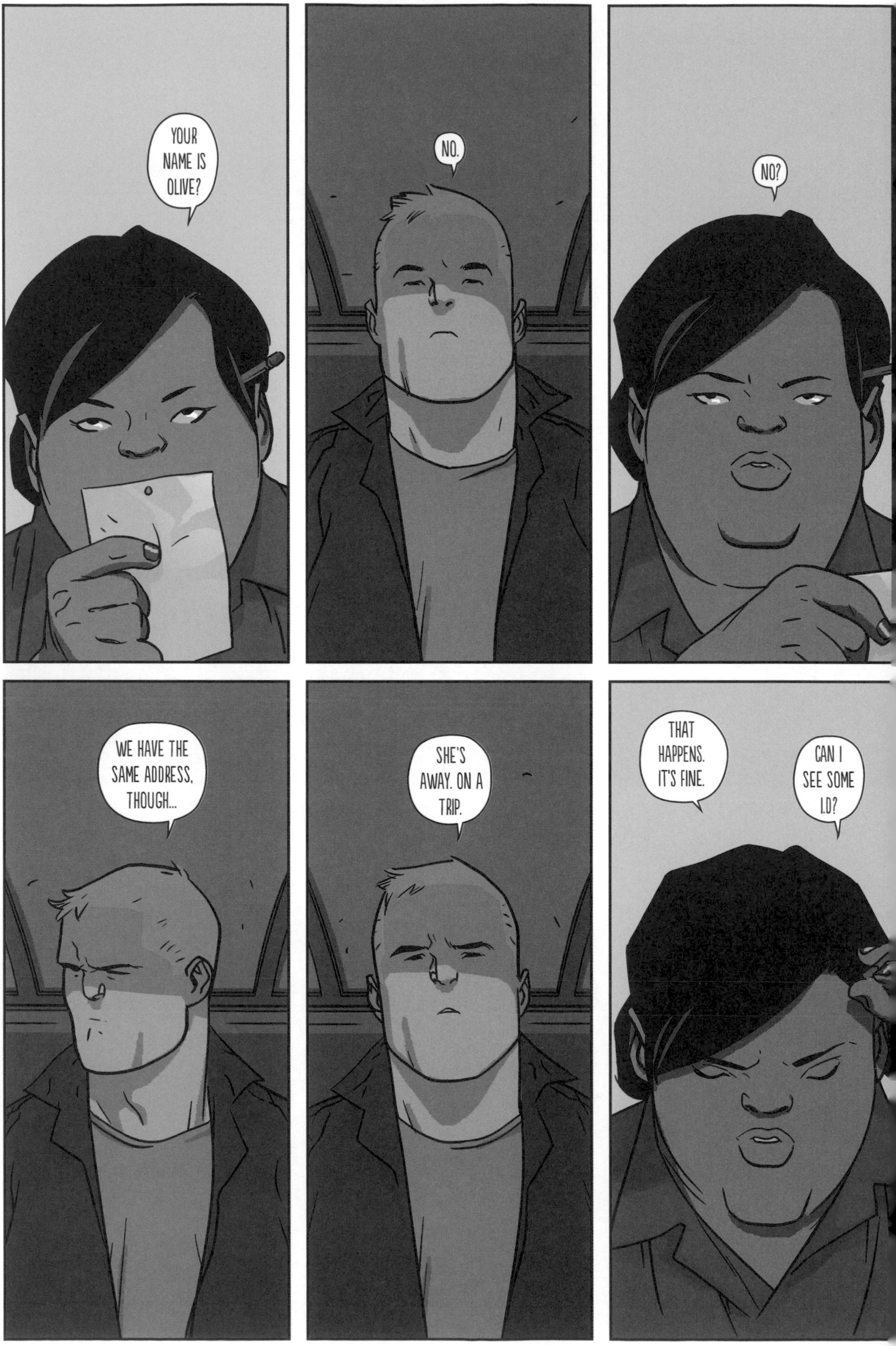
YOUR NAME IS OLIVE?
NO.
NO?
WE HAVE THE SAME ADDRESS, THOUGH...
SHE'S AWAY. ON A TRIP.
THAT HAPPENS. IT'S FINE.
CAN I SEE SOME I.D?

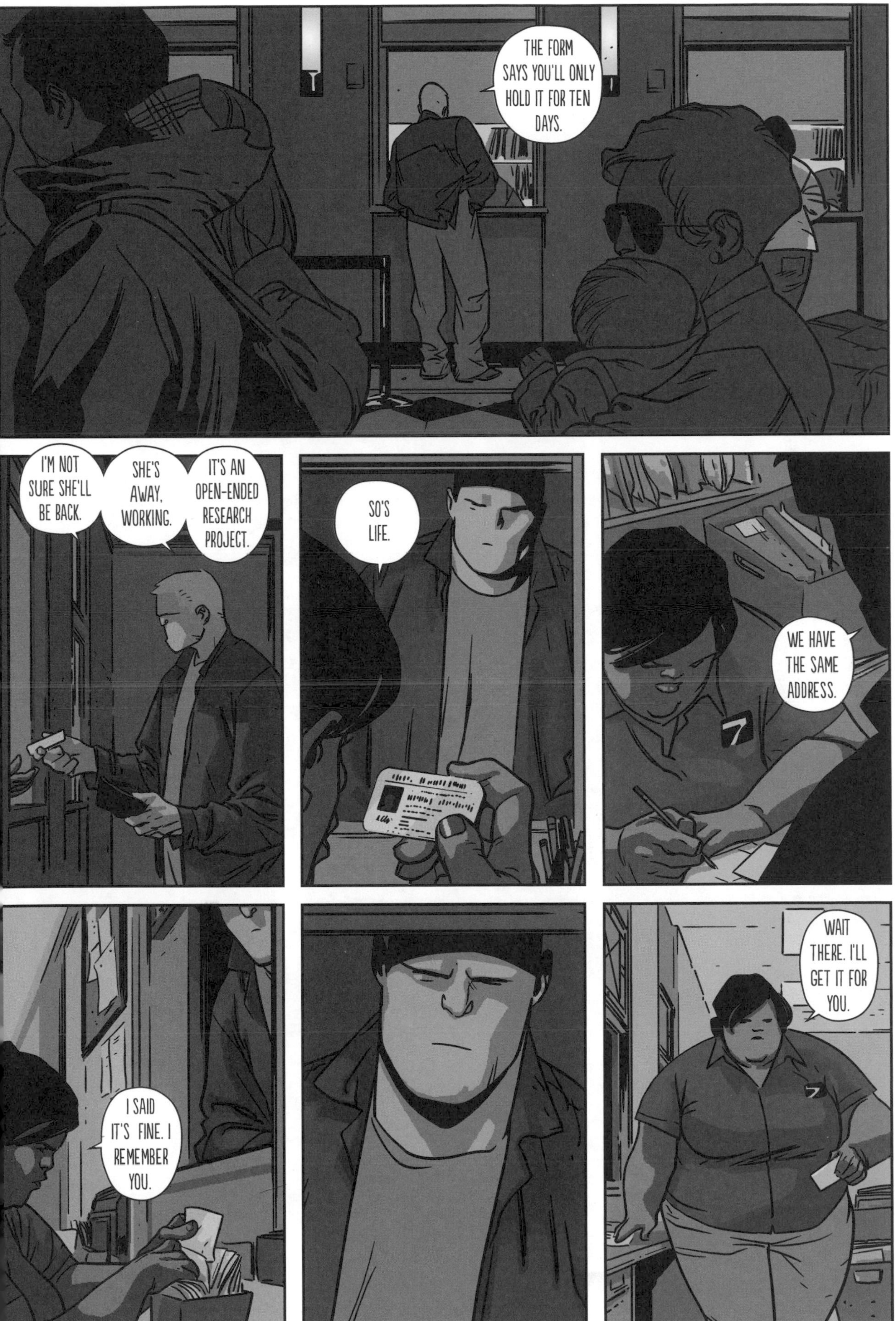
THE FORM SAYS YOU'LL ONLY HOLD IT FOR TEN DAYS.
I'M NOT SURE SHE'LL BE BACK.
SHE'S AWAY, WORKING.
IT'S AN OPEN-ENDED RESEARCH PROJECT.
SO'S LIFE.
WE HAVE THE SAME ADDRESS.
I SAID IT'S FINE. I REMEMBER YOU.
WAIT THERE. I'LL GET IT FOR YOU.

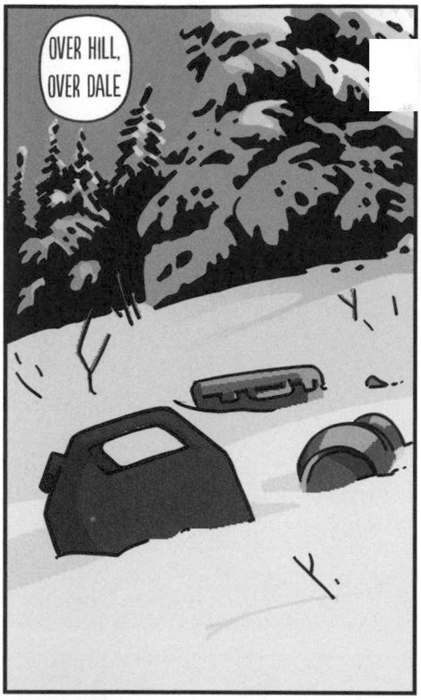
OVER HILL, OVER DALE

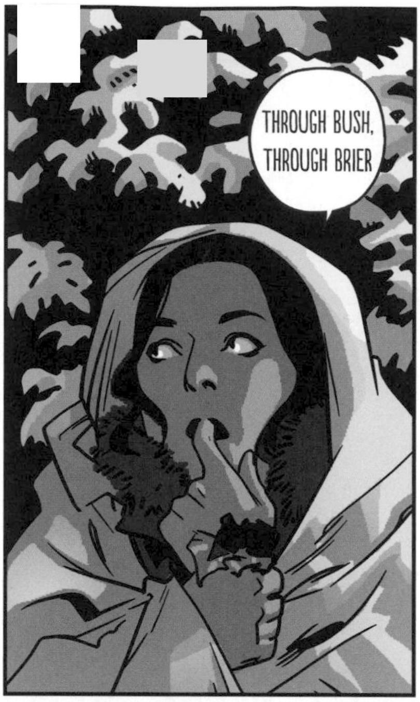
THROUGH BUSH, THROUGH BRIER

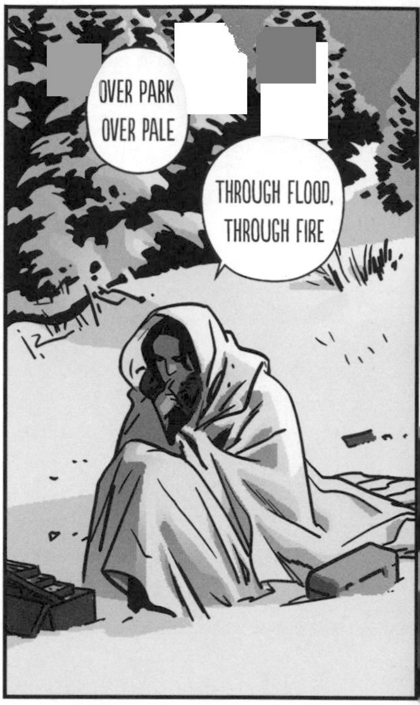
OVER PARK OVER PALE
THROUGH FLOOD, THROUGH FIRE

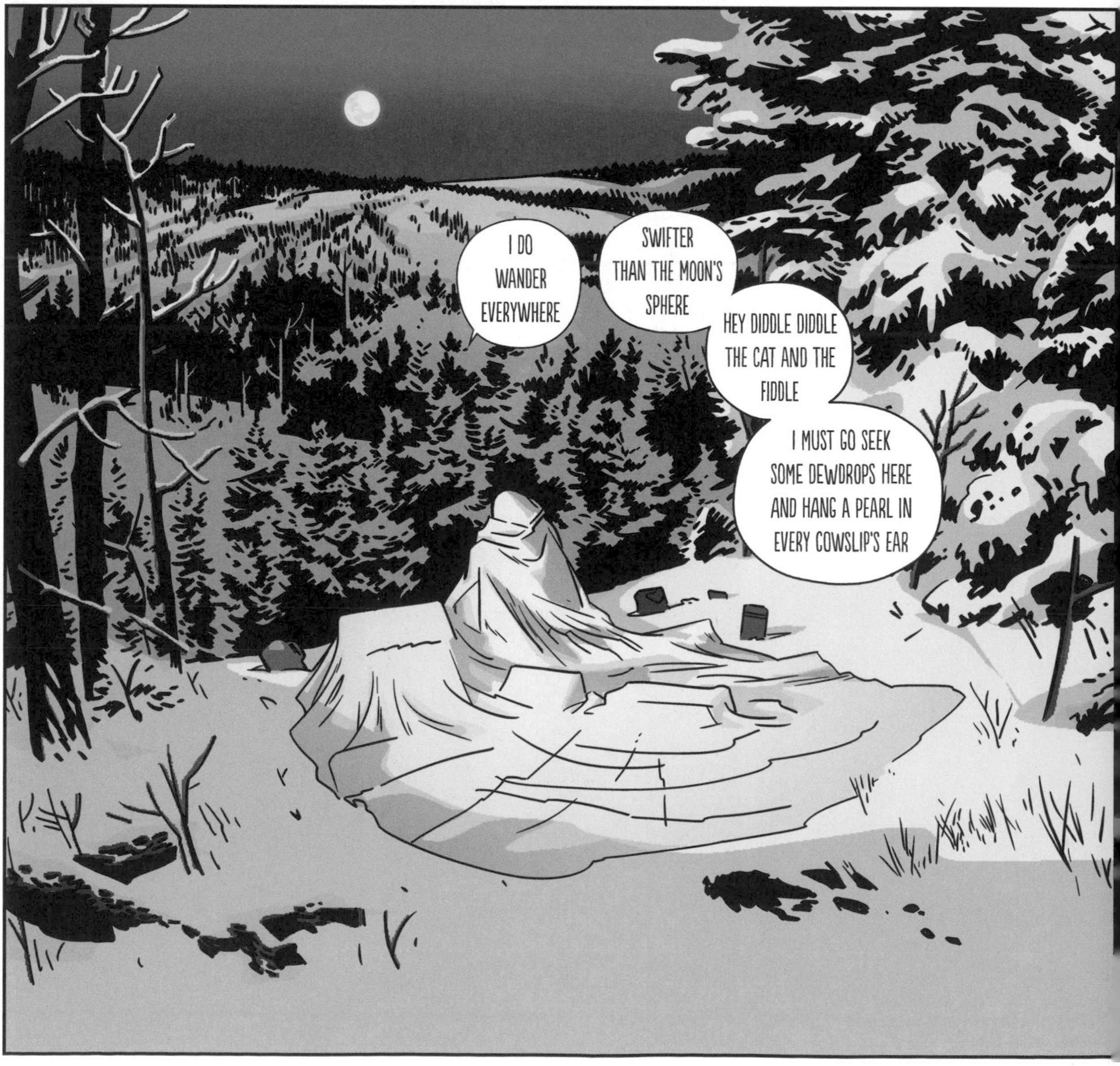
I DO WANDER EVERYWHERE
SWIFTER THAN THE MOON'S SPHERE
HEY DIDDLE DIDDLE THE CAT AND THE FIDDLE
I MUST GO SEEK SOME DEWDROPS HERE AND HANG A PEARL IN EVERY COWSLIP'S EAR

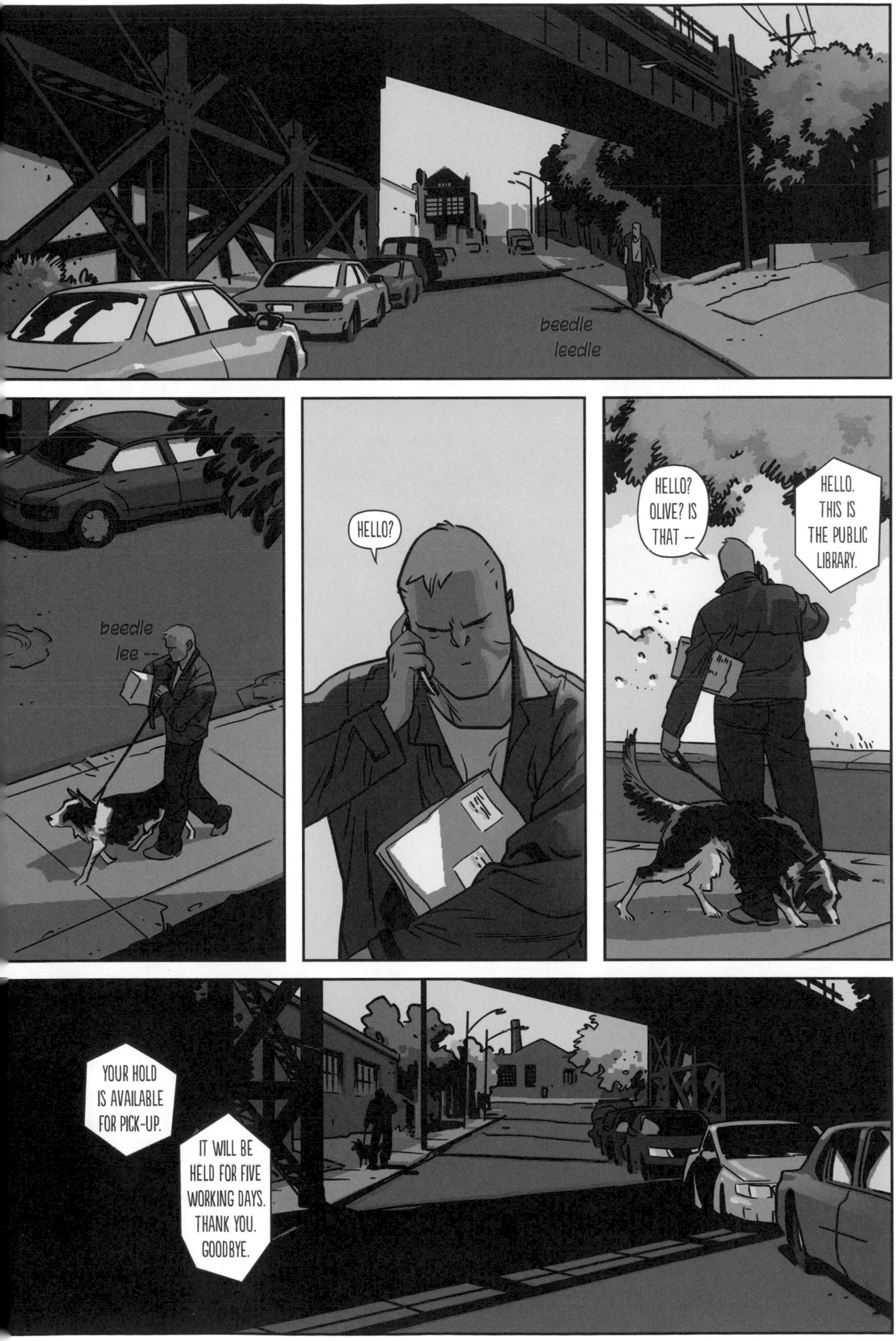

beedle
leedle
beedle
lee
HELLO?
HELLO? OLIVE? IS THAT --
HELLO. THIS IS THE PUBLIC LIBRARY.
YOUR HOLD IS AVAILABLE FOR PICK-UP.
IT WILL BE HELD FOR FIVE WORKING DAYS. THANK YOU. GOODBYE.

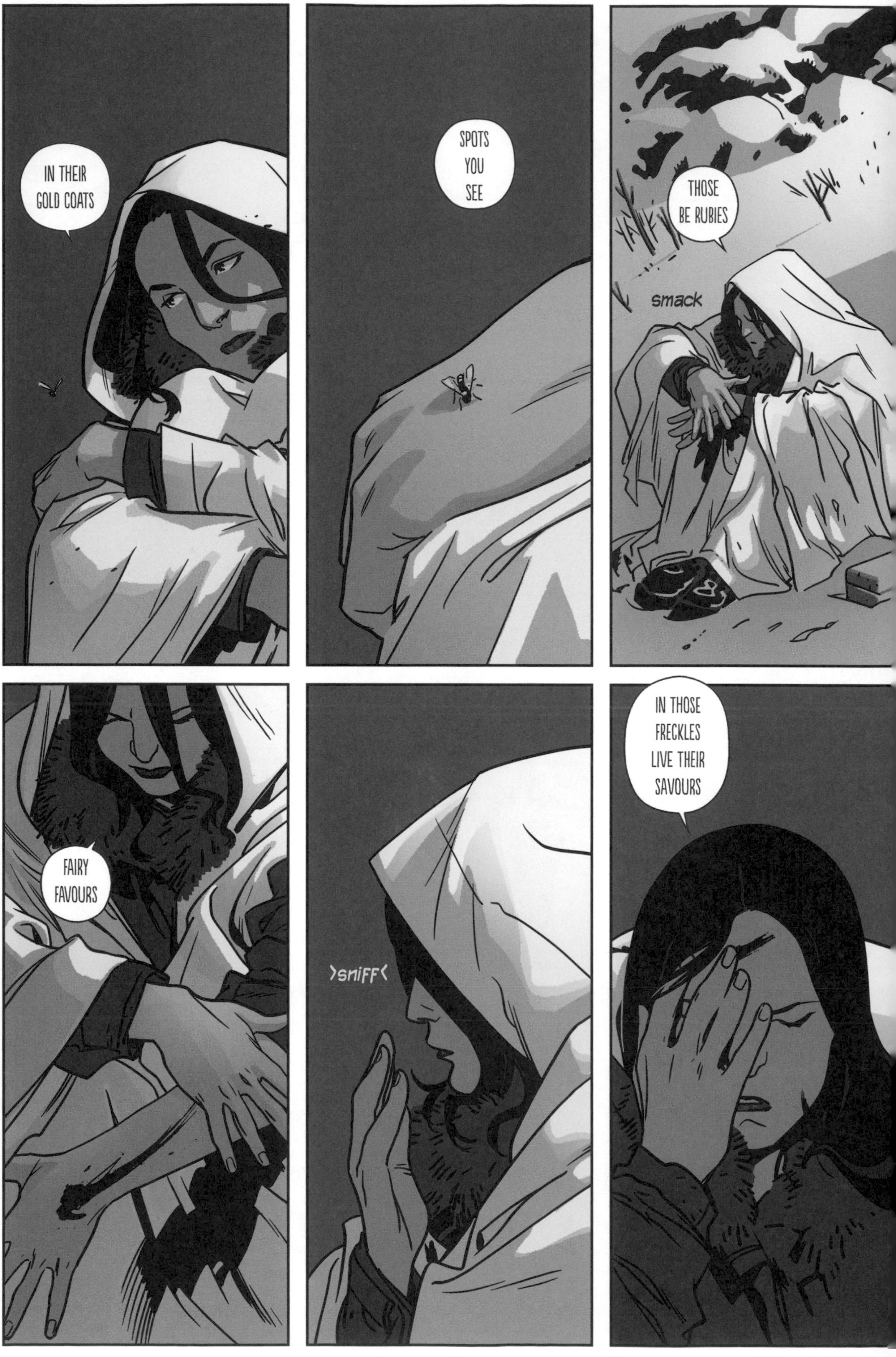

IN THEIR GOLD COATS
SPOTS YOU SEE
THOSE BE RUBIES
smack
FAIRY FAVOURS
>sniff<
IN THOSE FRECKLES LIVE THEIR SAVOURS

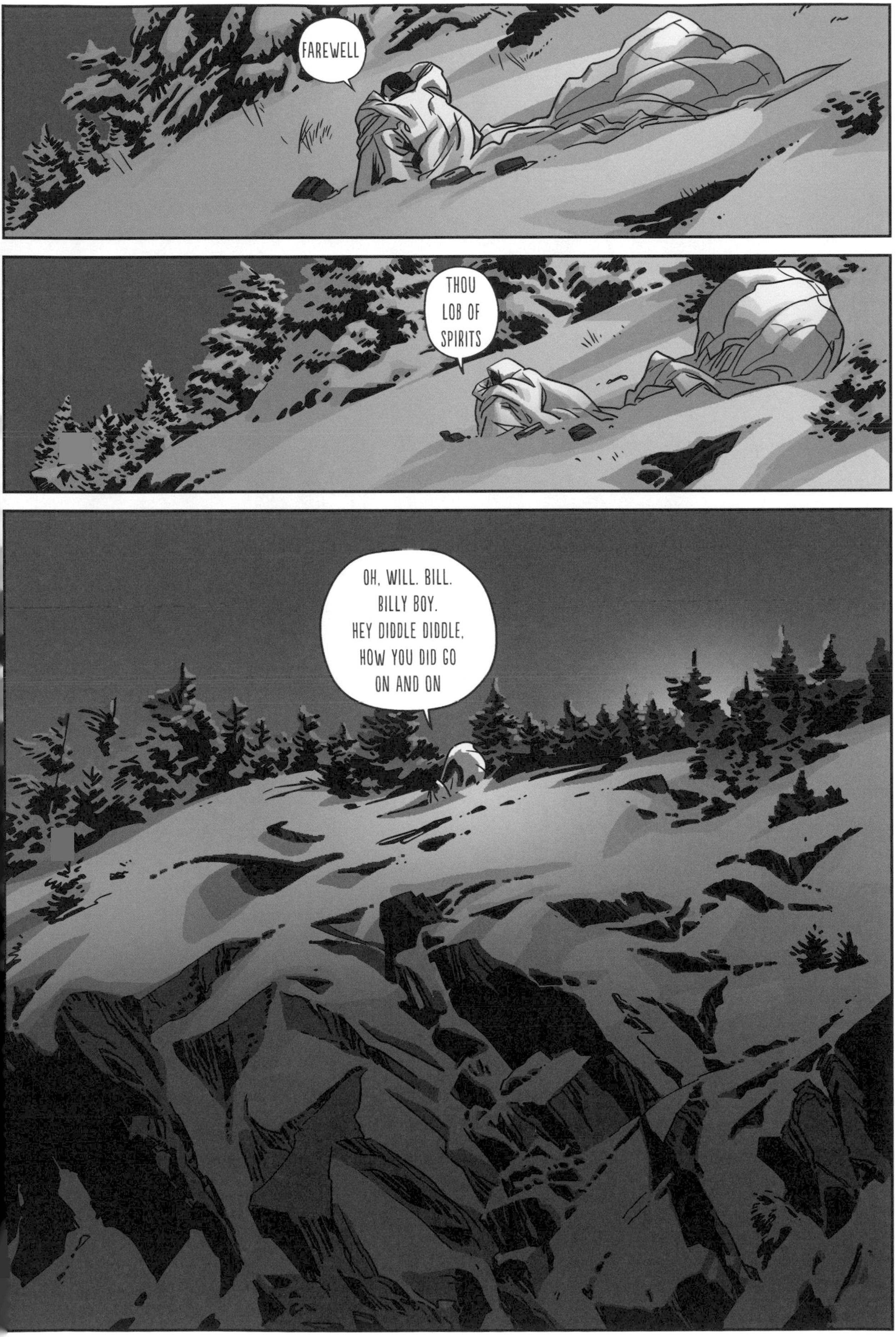
FAREWELL
THOU LOB OF SPIRITS
OH, WILL. BILL. BILLY BOY. HEY DIDDLE DIDDLE, HOW YOU DID GO ON AND ON

rattle
rattle

beep

OLIVE?

YOU HAVE ONE NEW MESSAGE.

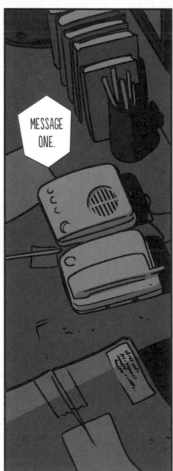

MESSAGE ONE.

GODDAMMIT RED, WHERE ARE YOU?

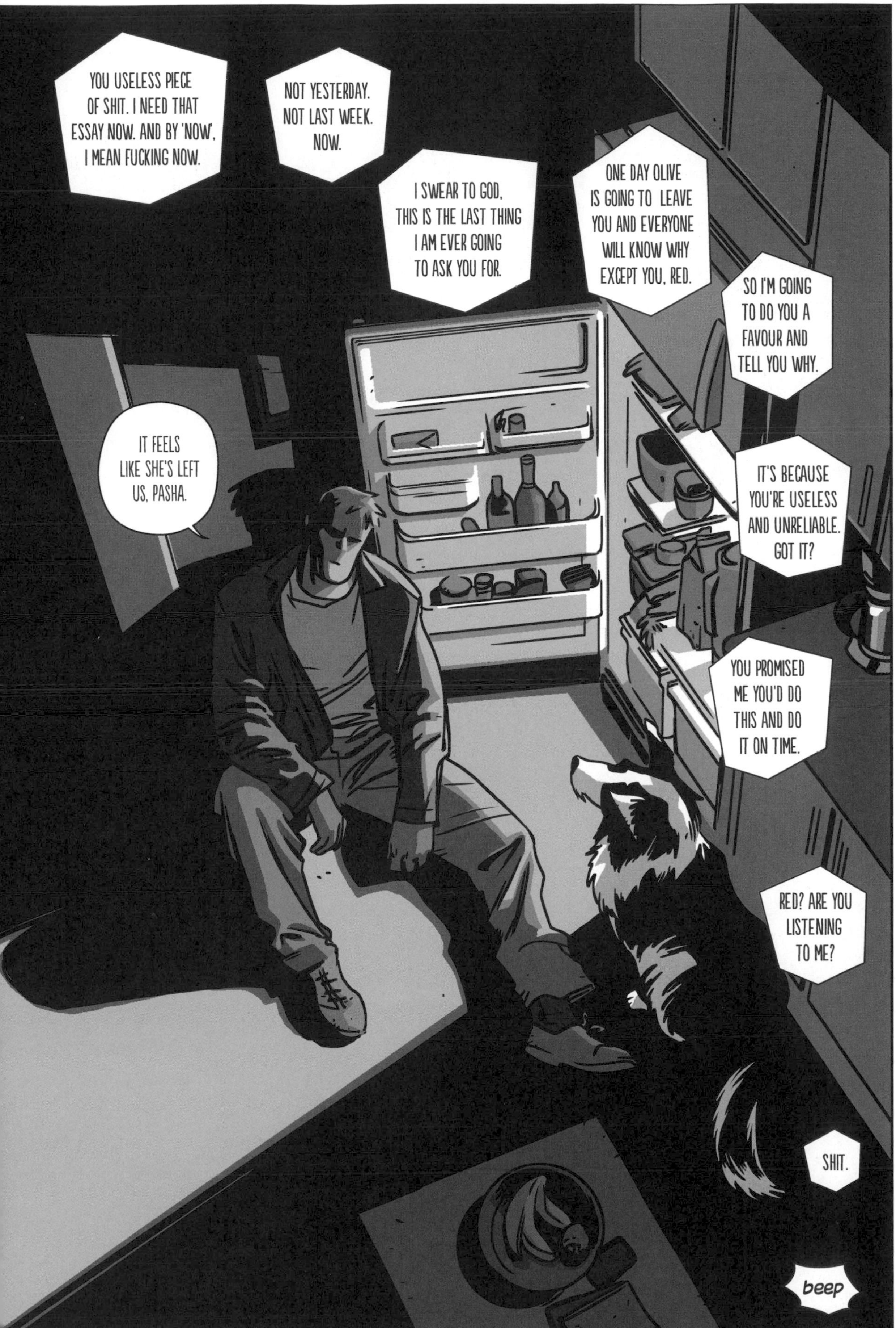
YOU USELESS PIECE OF SHIT. I NEED THAT ESSAY NOW. AND BY 'NOW', I MEAN FUCKING NOW.
NOT YESTERDAY. NOT LAST WEEK. NOW.
I SWEAR TO GOD, THIS IS THE LAST THING I AM EVER GOING TO ASK YOU FOR.
ONE DAY OLIVE IS GOING TO LEAVE YOU AND EVERYONE WILL KNOW WHY EXCEPT YOU, RED.
SO I'M GOING TO DO YOU A FAVOUR AND TELL YOU WHY.
IT FEELS LIKE SHE'S LEFT US, PASHA.
IT'S BECAUSE YOU'RE USELESS AND UNRELIABLE. GOT IT?
YOU PROMISED ME YOU'D DO THIS AND DO IT ON TIME.
RED? ARE YOU LISTENING TO ME?
SHIT.
beep

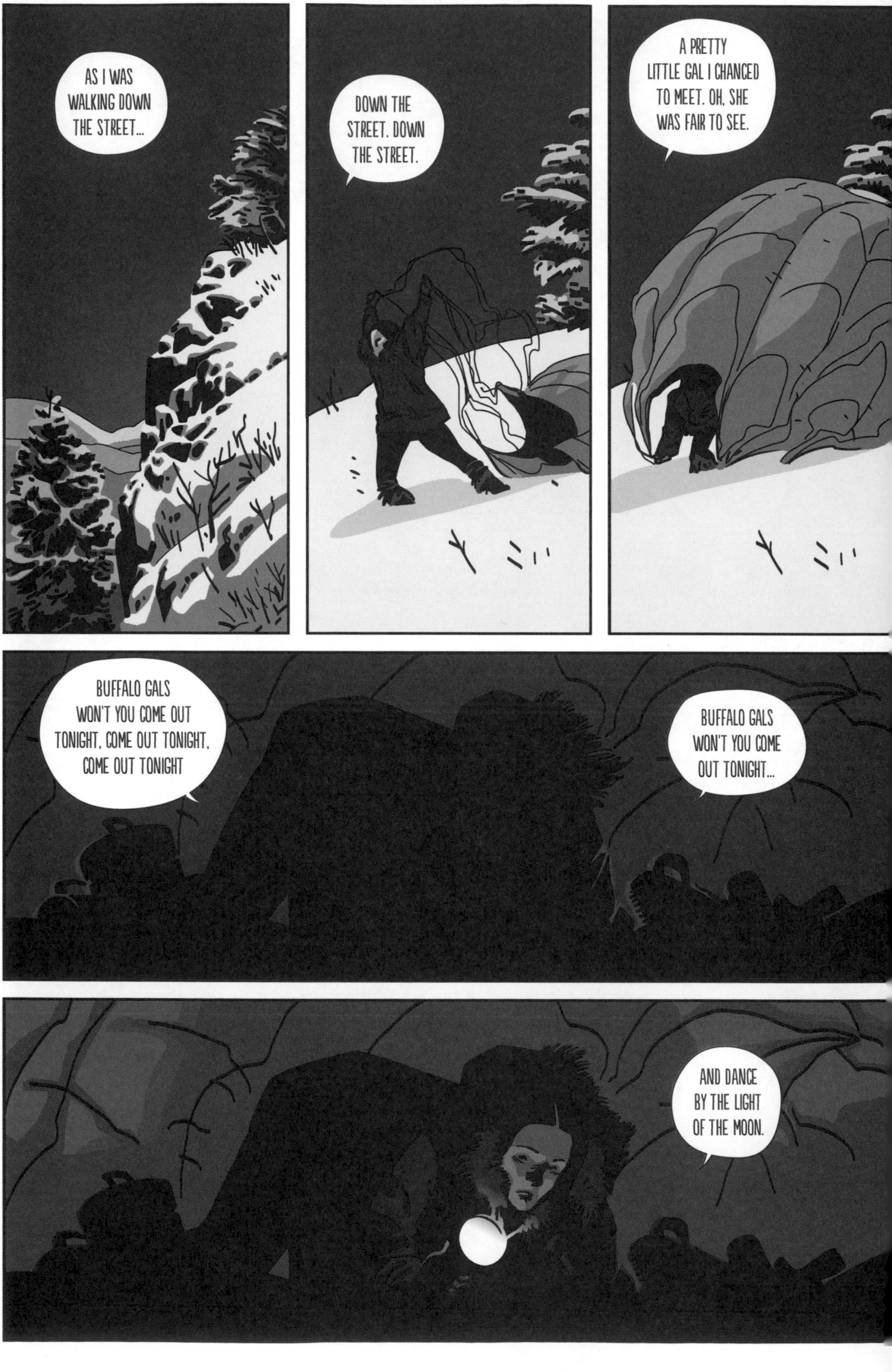

AS I WAS WALKING DOWN THE STREET...
DOWN THE STREET. DOWN THE STREET.
A PRETTY LITTLE GAL I CHANCED TO MEET. OH, SHE WAS FAIR TO SEE.
BUFFALO GALS WON'T YOU COME OUT TONIGHT, COME OUT TONIGHT, COME OUT TONIGHT
BUFFALO GALS WON'T YOU COME OUT TONIGHT...
AND DANCE BY THE LIGHT OF THE MOON.

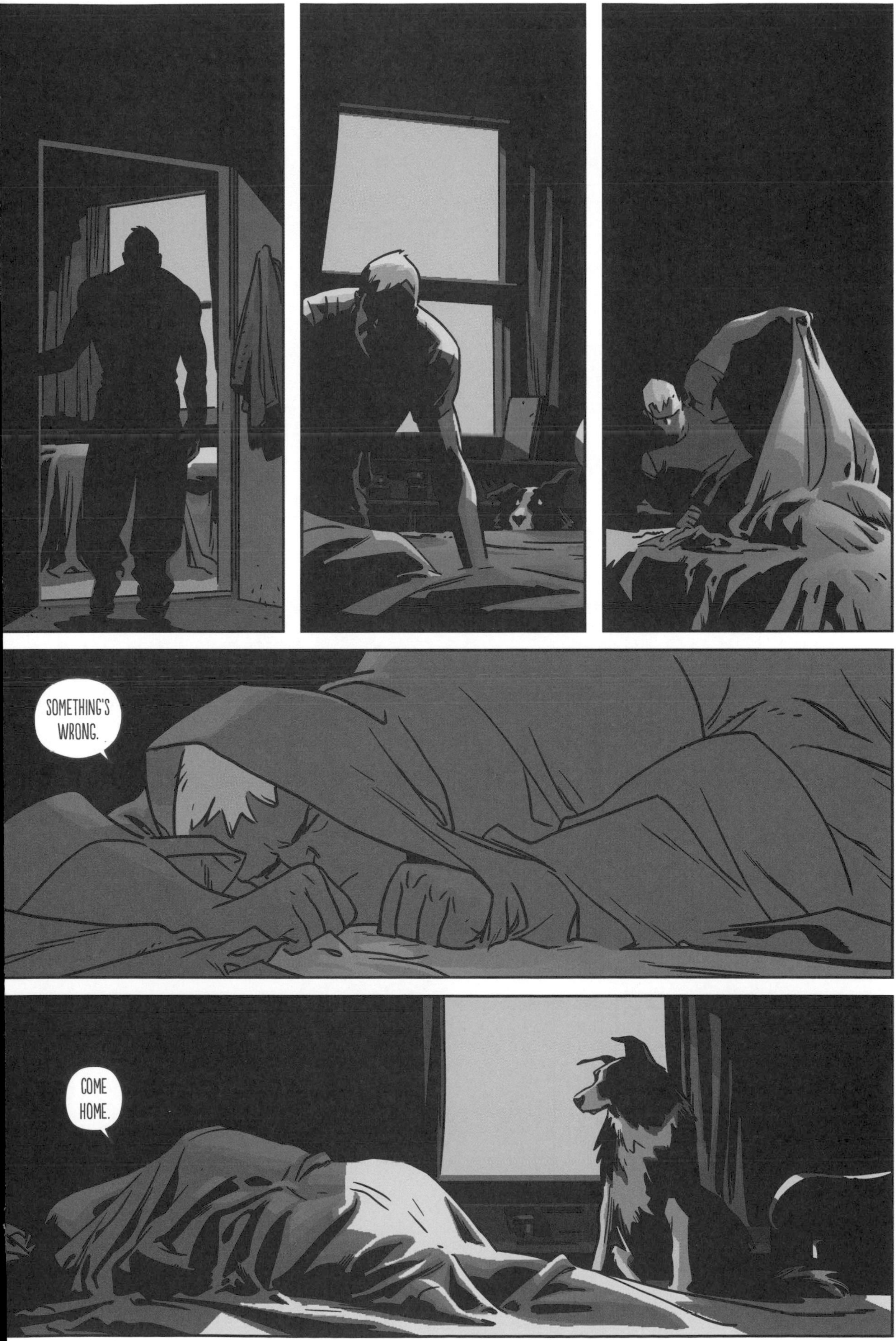
SOMETHING'S WRONG.
COME HOME.

IV

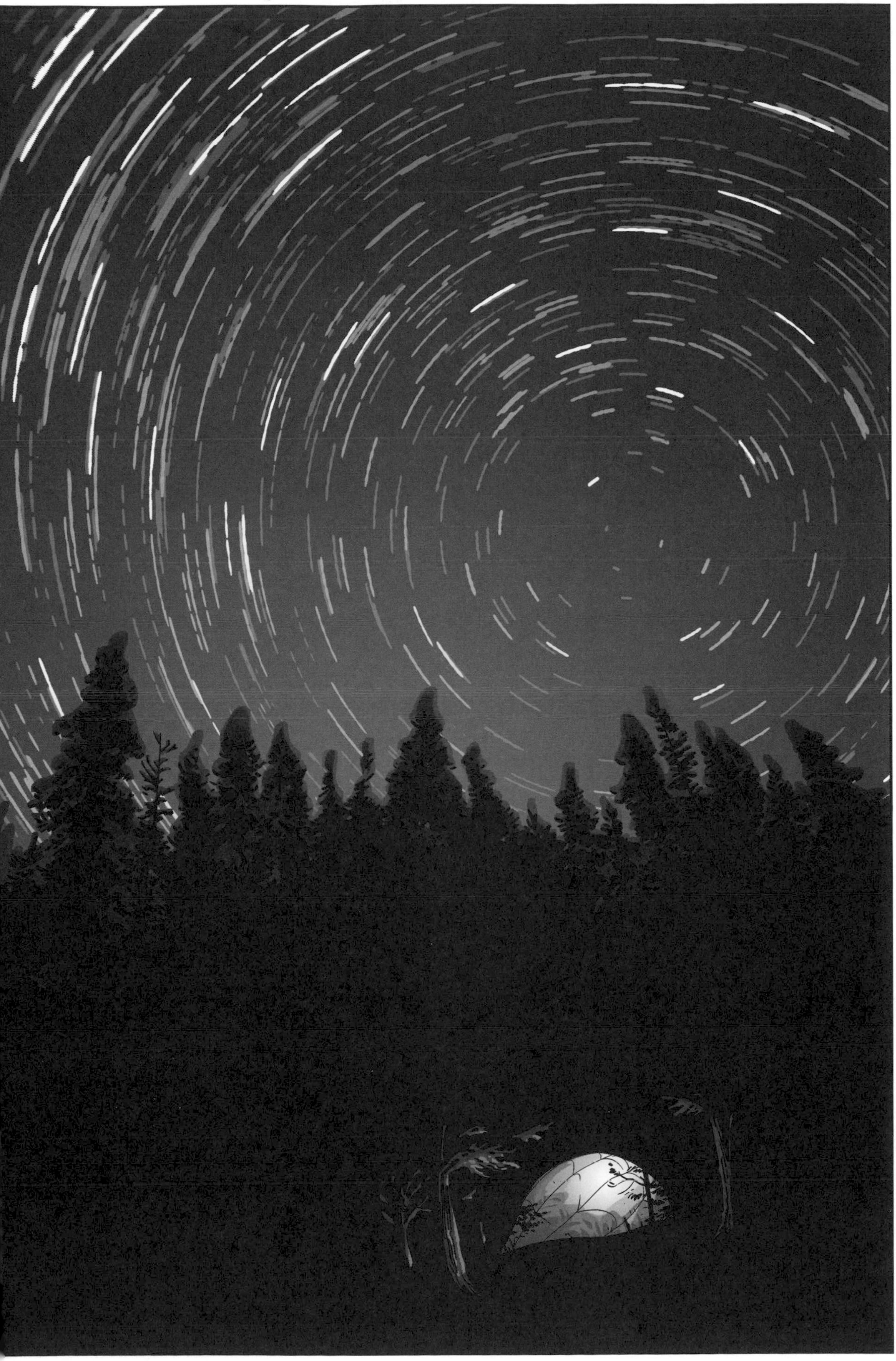

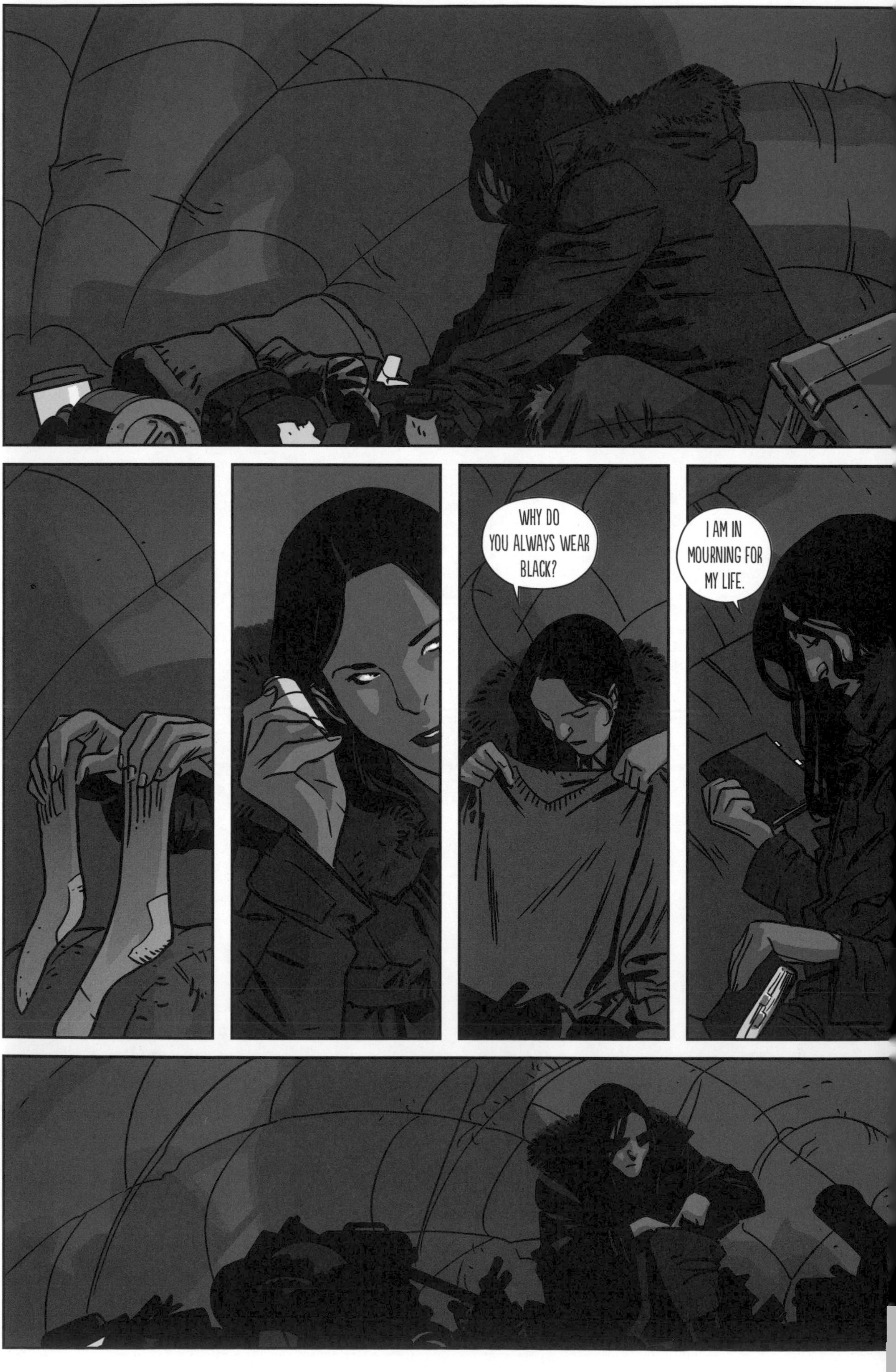
WHY DO YOU ALWAYS WEAR BLACK?
I AM IN MOURNING FOR MY LIFE.

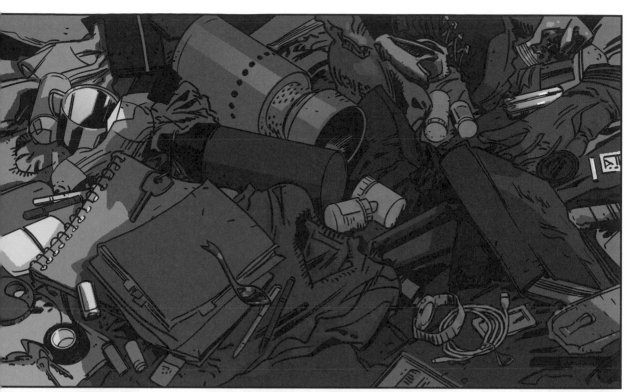

"BUT HOW ARE YOU GOING TO WRITE TO HER?" SAYS THE LANDLADY.

SHE NEVER TOLD US HER SURNAME.

ОСТРОВЪ САХАЛИНЪ

АНТОН ПАВЛОВИЧ

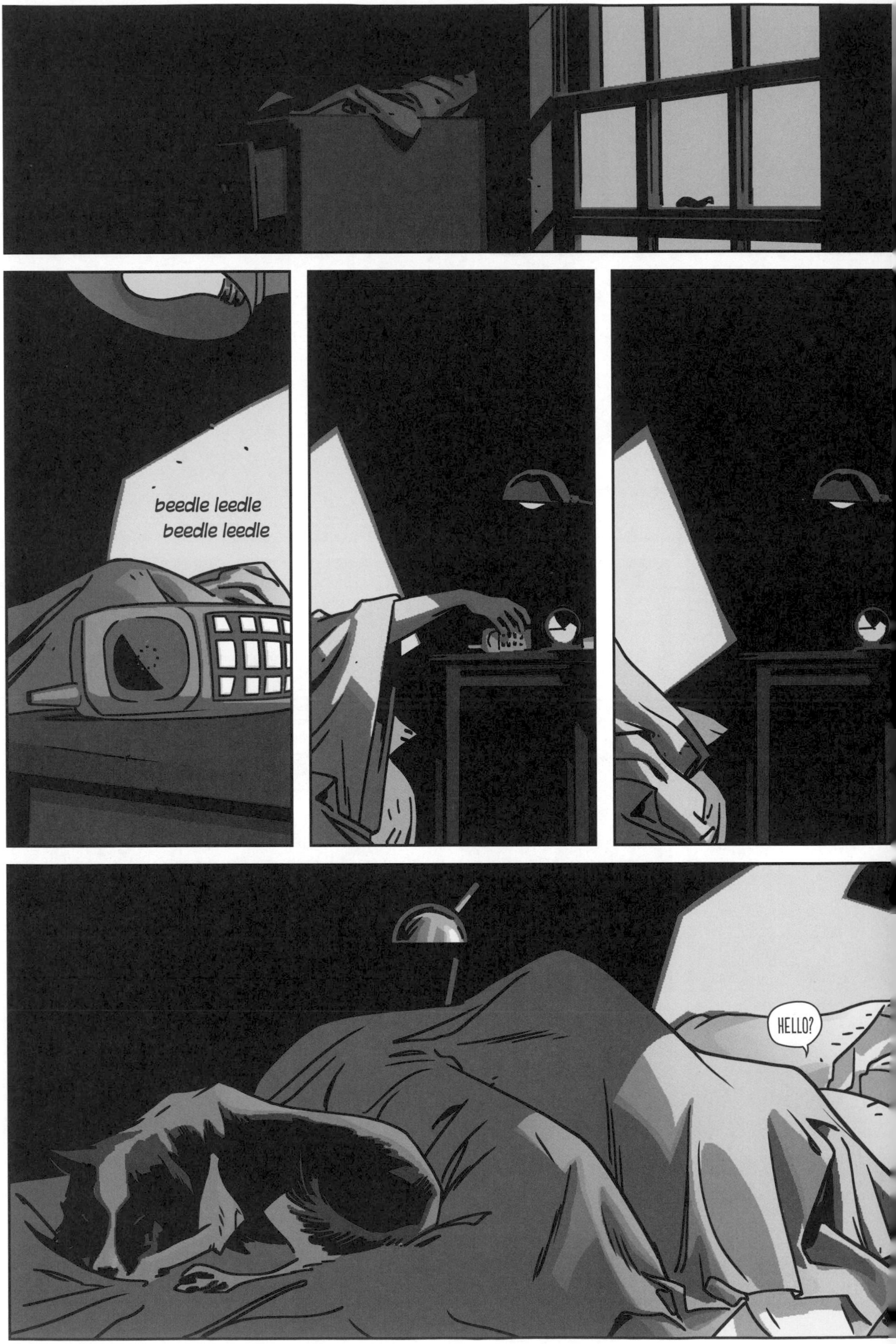
beedle leedle
beedle leedle
HELLO?

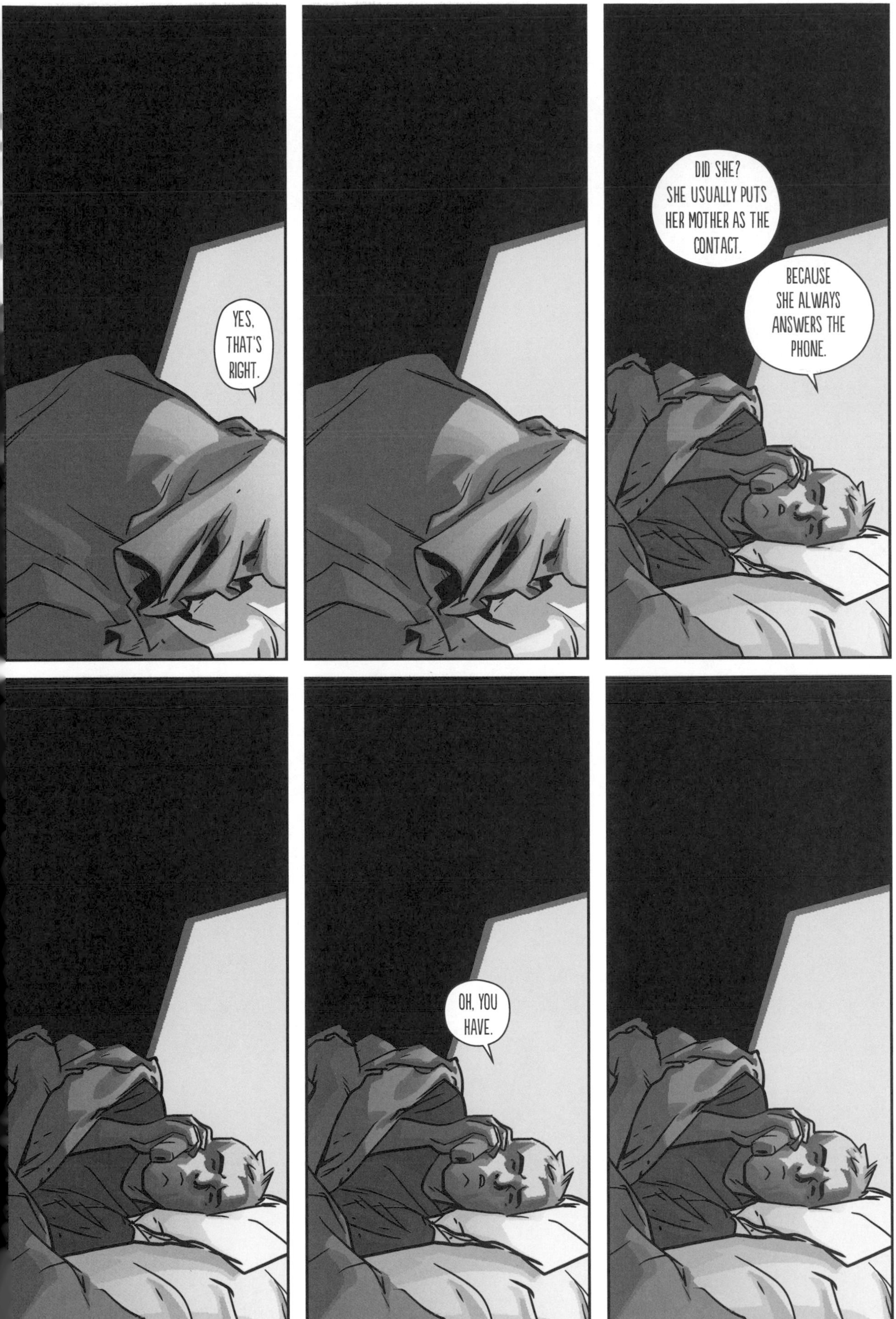
YES, THAT'S RIGHT.
DID SHE? SHE USUALLY PUTS HER MOTHER AS THE CONTACT.
BECAUSE SHE ALWAYS ANSWERS THE PHONE.
OH, YOU HAVE.

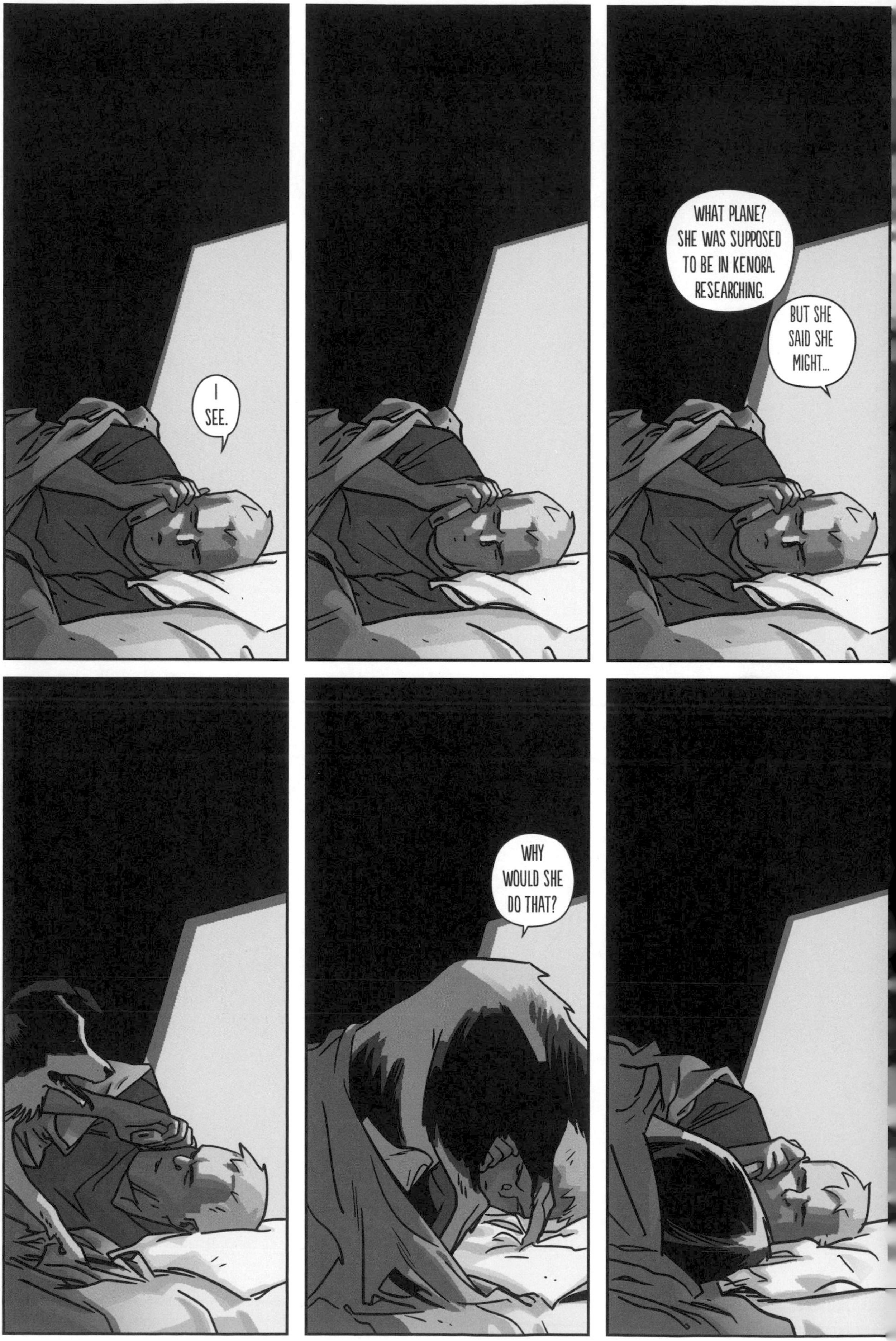
I SEE.
WHAT PLANE? SHE WAS SUPPOSED TO BE IN KENORA. RESEARCHING.
BUT SHE SAID SHE MIGHT...
WHY WOULD SHE DO THAT?

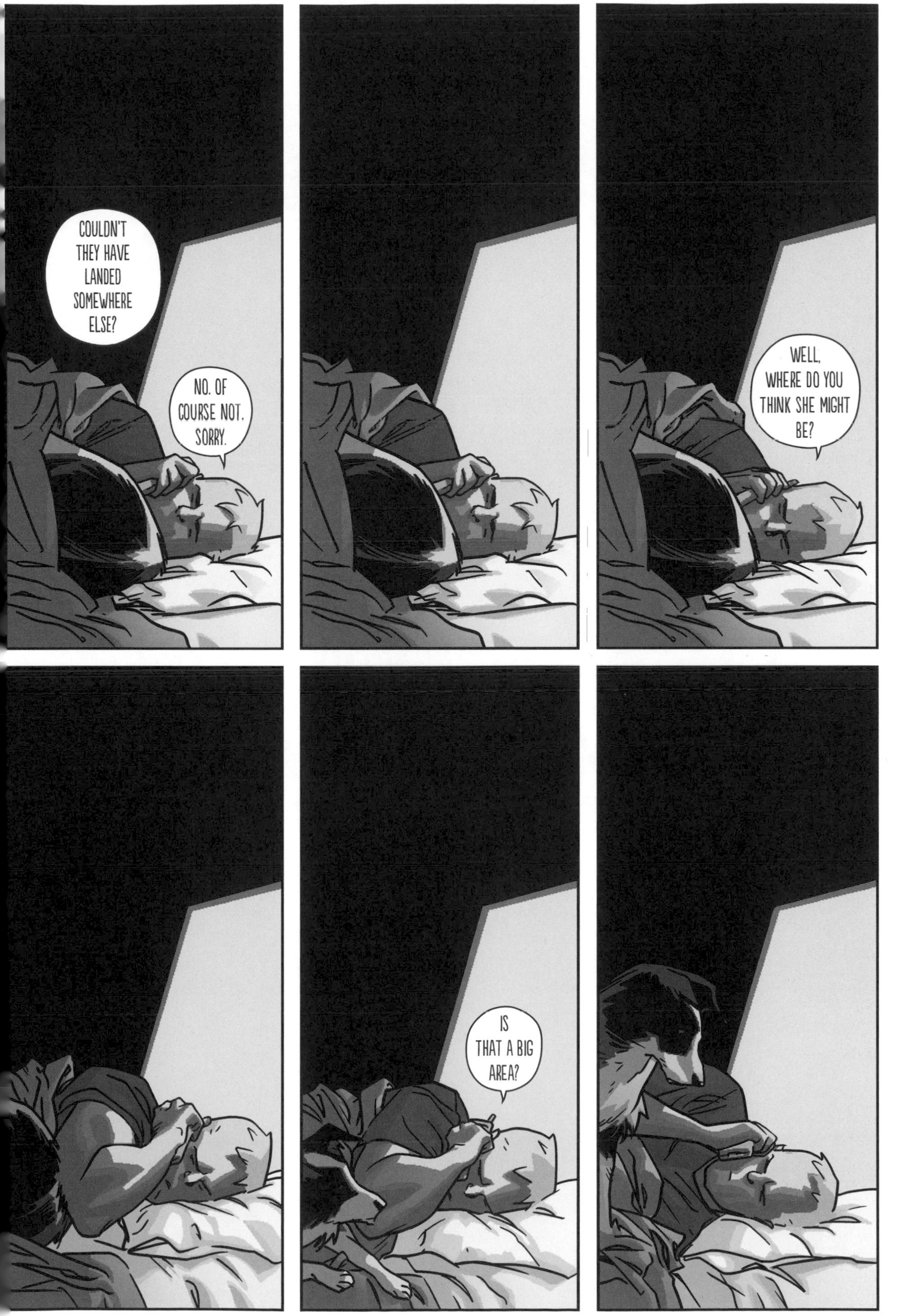
COULDN'T THEY HAVE LANDED SOMEWHERE ELSE?
NO. OF COURSE NOT. SORRY.
WELL, WHERE DO YOU THINK SHE MIGHT BE?
IS THAT A BIG AREA?

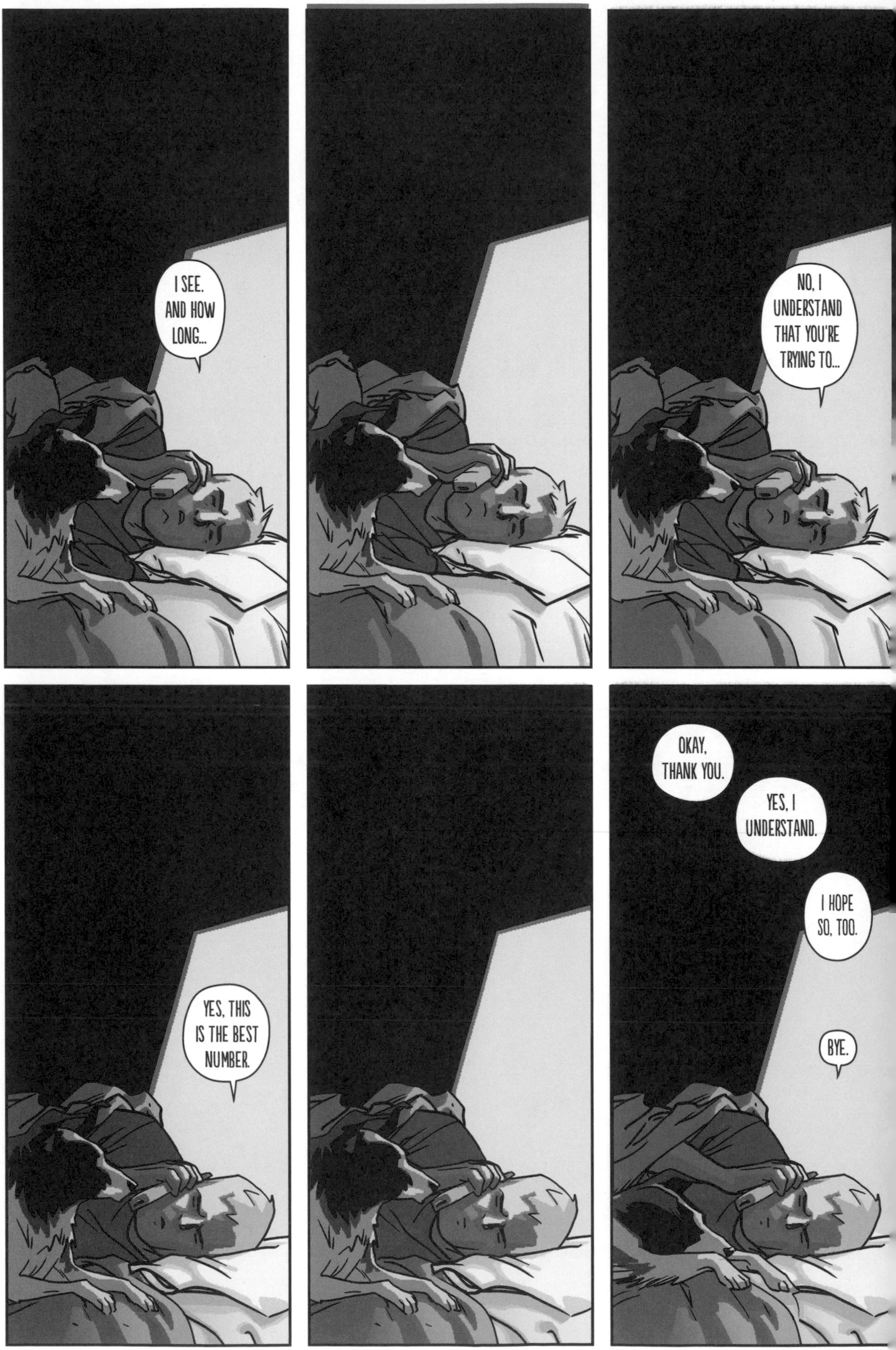
I SEE. AND HOW LONG...
NO, I UNDERSTAND THAT YOU'RE TRYING TO...
YES, THIS IS THE BEST NUMBER.
OKAY, THANK YOU.
YES, I UNDERSTAND.
I HOPE SO, TOO.
BYE.

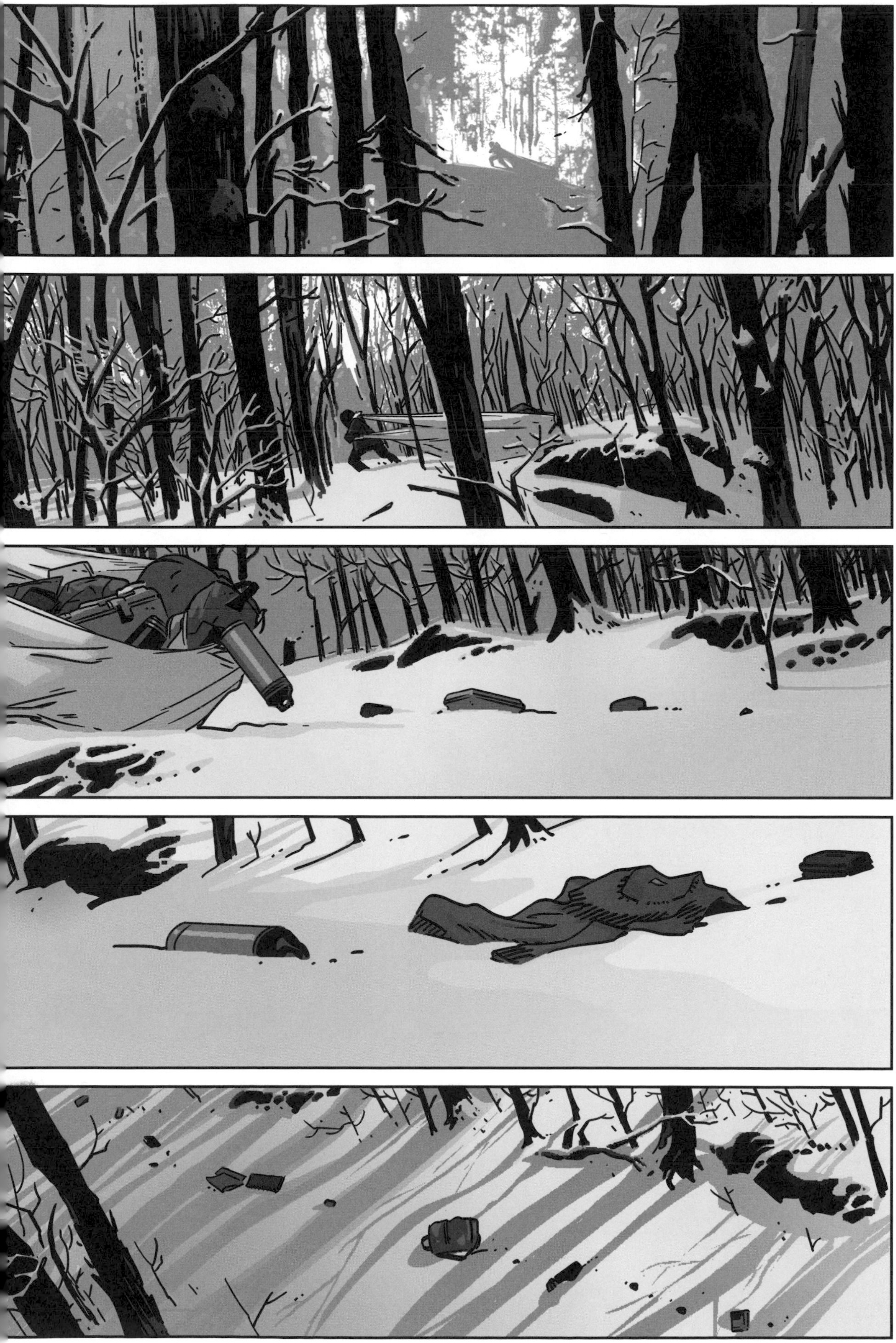

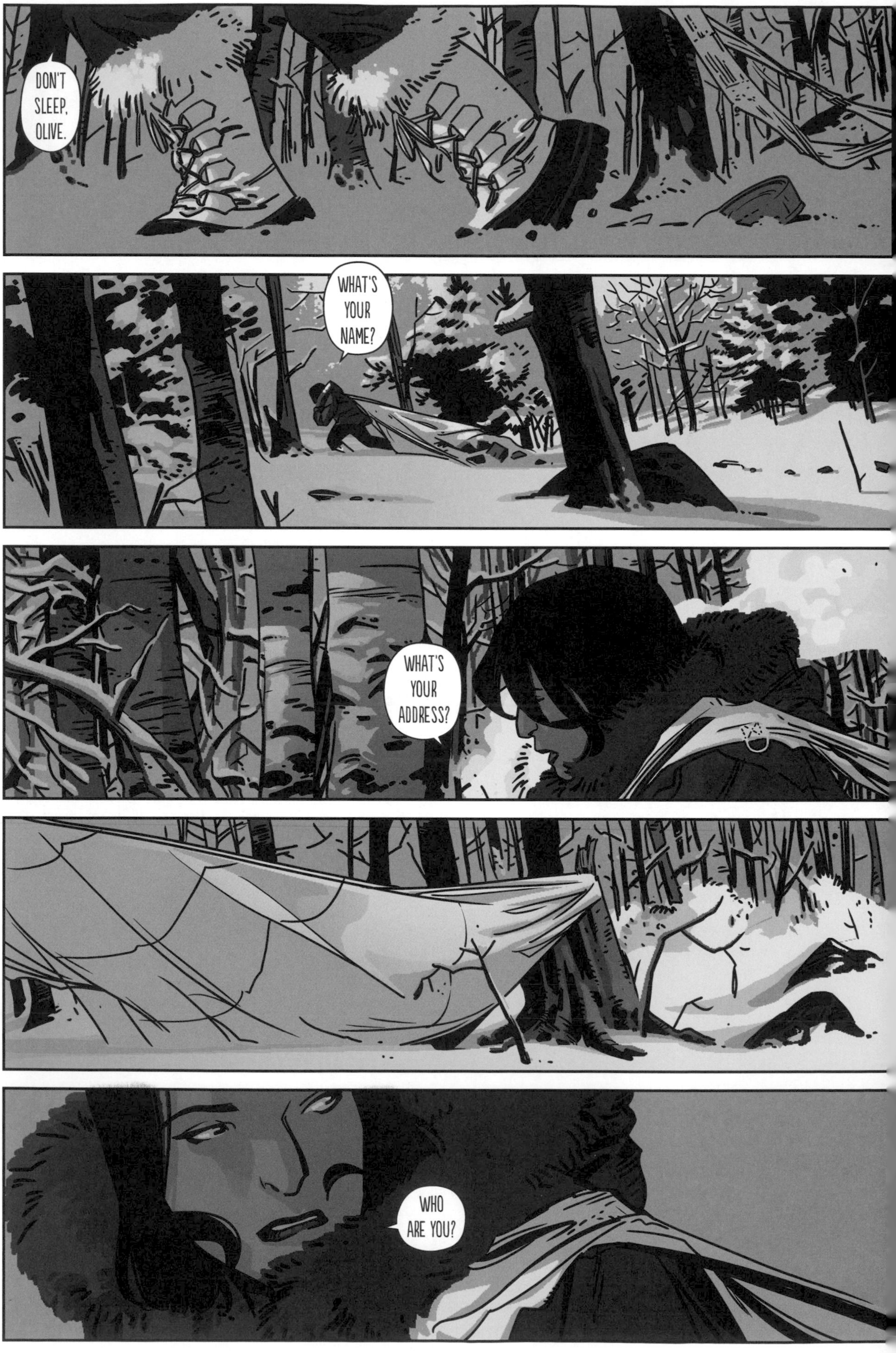
DON'T SLEEP, OLIVE.
WHAT'S YOUR NAME?
WHAT'S YOUR ADDRESS?
WHO ARE YOU?

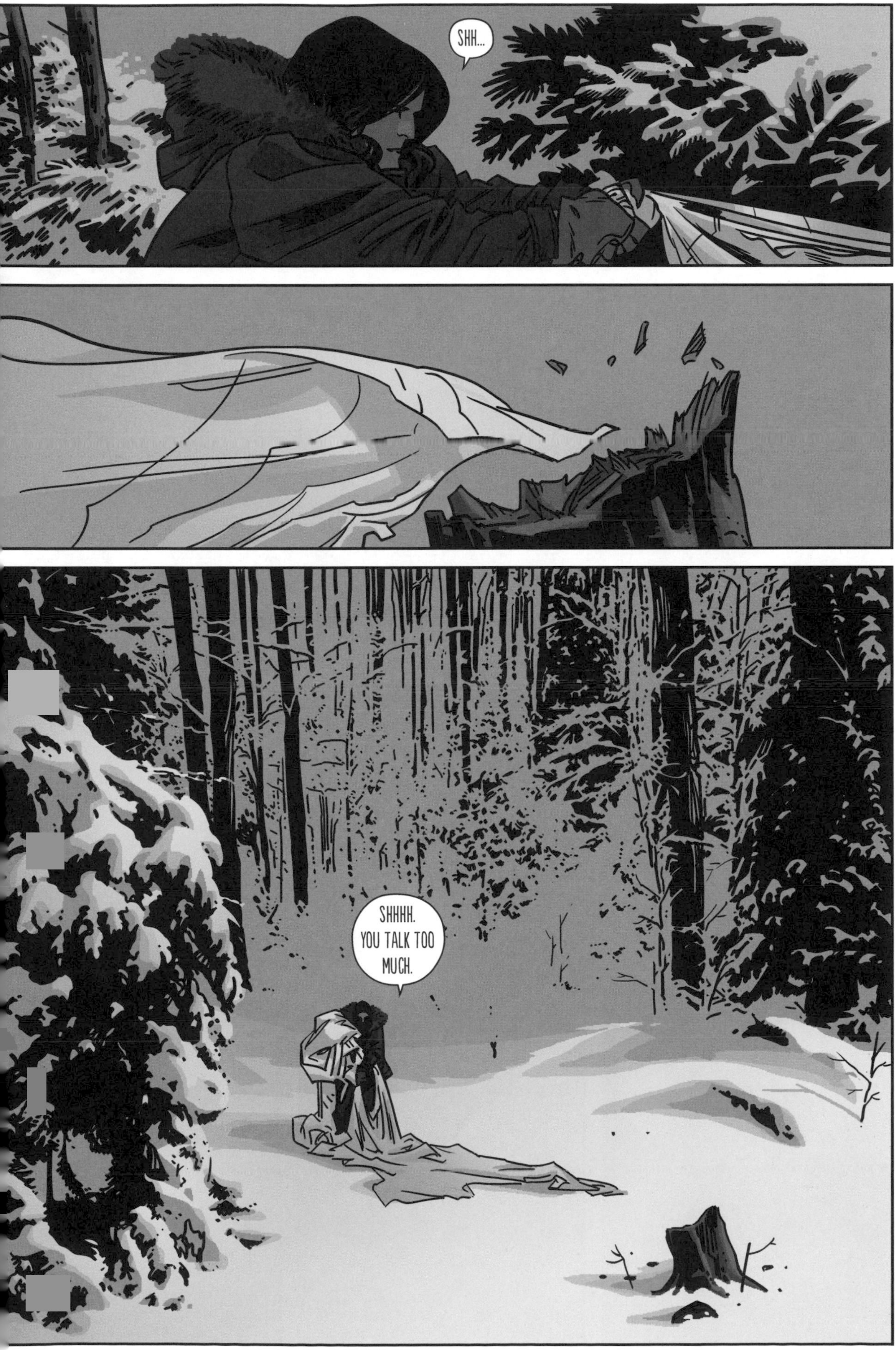
SHH...
SHHHH. YOU TALK TOO MUCH.

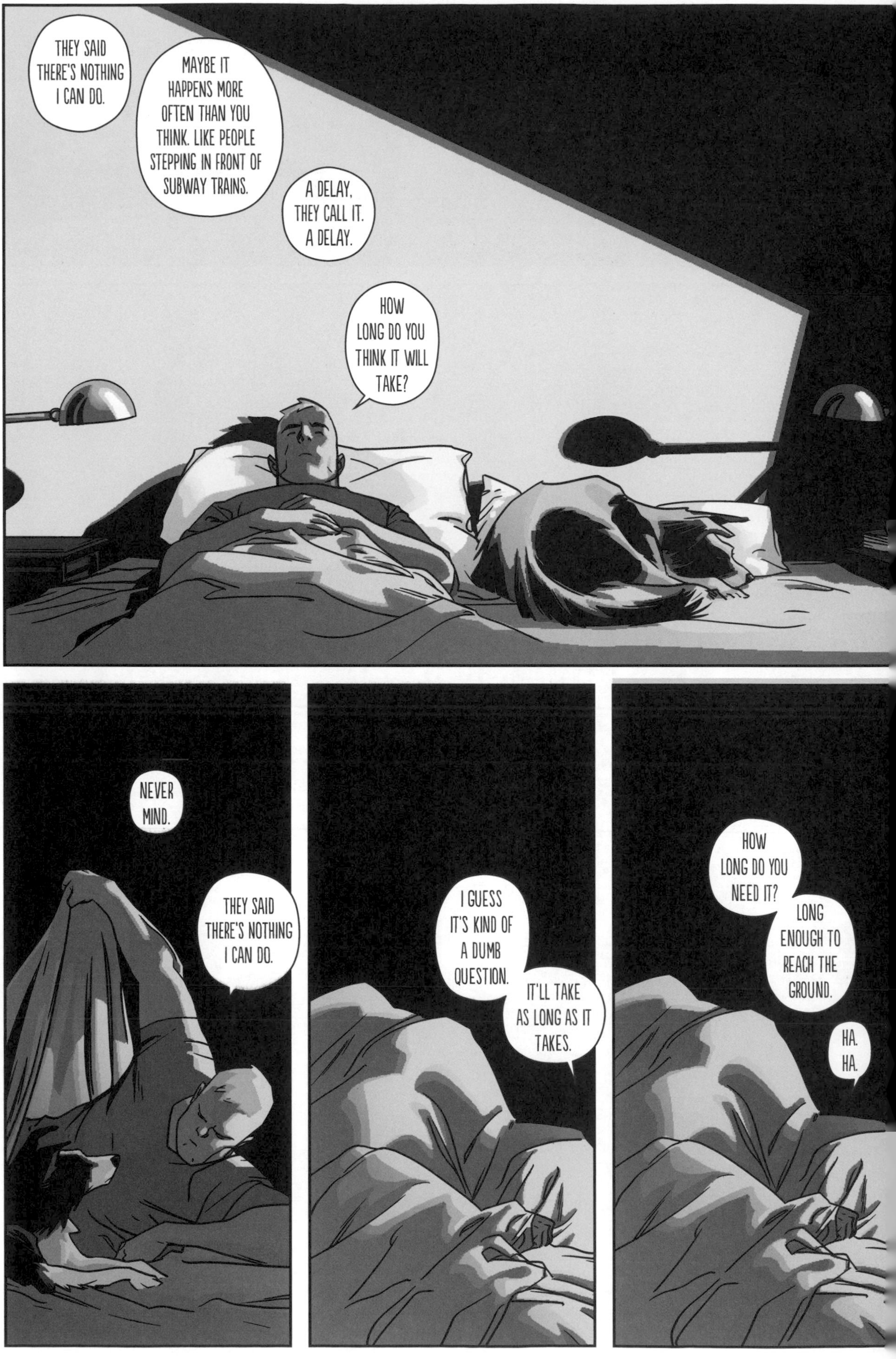
THEY SAID THERE'S NOTHING I CAN DO.
MAYBE IT HAPPENS MORE OFTEN THAN YOU THINK. LIKE PEOPLE STEPPING IN FRONT OF SUBWAY TRAINS.
A DELAY, THEY CALL IT. A DELAY.
HOW LONG DO YOU THINK IT WILL TAKE?
NEVER MIND.
THEY SAID THERE'S NOTHING I CAN DO.
I GUESS IT'S KIND OF A DUMB QUESTION.
IT'LL TAKE AS LONG AS IT TAKES.
HOW LONG DO YOU NEED IT?
LONG ENOUGH TO REACH THE GROUND.
HA. HA.

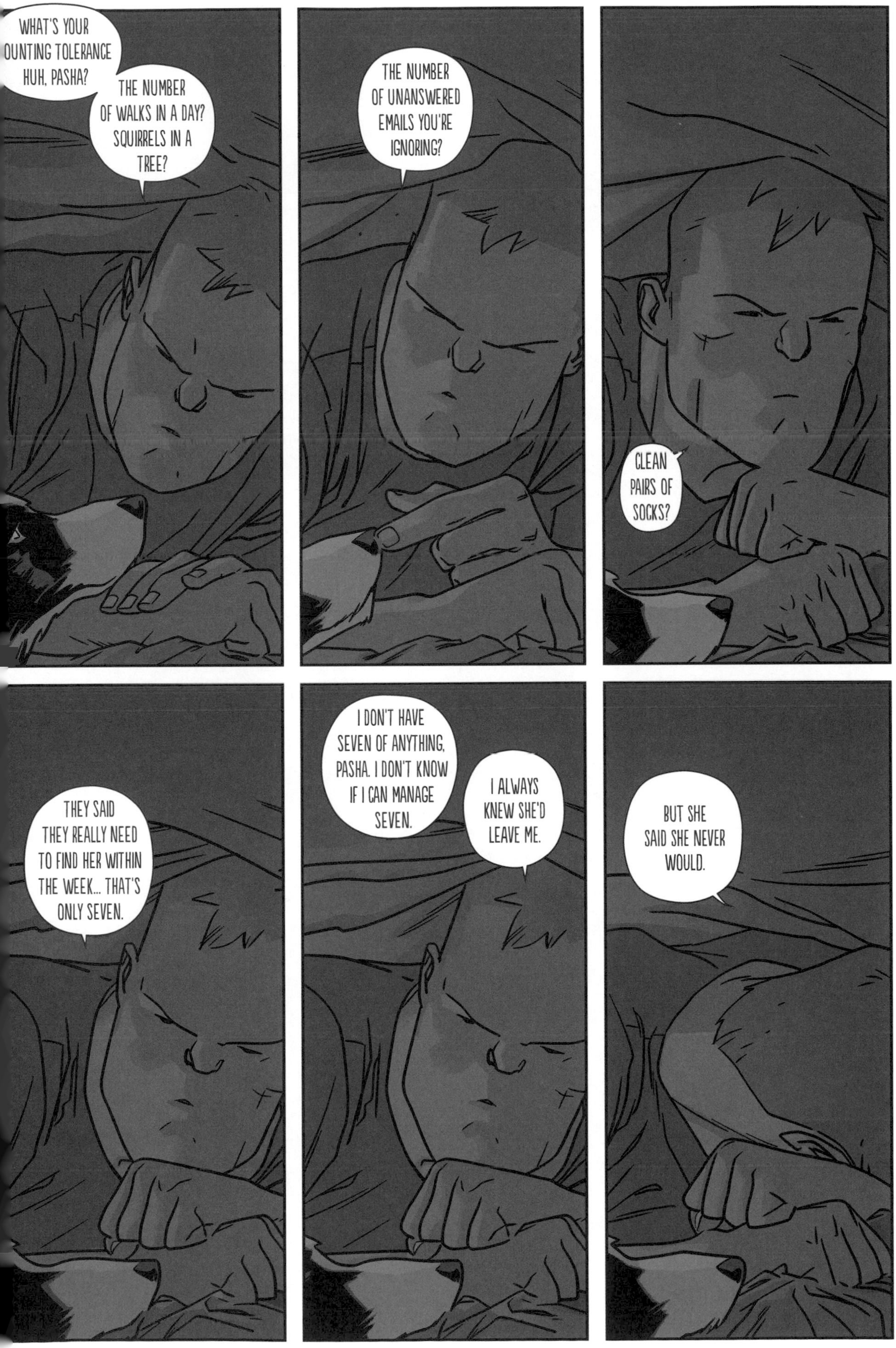
WHAT'S YOUR OUNTING TOLERANCE HUH, PASHA?
THE NUMBER OF WALKS IN A DAY? SQUIRRELS IN A TREE?
THE NUMBER OF UNANSWERED EMAILS YOU'RE IGNORING?
CLEAN PAIRS OF SOCKS?
THEY SAID THEY REALLY NEED TO FIND HER WITHIN THE WEEK... THAT'S ONLY SEVEN.
I DON'T HAVE SEVEN OF ANYTHING, PASHA. I DON'T KNOW IF I CAN MANAGE SEVEN.
I ALWAYS KNEW SHE'D LEAVE ME.
BUT SHE SAID SHE NEVER WOULD.

V

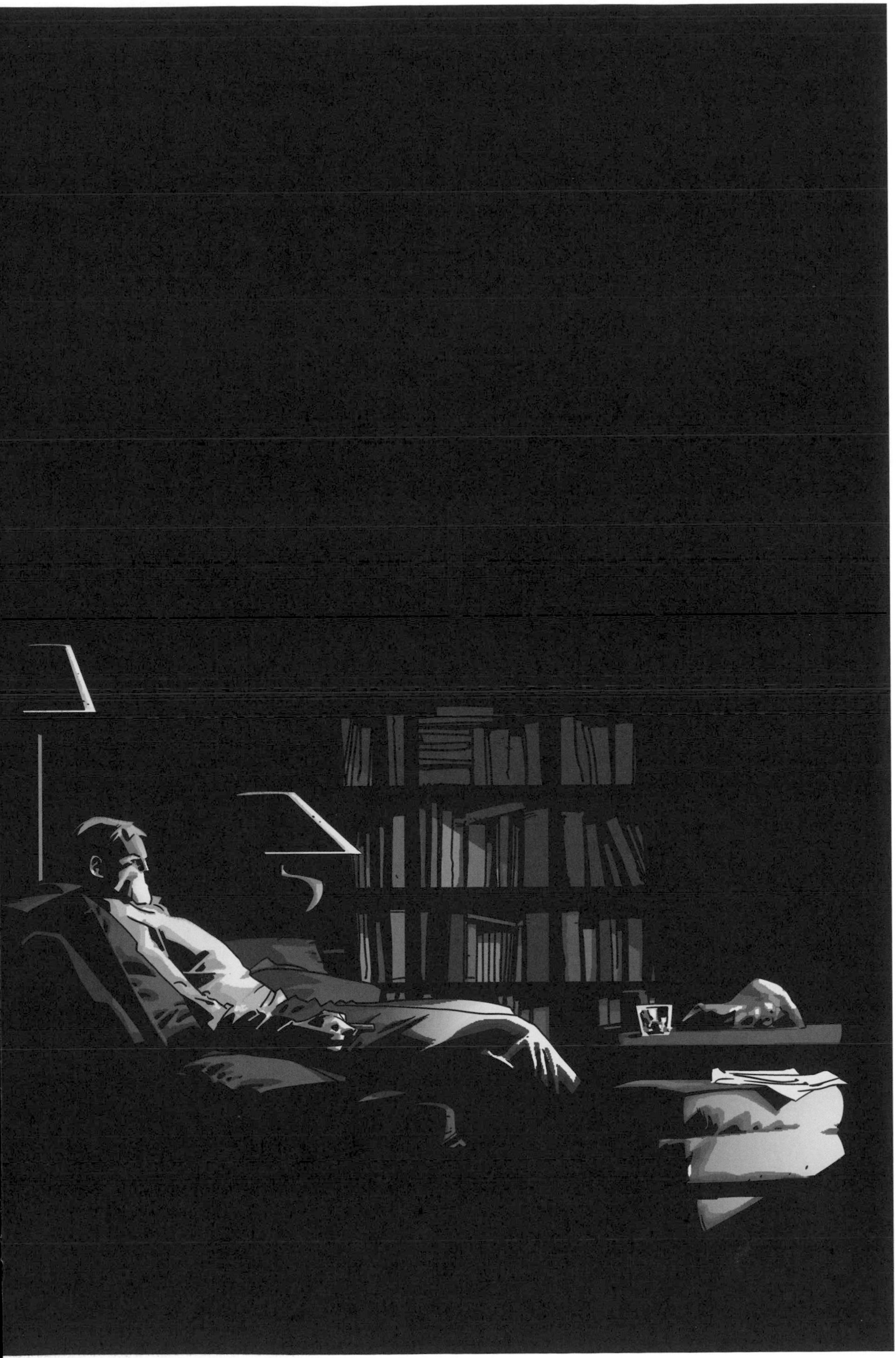

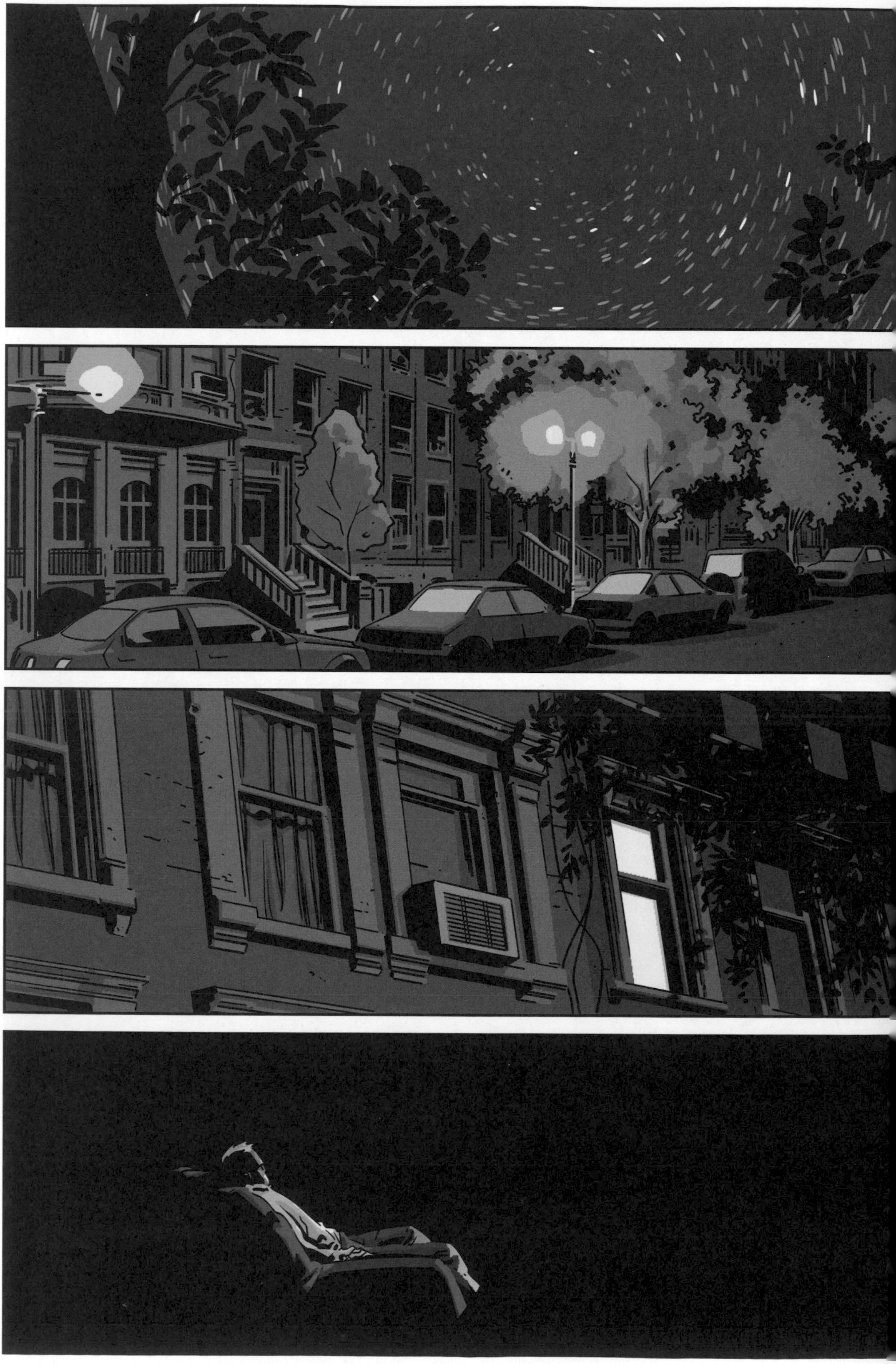

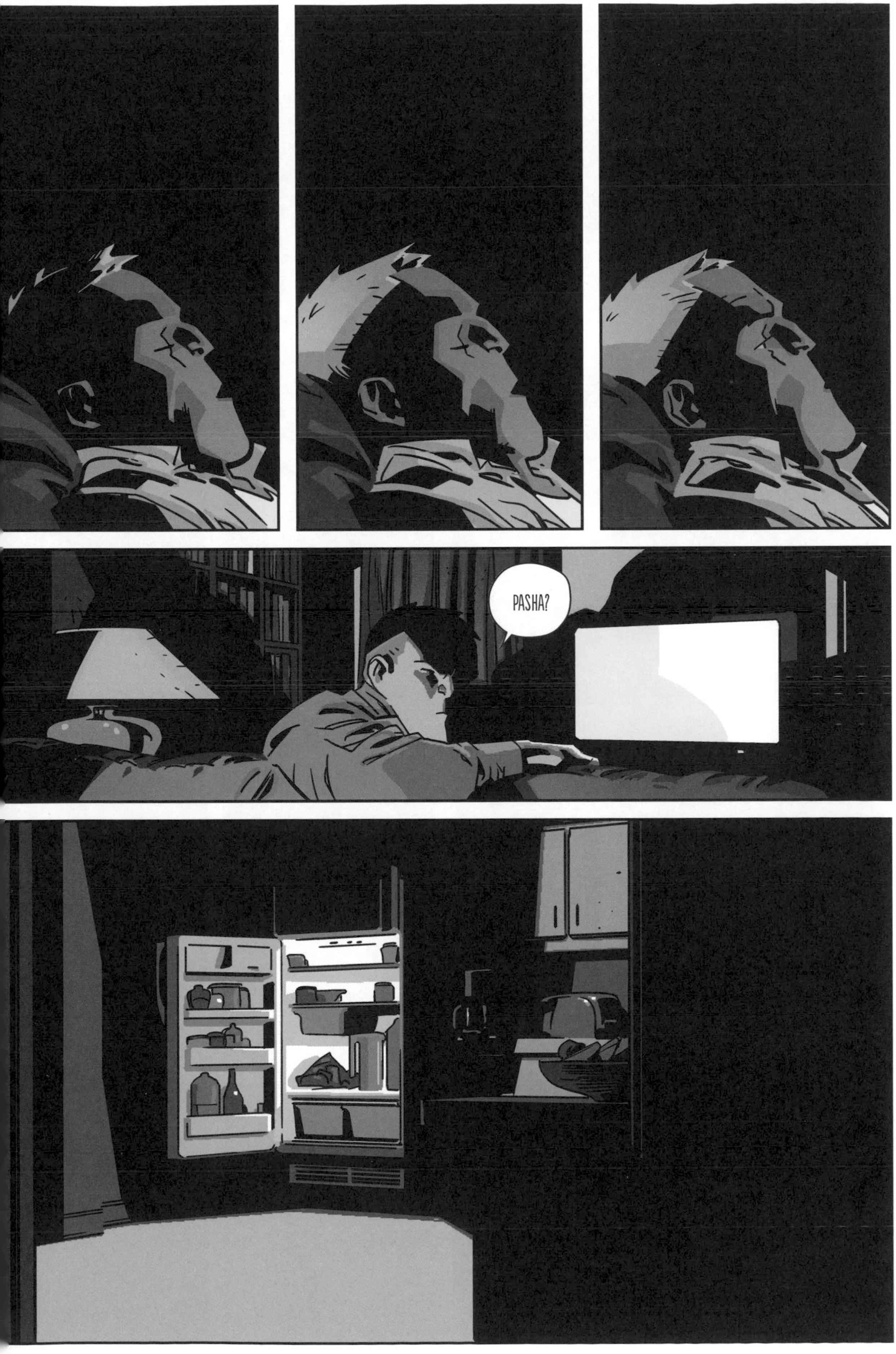
PASHA?

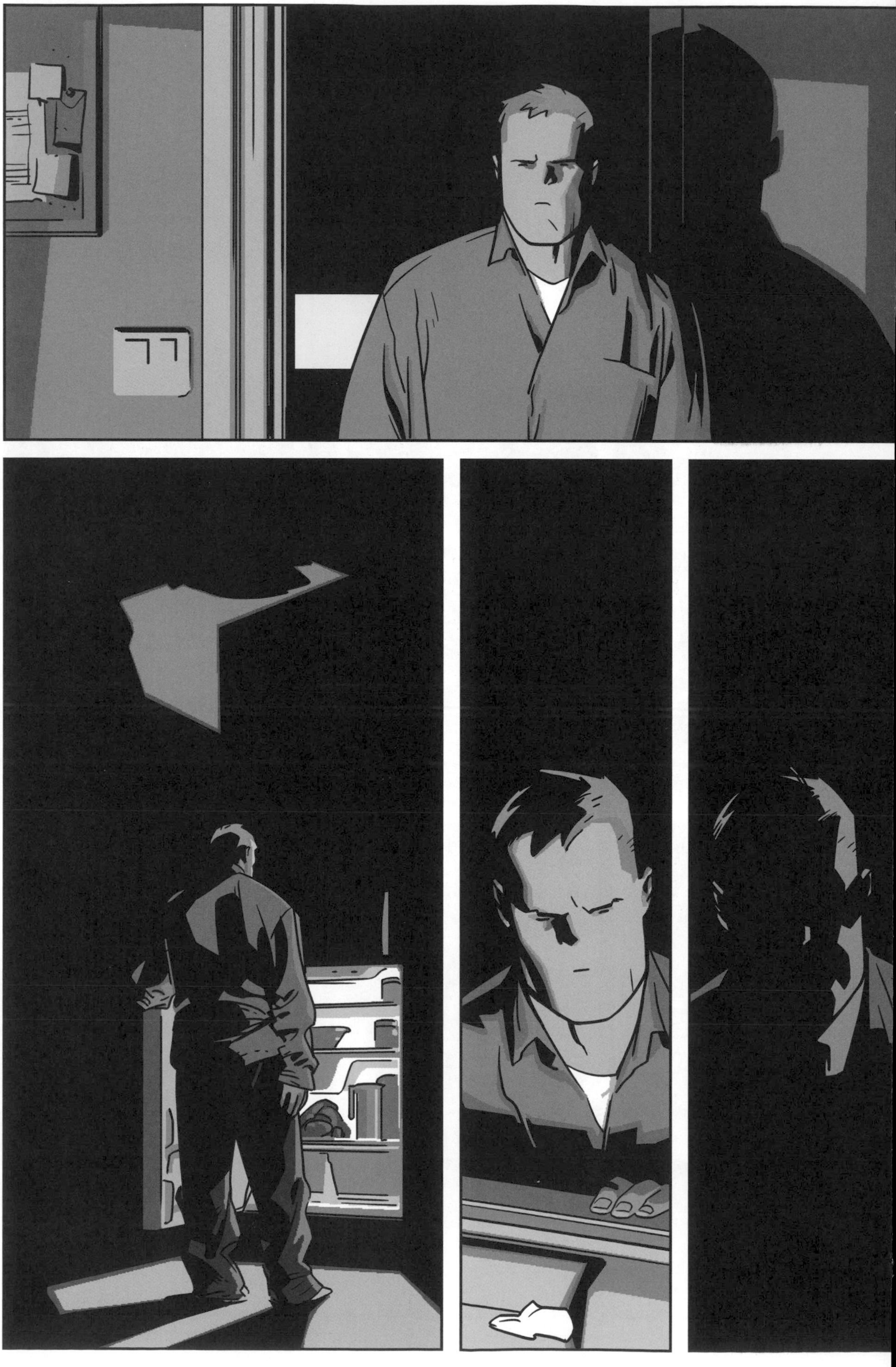

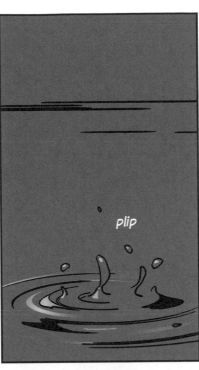

plip

plup

DID YOU KNOW THAT THERE ARE PEOPLE LIVING IN MAINE WHO ARE CLOSER TO MOSCOW THAN PEOPLE LIVING IN SOME PARTS OF SIBERIA?

plup

DID YOU KNOW THAT SIBERIA HAS THE LONGEST RAILROAD? THE FLATTEST PLAIN? THE LARGEST PEAT BOG?

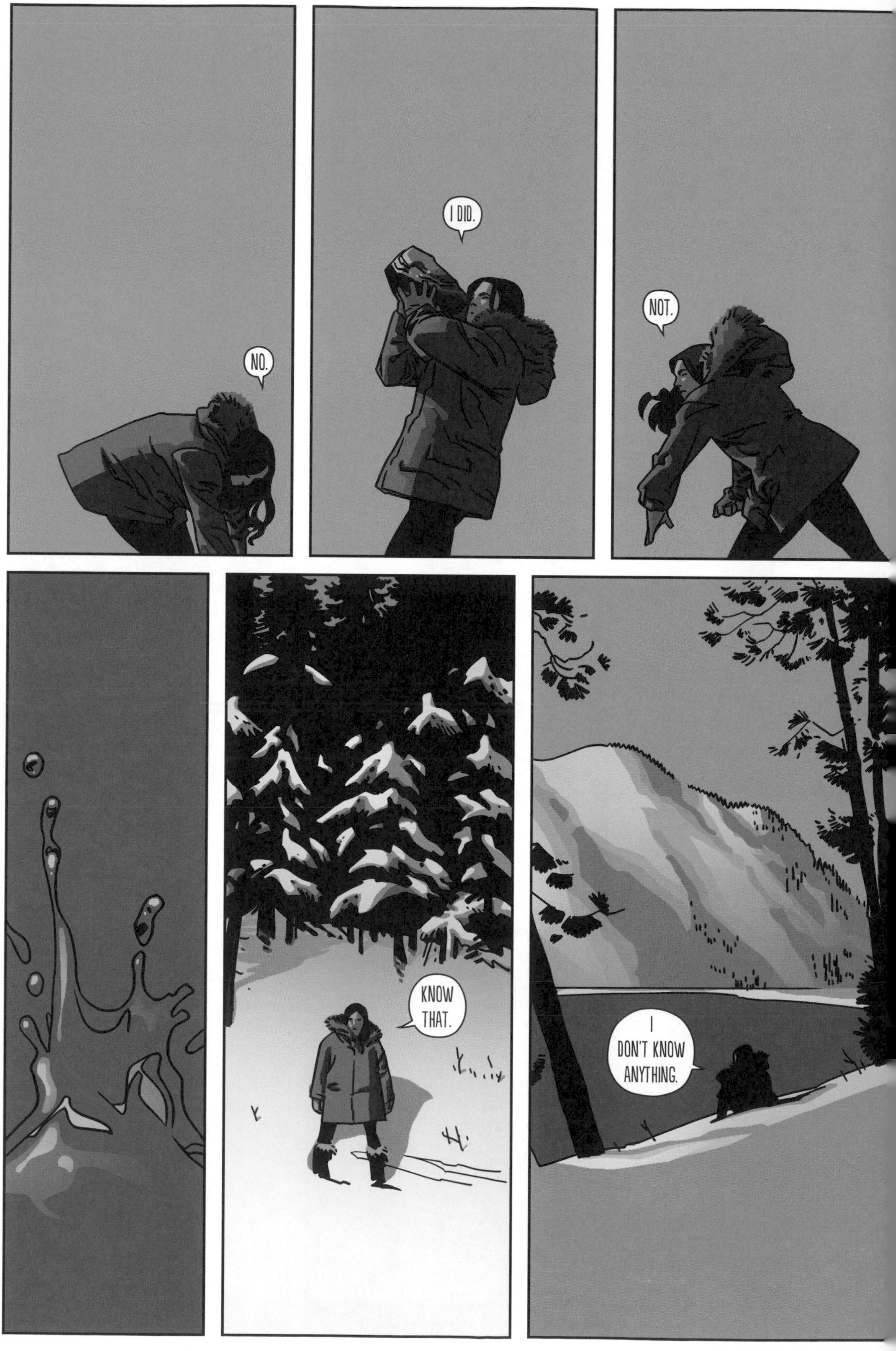
NO.
I DID.
NOT.
KNOW THAT.
I DON'T KNOW ANYTHING.

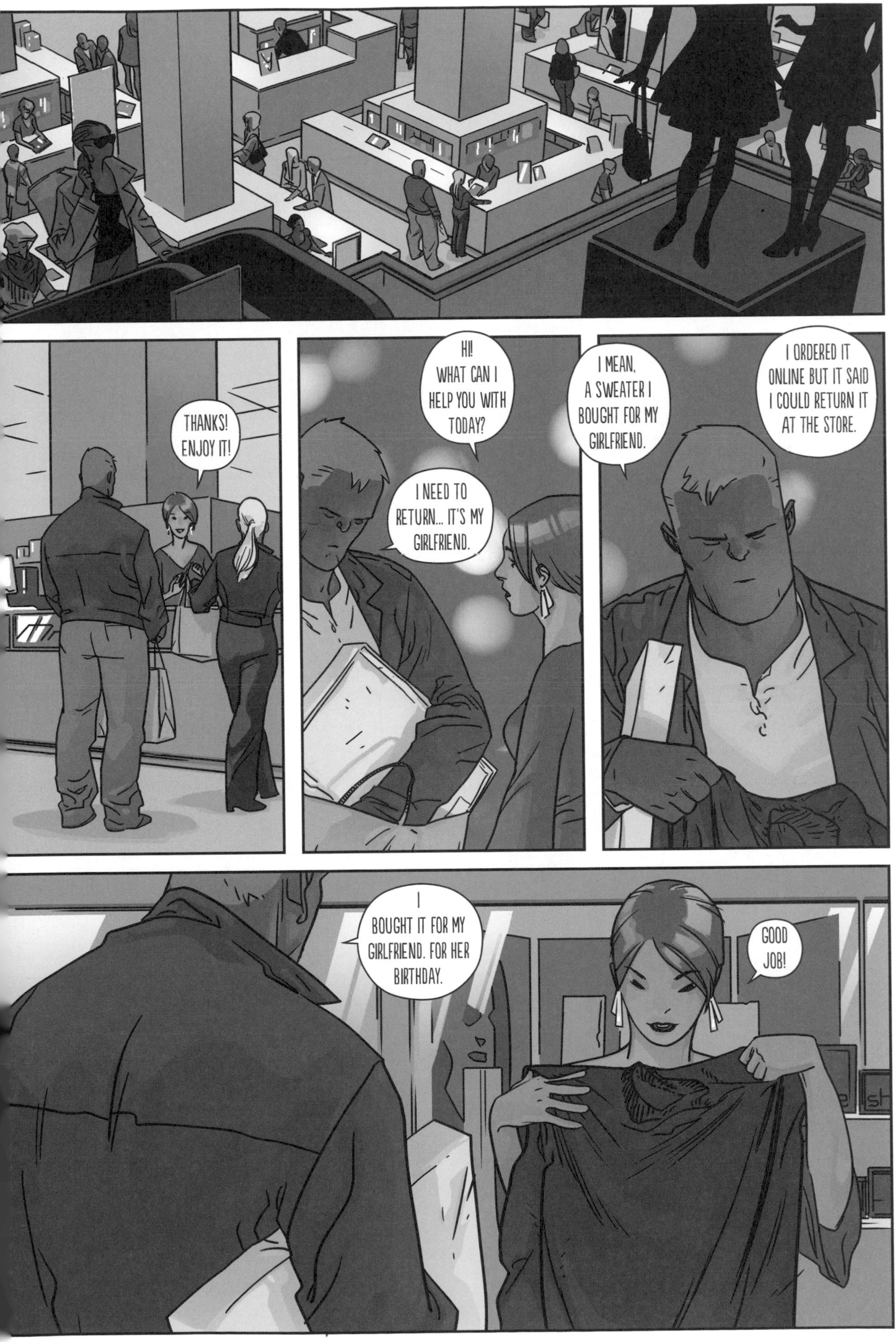
THANKS! ENJOY IT!
HI! WHAT CAN I HELP YOU WITH TODAY?
I NEED TO RETURN... IT'S MY GIRLFRIEND.
I MEAN, A SWEATER I BOUGHT FOR MY GIRLFRIEND.
I ORDERED IT ONLINE BUT IT SAID I COULD RETURN IT AT THE STORE.
I BOUGHT IT FOR MY GIRLFRIEND. FOR HER BIRTHDAY.
GOOD JOB!

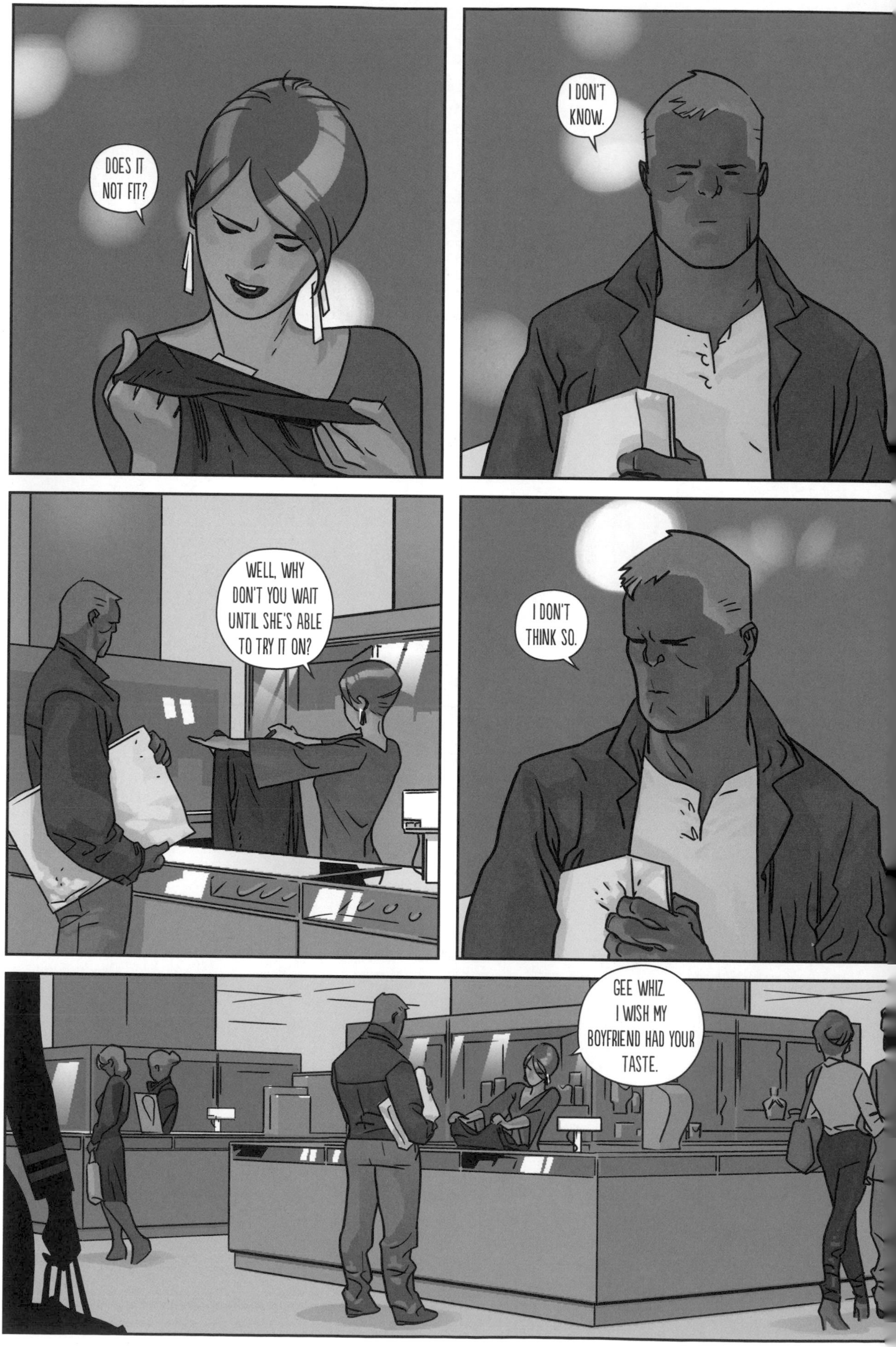
DOES IT NOT FIT?
I DON'T KNOW.
WELL, WHY DON'T YOU WAIT UNTIL SHE'S ABLE TO TRY IT ON?
I DON'T THINK SO.
GEE WHIZ. I WISH MY BOYFRIEND HAD YOUR TASTE.

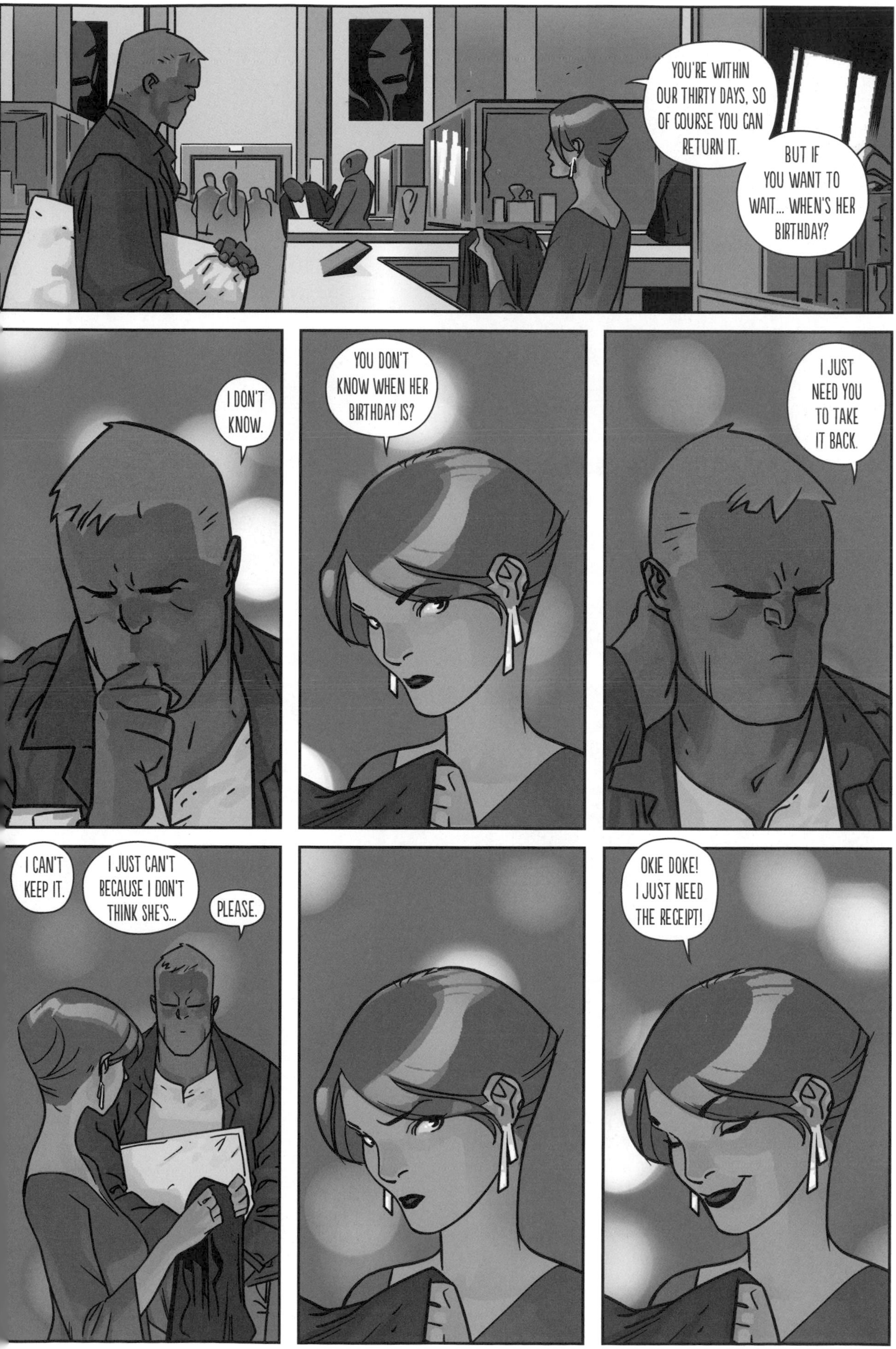
YOU'RE WITHIN OUR THIRTY DAYS, SO OF COURSE YOU CAN RETURN IT.
BUT IF YOU WANT TO WAIT... WHEN'S HER BIRTHDAY?
I DON'T KNOW.
YOU DON'T KNOW WHEN HER BIRTHDAY IS?
I JUST NEED YOU TO TAKE IT BACK.
I CAN'T KEEP IT.
I JUST CAN'T BECAUSE I DON'T THINK SHE'S...
PLEASE.
OKIE DOKE! I JUST NEED THE RECEIPT!

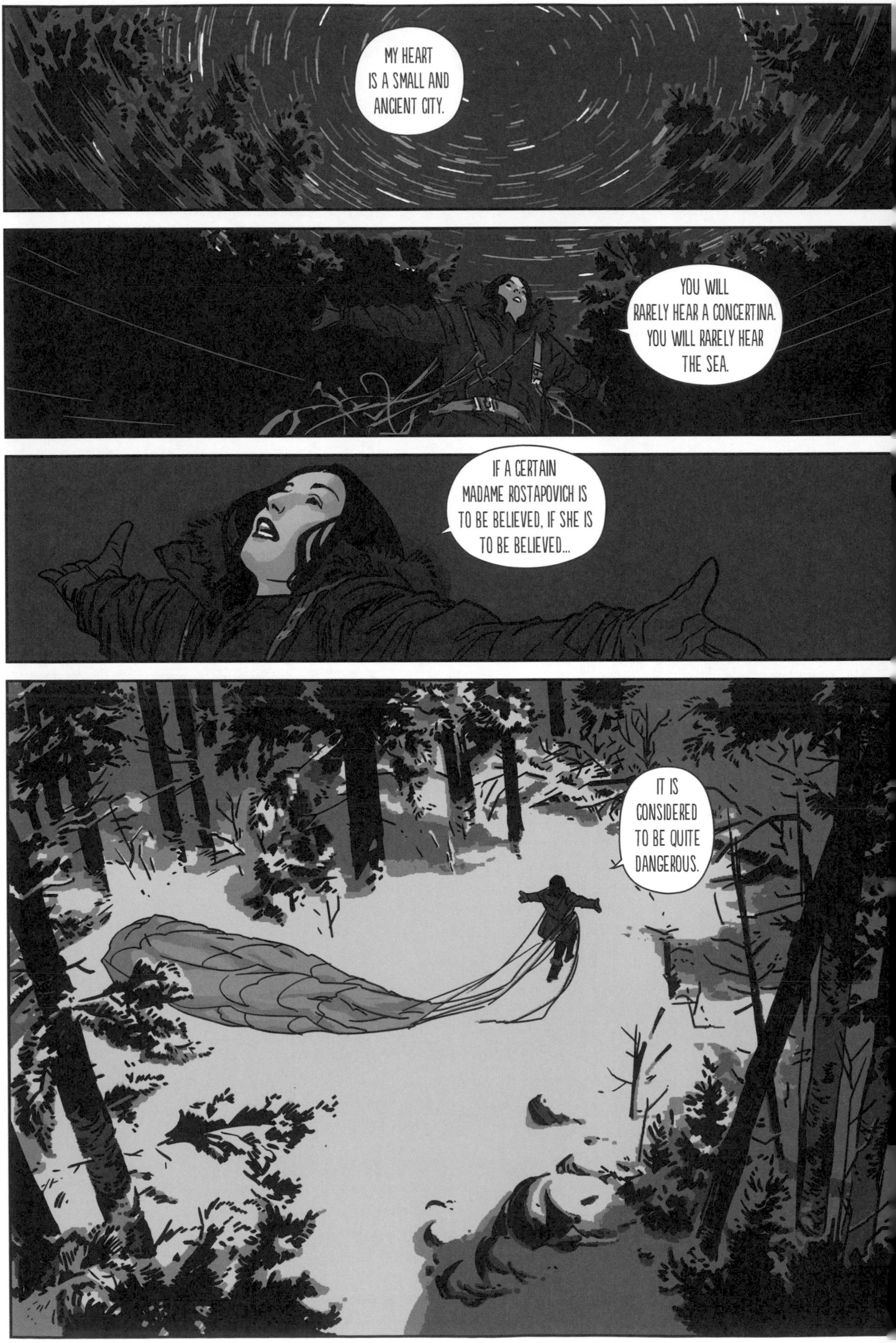
MY HEART IS A SMALL AND ANCIENT CITY.
YOU WILL RARELY HEAR A CONCERTINA. YOU WILL RARELY HEAR THE SEA.
IF A CERTAIN MADAME ROSTAPOVICH IS TO BE BELIEVED, IF SHE IS TO BE BELIEVED...
IT IS CONSIDERED TO BE QUITE DANGEROUS.

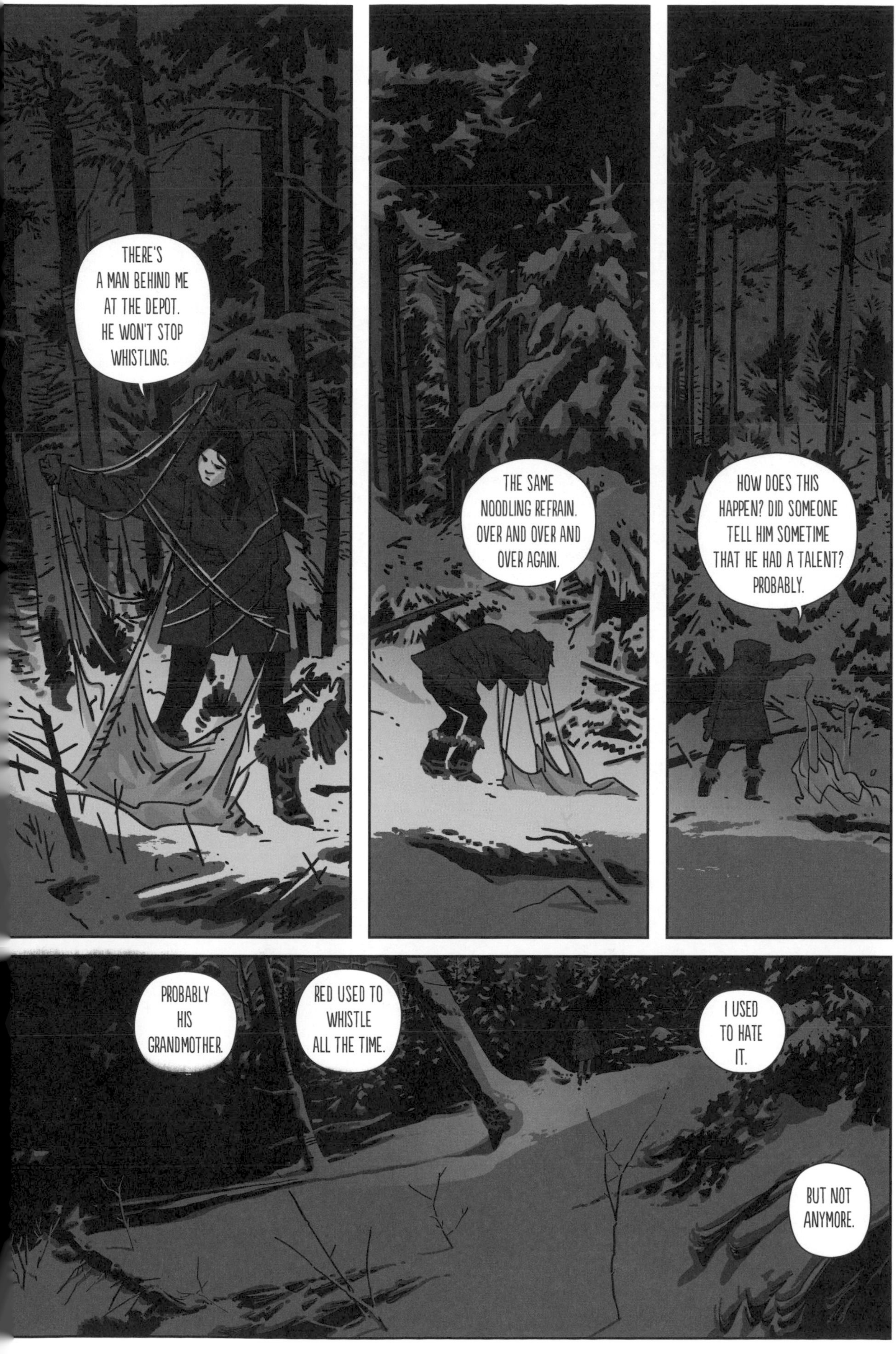
THERE'S A MAN BEHIND ME AT THE DEPOT. HE WON'T STOP WHISTLING.
THE SAME NOODLING REFRAIN. OVER AND OVER AND OVER AGAIN.
HOW DOES THIS HAPPEN? DID SOMEONE TELL HIM SOMETIME THAT HE HAD A TALENT? PROBABLY.
PROBABLY HIS GRANDMOTHER.
RED USED TO WHISTLE ALL THE TIME.
I USED TO HATE IT.
BUT NOT ANYMORE.

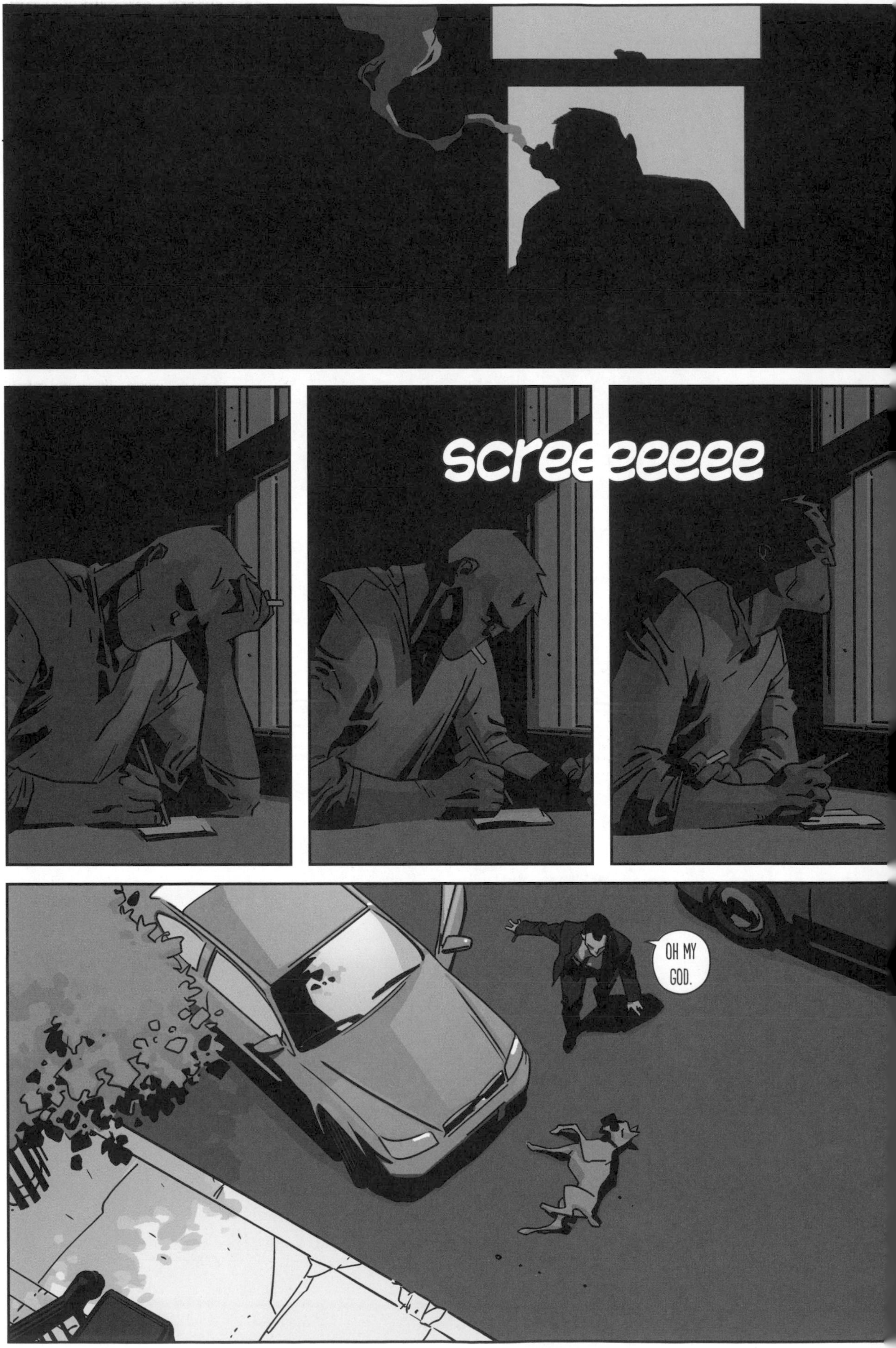
screeeeeeee
OH MY GOD.

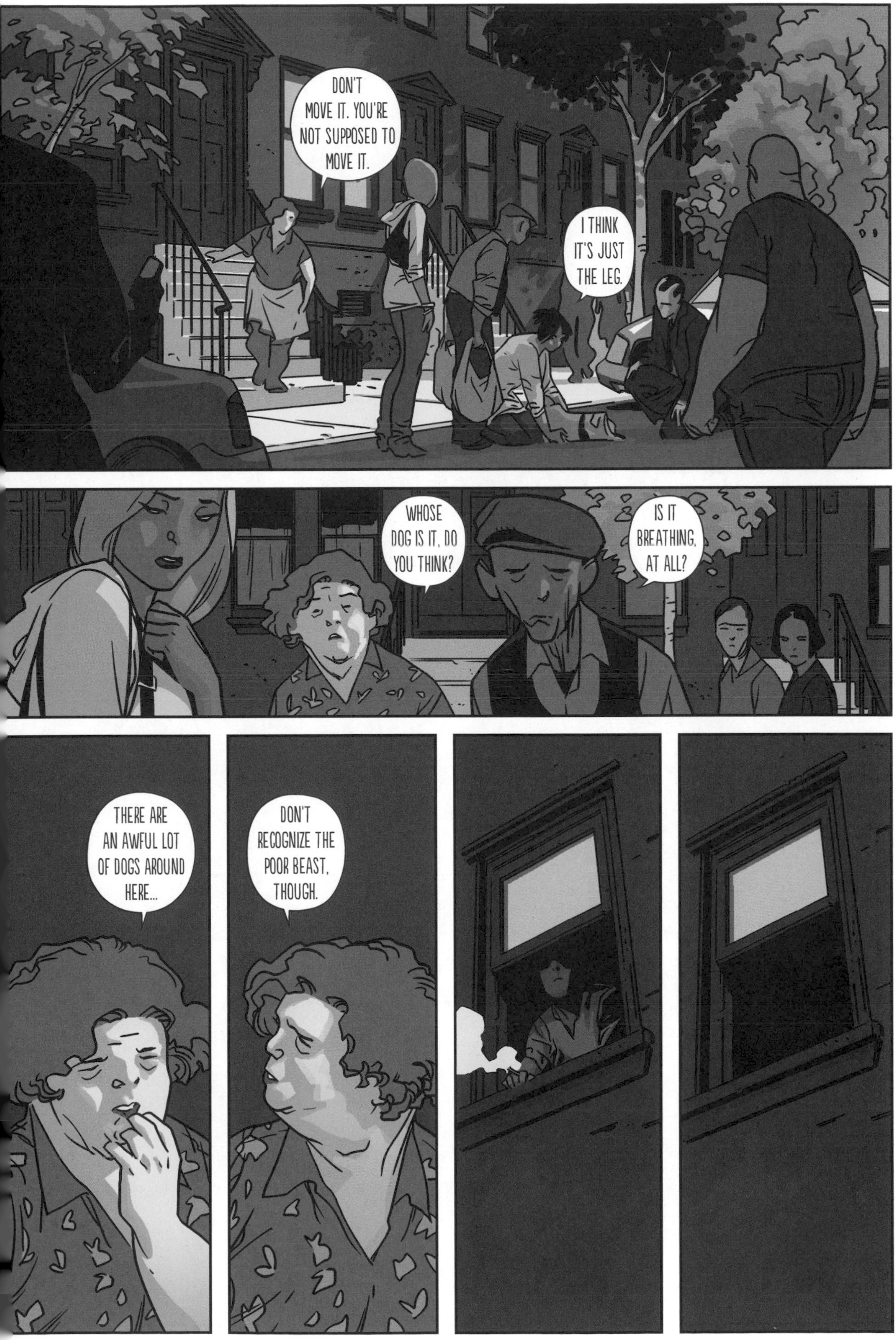
DON'T MOVE IT. YOU'RE NOT SUPPOSED TO MOVE IT.
I THINK IT'S JUST THE LEG.
WHOSE DOG IS IT, DO YOU THINK?
IS IT BREATHING, AT ALL?
THERE ARE AN AWFUL LOT OF DOGS AROUND HERE...
DON'T RECOGNIZE THE POOR BEAST, THOUGH.

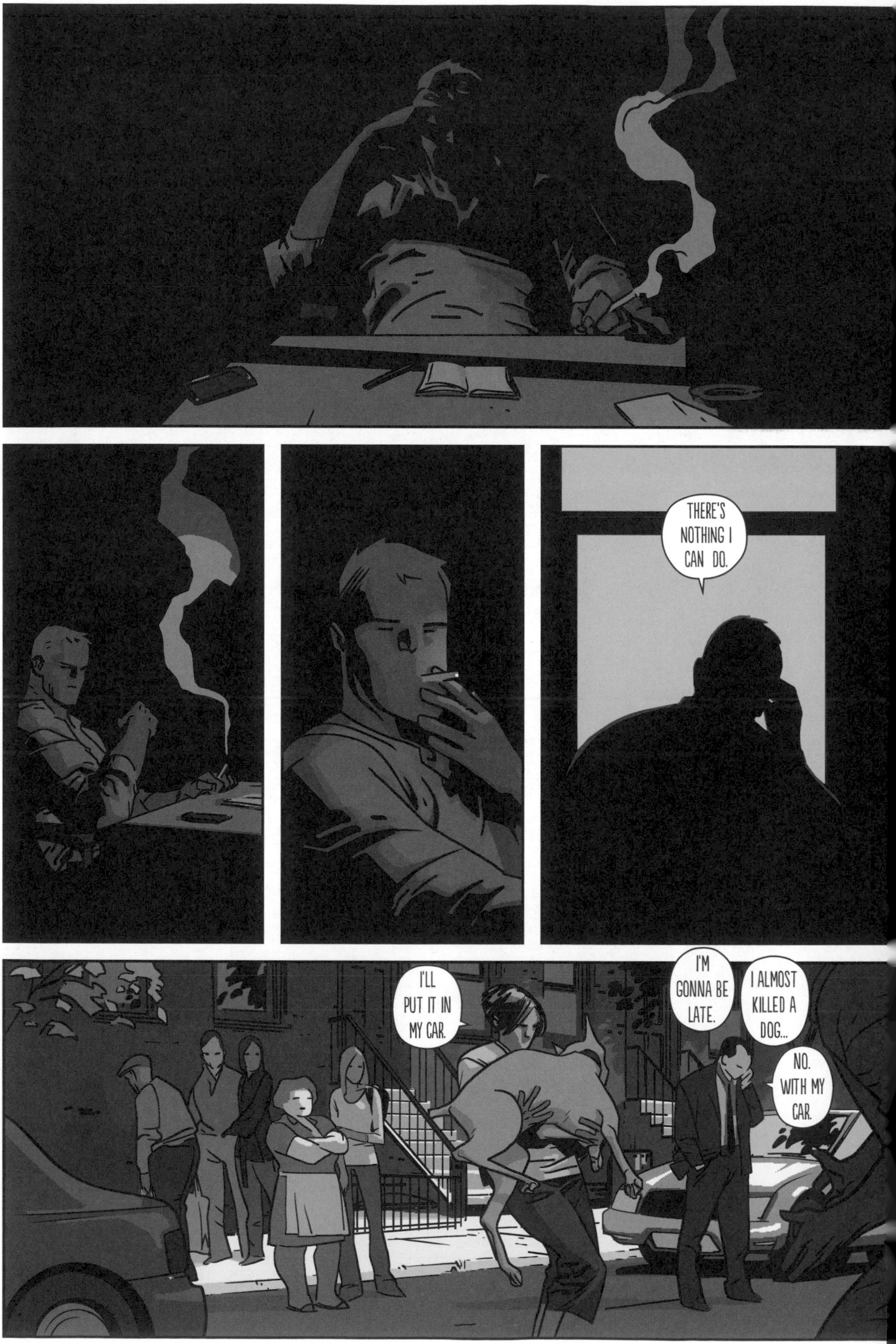
THERE'S NOTHING I CAN DO.
I'LL PUT IT IN MY CAR.
I'M GONNA BE LATE.
I ALMOST KILLED A DOG...
NO. WITH MY CAR.

VI

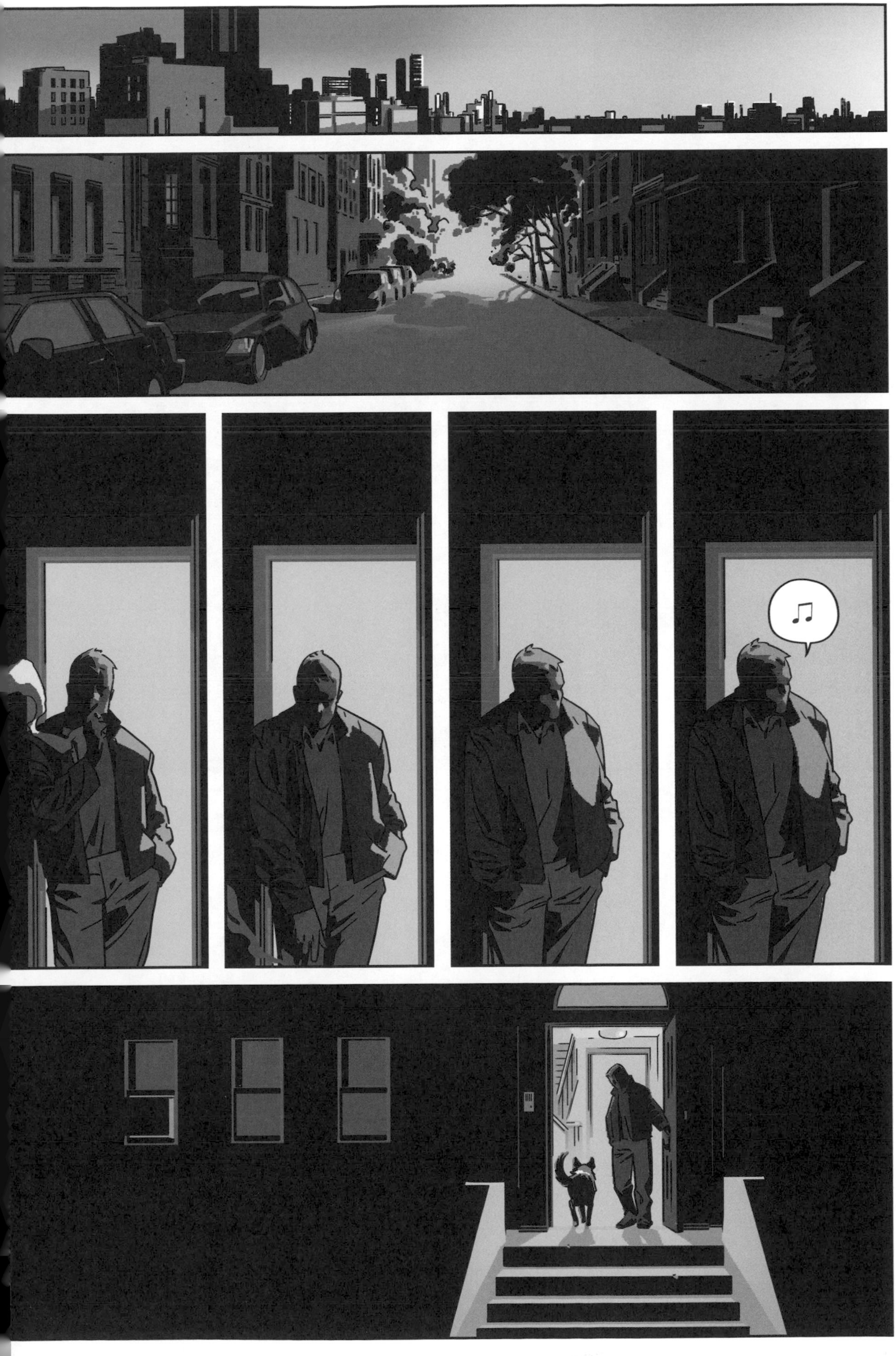

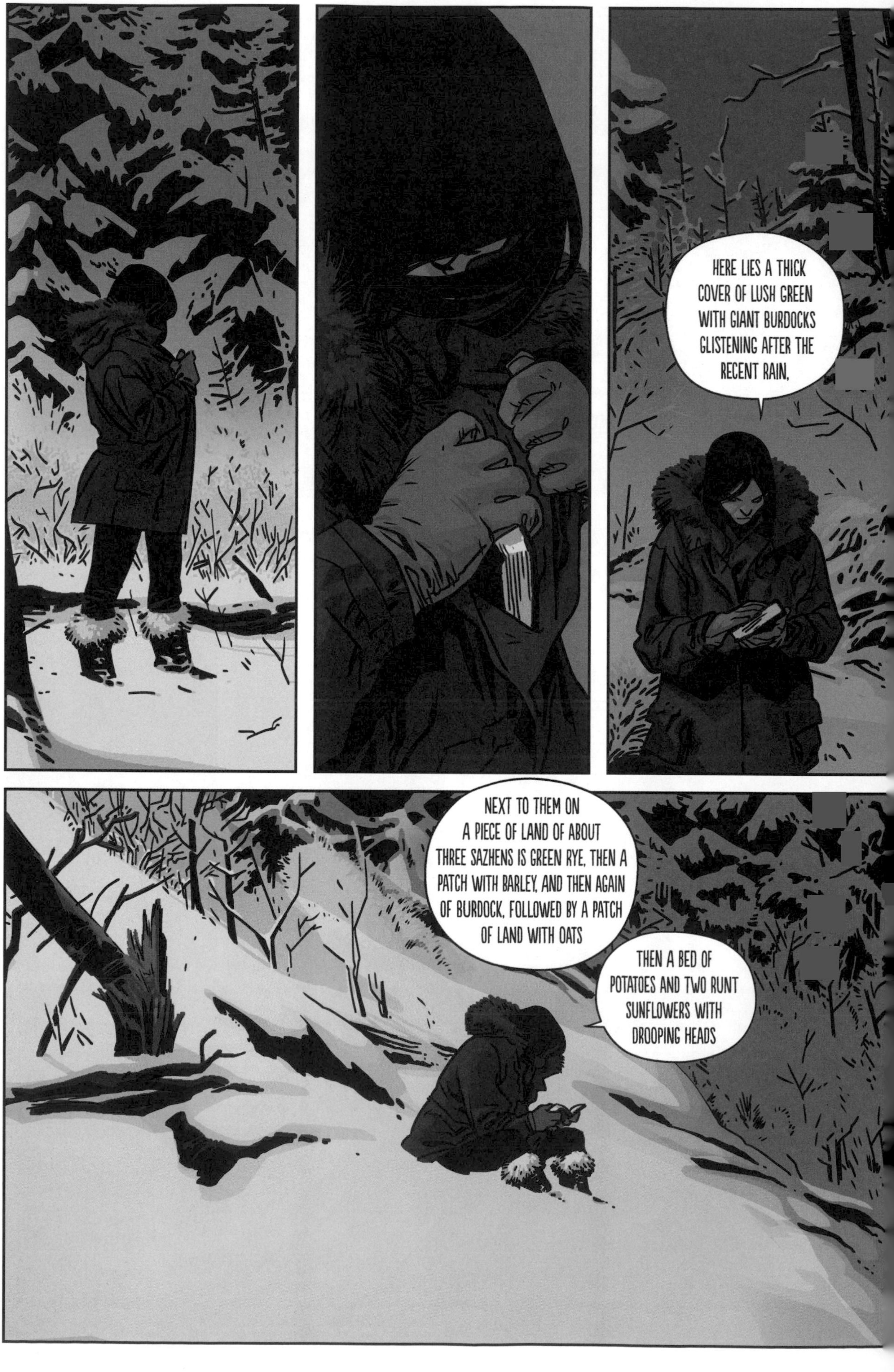
HERE LIES A THICK COVER OF LUSH GREEN WITH GIANT BURDOCKS GLISTENING AFTER THE RECENT RAIN,
NEXT TO THEM ON A PIECE OF LAND OF ABOUT THREE SAZHENS IS GREEN RYE, THEN A PATCH WITH BARLEY, AND THEN AGAIN OF BURDOCK, FOLLOWED BY A PATCH OF LAND WITH OATS
THEN A BED OF POTATOES AND TWO RUNT SUNFLOWERS WITH DROOPING HEADS

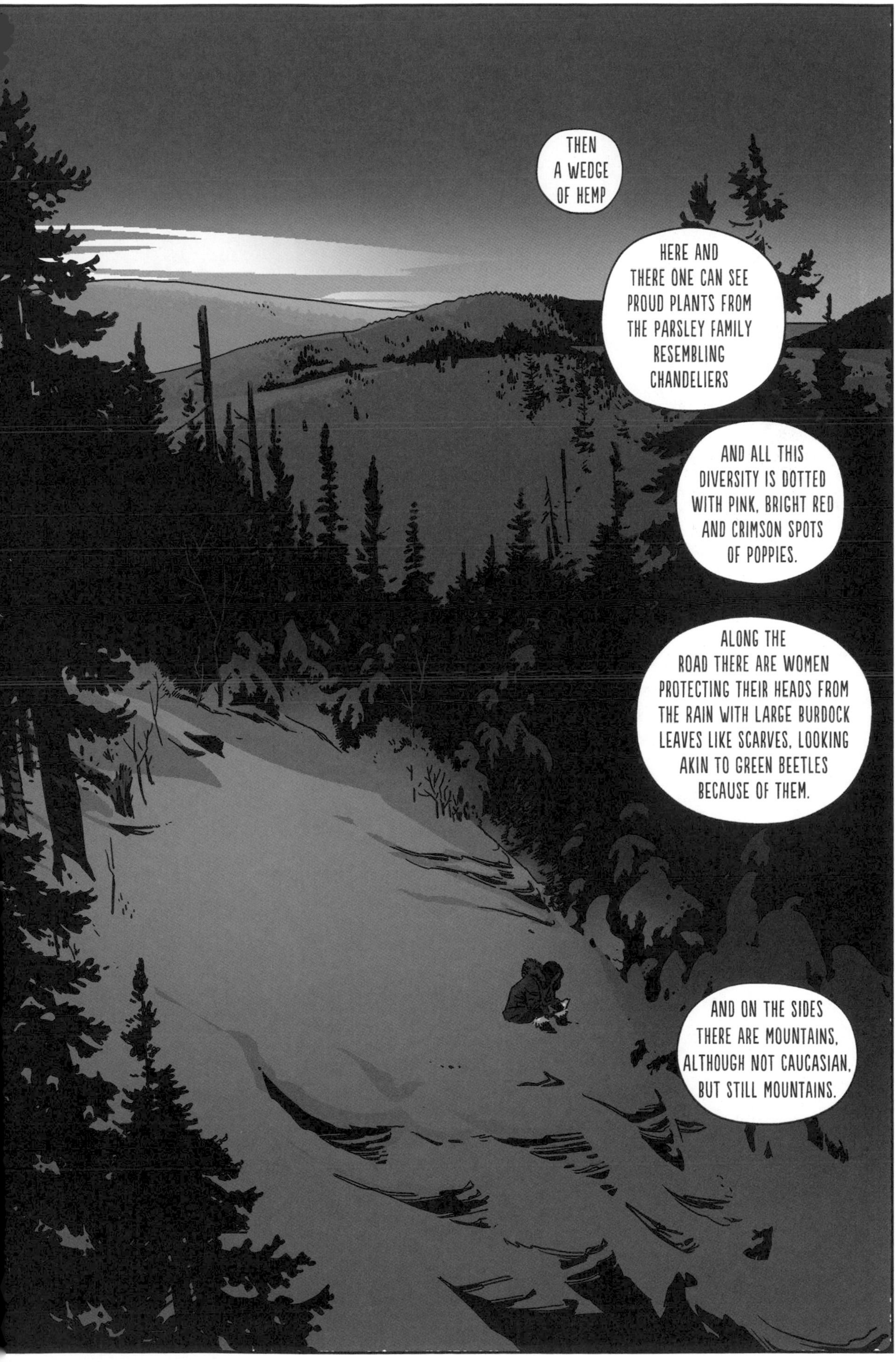
THEN A WEDGE OF HEMP
HERE AND THERE ONE CAN SEE PROUD PLANTS FROM THE PARSLEY FAMILY RESEMBLING CHANDELIERS
AND ALL THIS DIVERSITY IS DOTTED WITH PINK, BRIGHT RED AND CRIMSON SPOTS OF POPPIES.
ALONG THE ROAD THERE ARE WOMEN PROTECTING THEIR HEADS FROM THE RAIN WITH LARGE BURDOCK LEAVES LIKE SCARVES, LOOKING AKIN TO GREEN BEETLES BECAUSE OF THEM.
AND ON THE SIDES THERE ARE MOUNTAINS, ALTHOUGH NOT CAUCASIAN, BUT STILL MOUNTAINS.

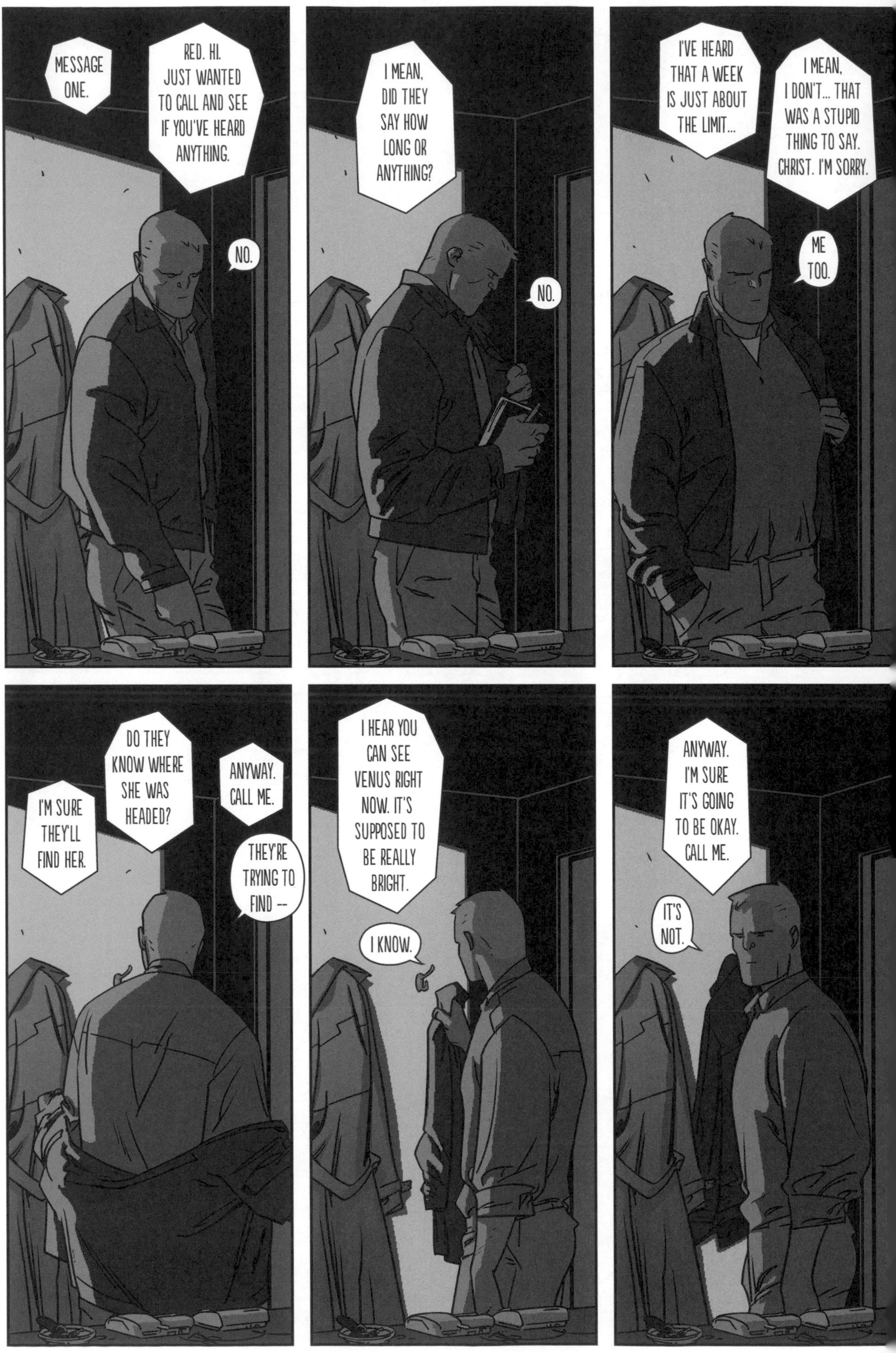
MESSAGE ONE.
RED. HI. JUST WANTED TO CALL AND SEE IF YOU'VE HEARD ANYTHING.
NO.
I MEAN, DID THEY SAY HOW LONG OR ANYTHING?
NO.
I'VE HEARD THAT A WEEK IS JUST ABOUT THE LIMIT...
I MEAN, I DON'T... THAT WAS A STUPID THING TO SAY. CHRIST. I'M SORRY.
ME TOO.
I'M SURE THEY'LL FIND HER.
DO THEY KNOW WHERE SHE WAS HEADED?
ANYWAY. CALL ME.
THEY'RE TRYING TO FIND --
I HEAR YOU CAN SEE VENUS RIGHT NOW. IT'S SUPPOSED TO BE REALLY BRIGHT.
I KNOW.
ANYWAY. I'M SURE IT'S GOING TO BE OKAY. CALL ME.
IT'S NOT.

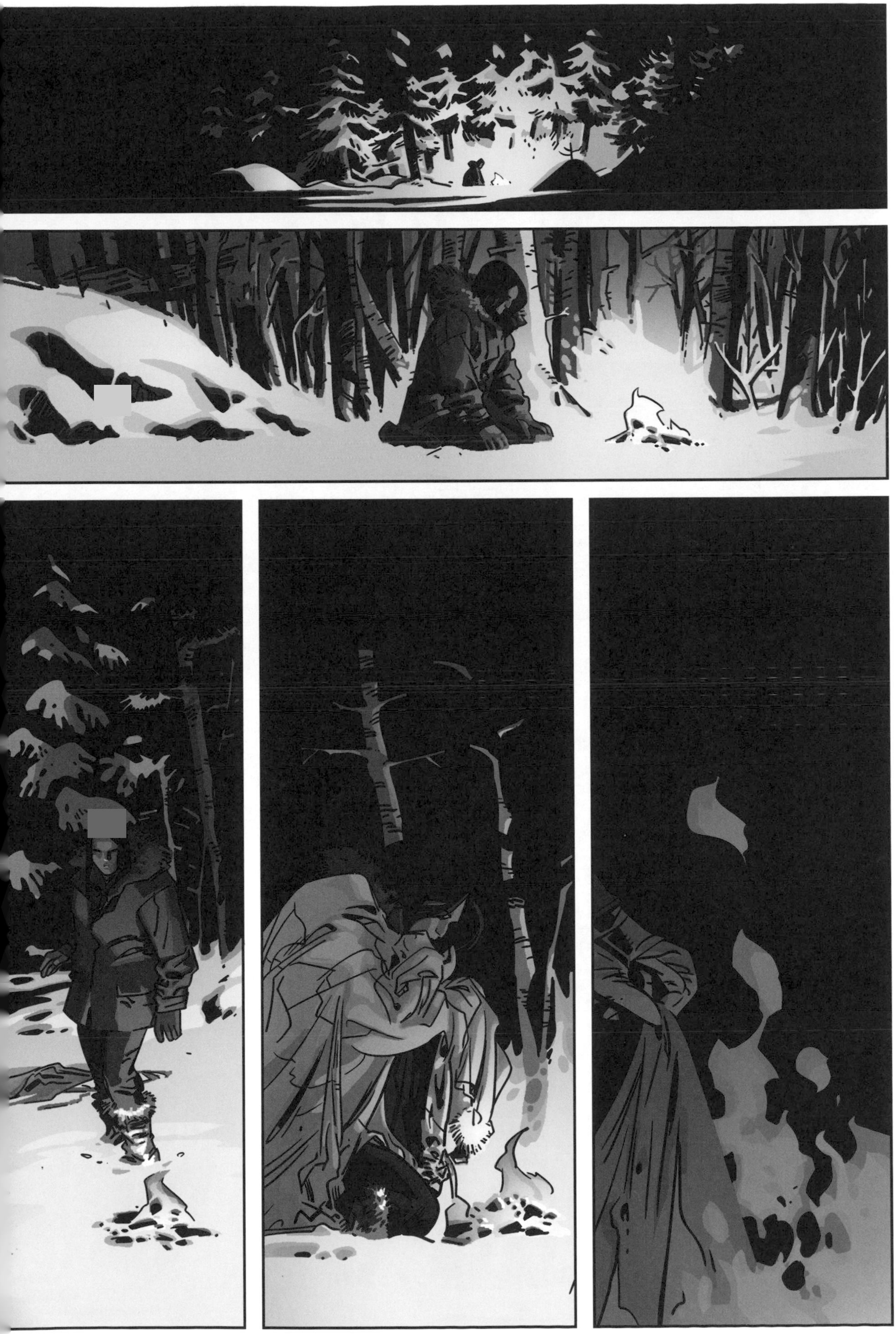

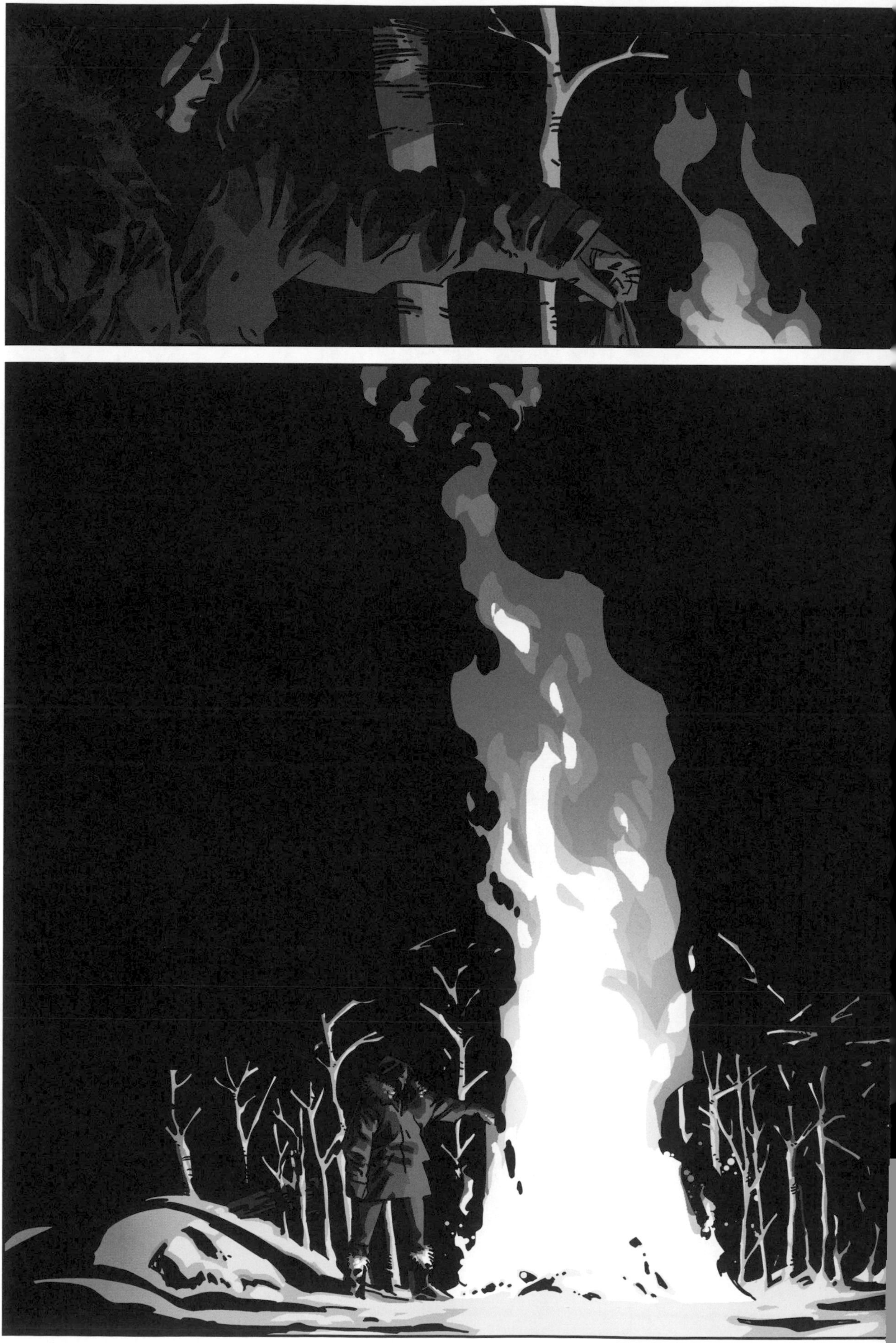

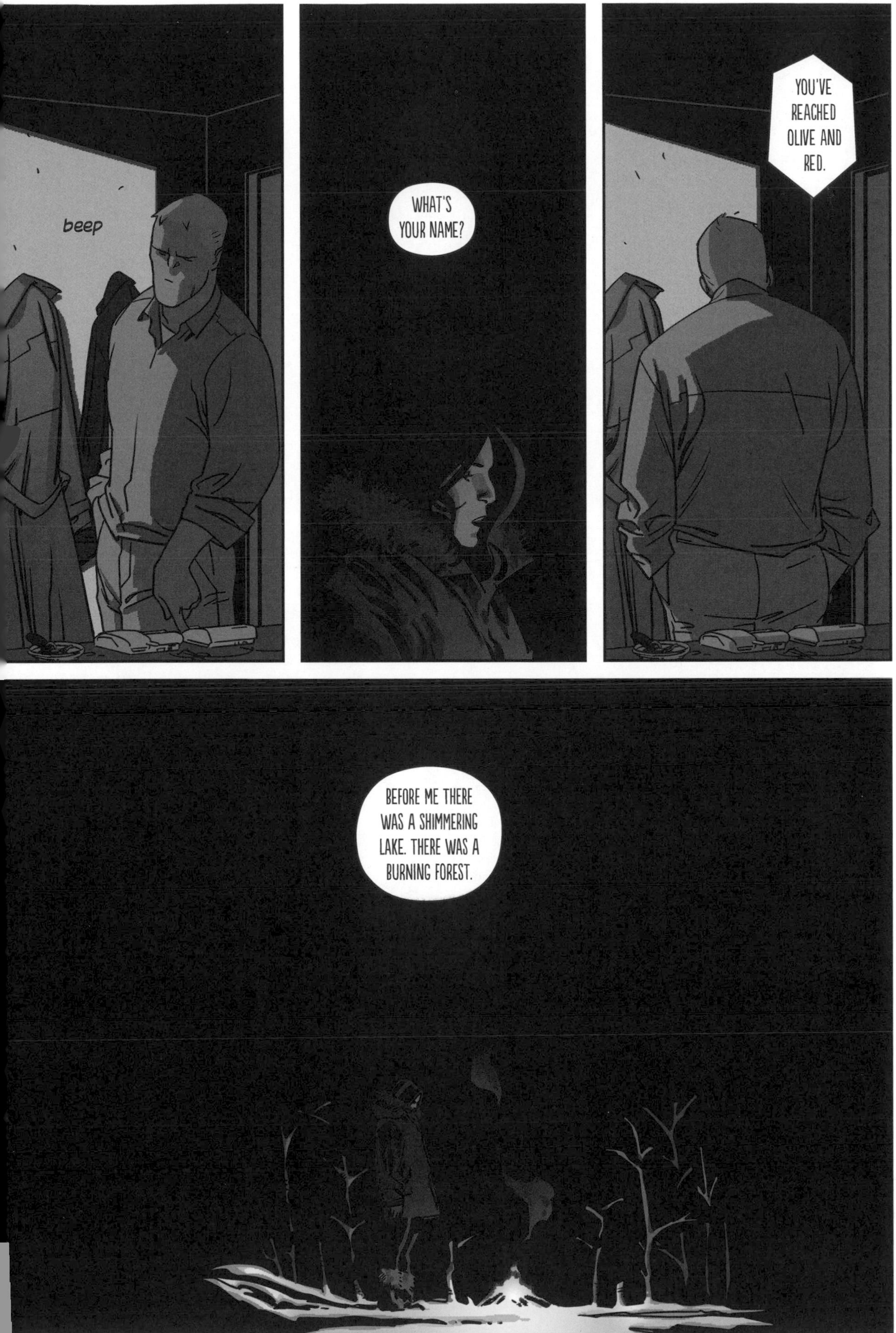
beep
WHAT'S YOUR NAME?
YOU'VE REACHED OLIVE AND RED.
BEFORE ME THERE WAS A SHIMMERING LAKE. THERE WAS A BURNING FOREST.

WHERE DO YOU LIVE?

WE'RE NOT HOME RIGHT NOW --

SO LEAVE A MESSAGE!

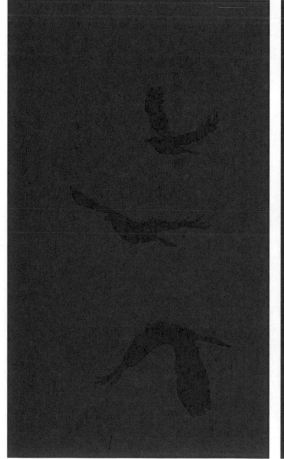

PLACED BEFORE ME WAS AN UNIMAGINABLE TASK...

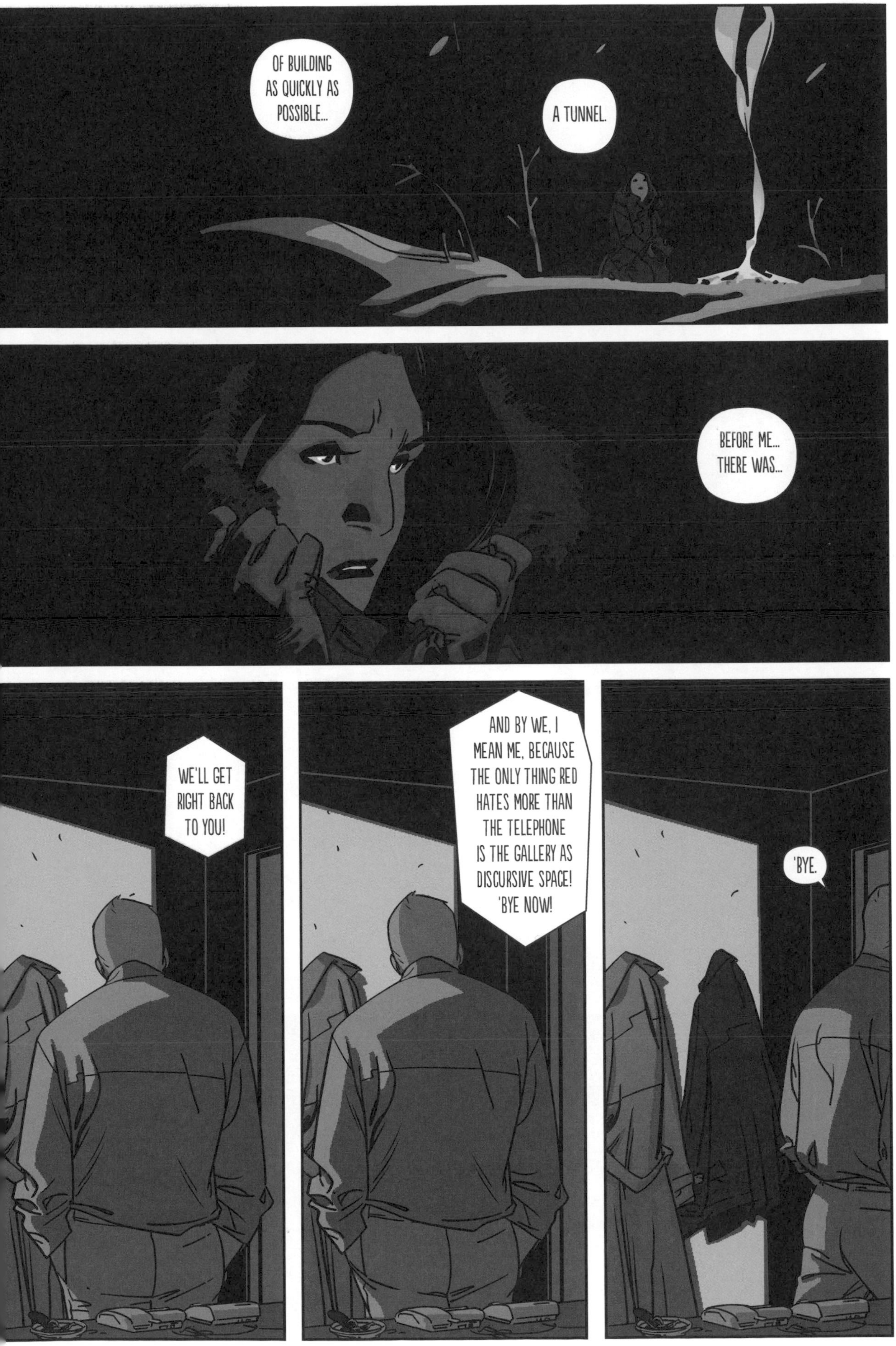
OF BUILDING AS QUICKLY AS POSSIBLE...
A TUNNEL.
BEFORE ME... THERE WAS...
WE'LL GET RIGHT BACK TO YOU!
AND BY WE, I MEAN ME, BECAUSE THE ONLY THING RED HATES MORE THAN THE TELEPHONE IS THE GALLERY AS DISCURSIVE SPACE! 'BYE NOW!
'BYE.

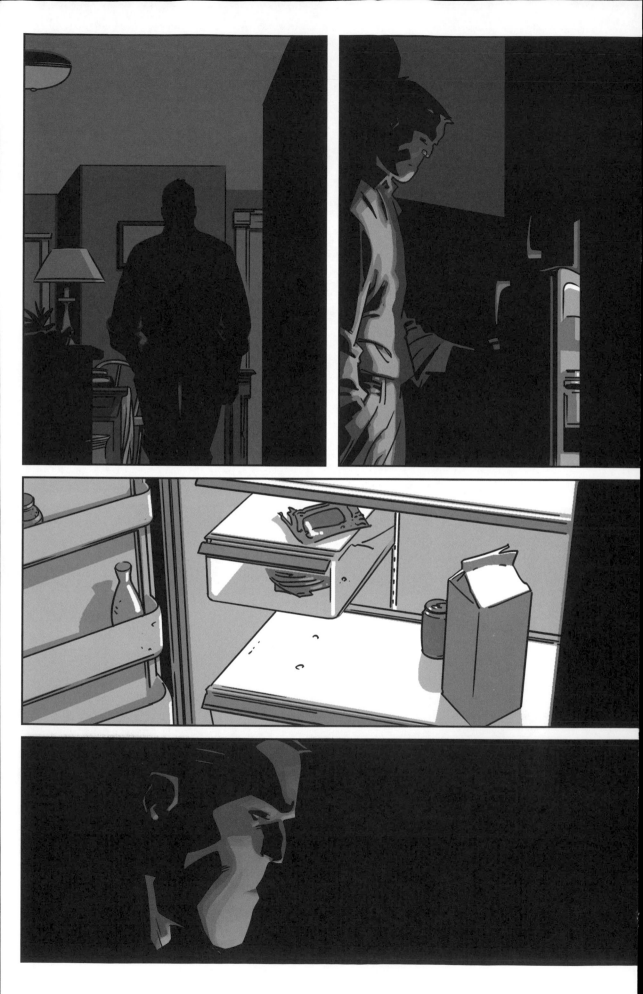

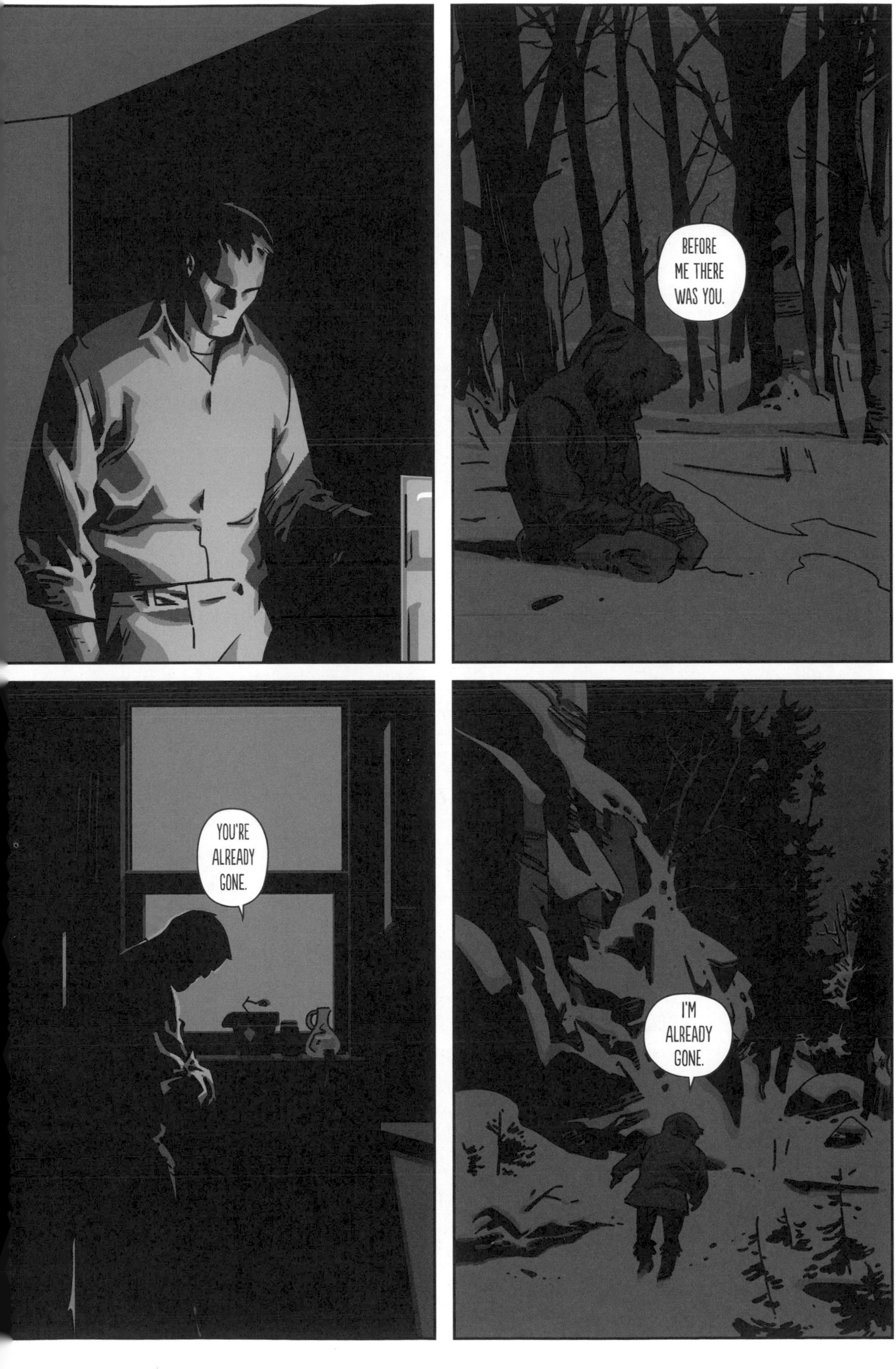
BEFORE ME THERE WAS YOU.
YOU'RE ALREADY GONE.
I'M ALREADY GONE.

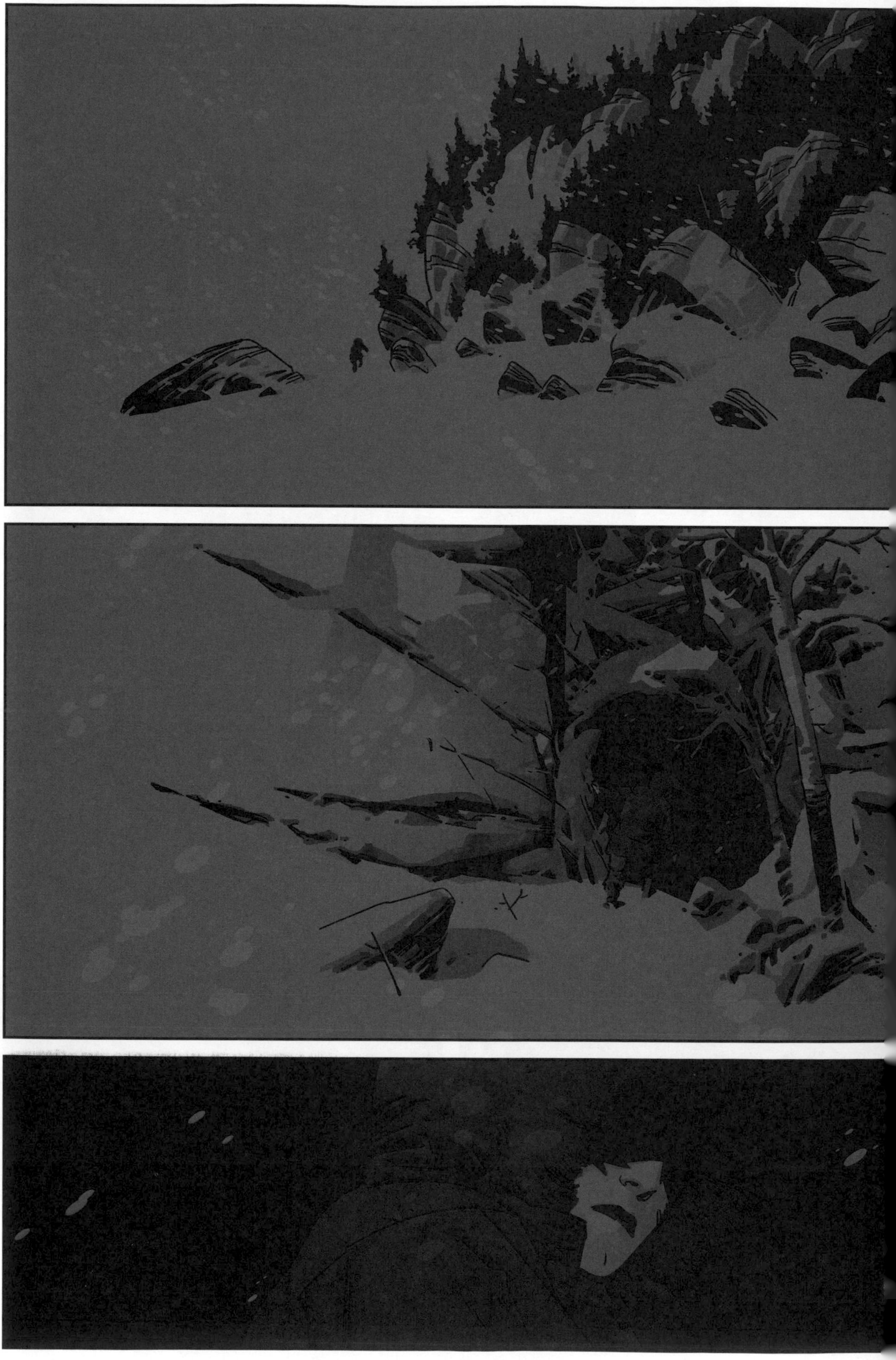

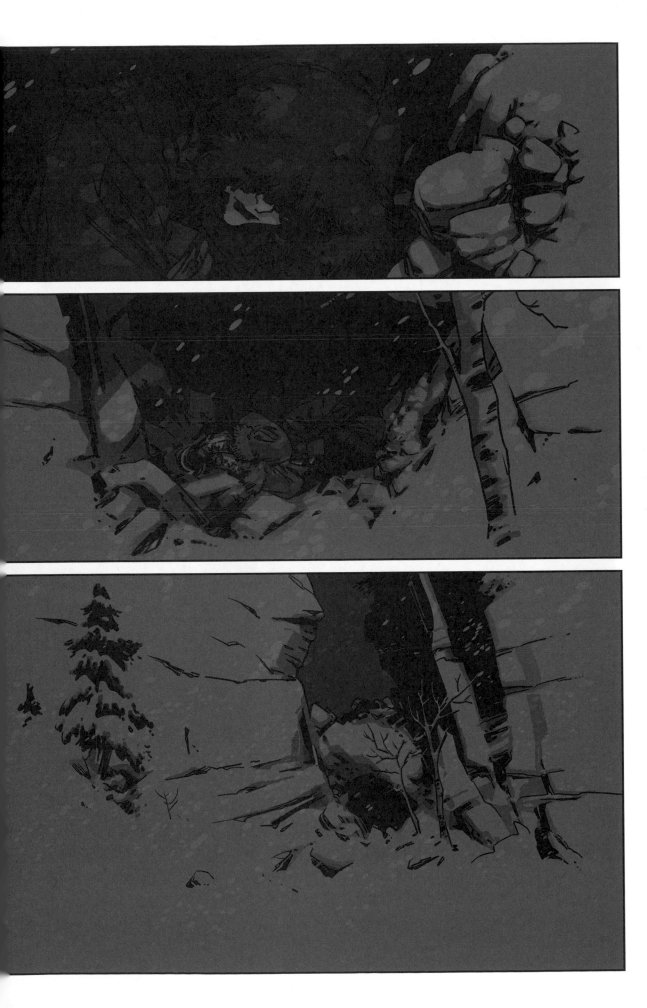

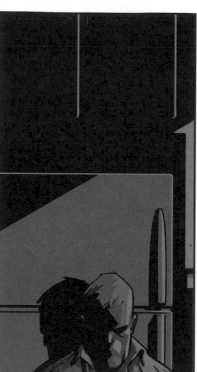
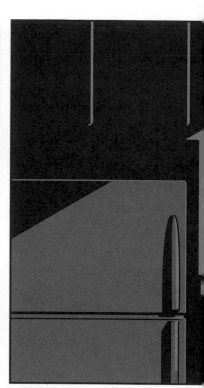

DON'T LEAVE ME.

I WANTED TO TELL YOU SOMETHING.

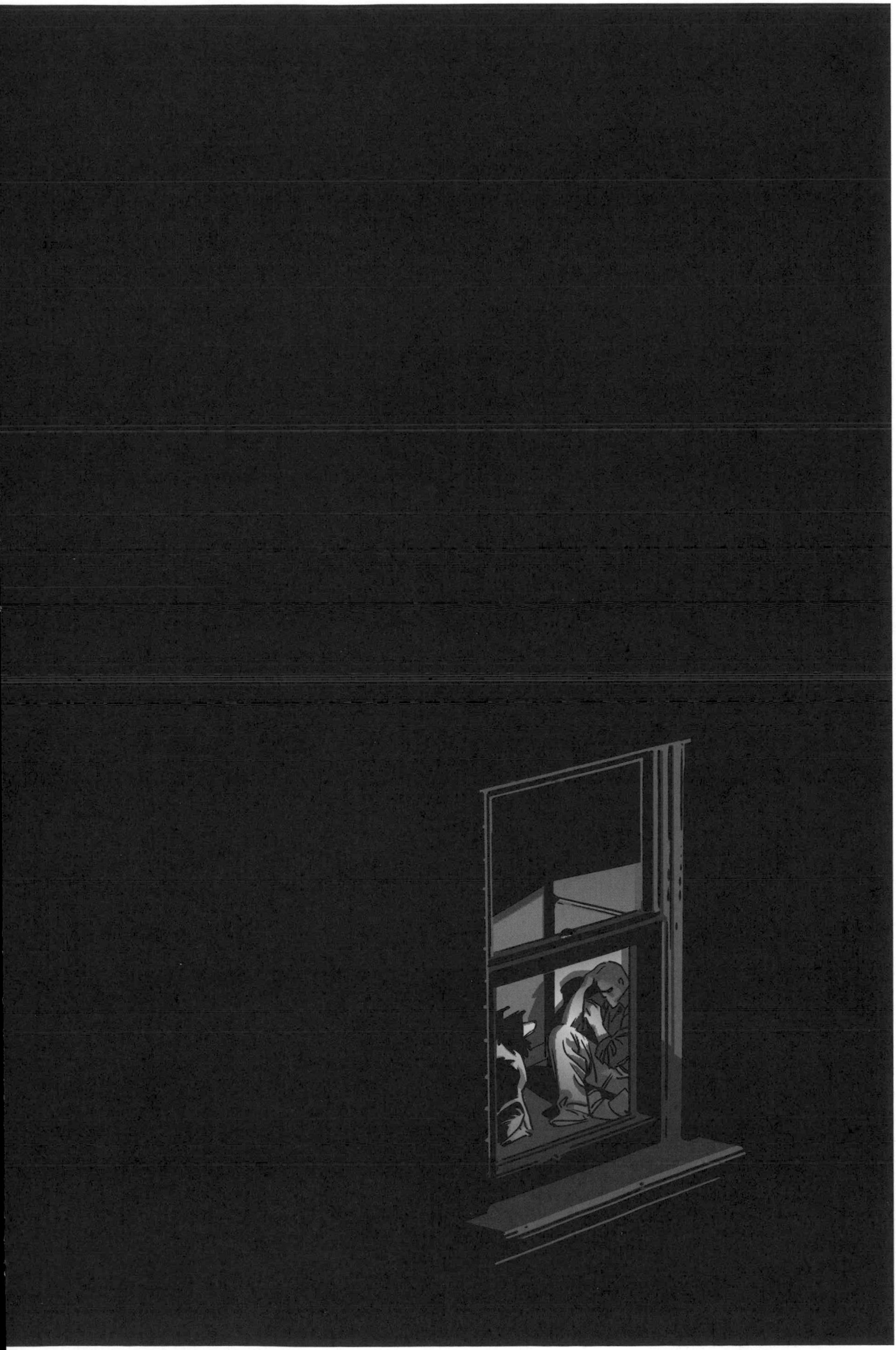

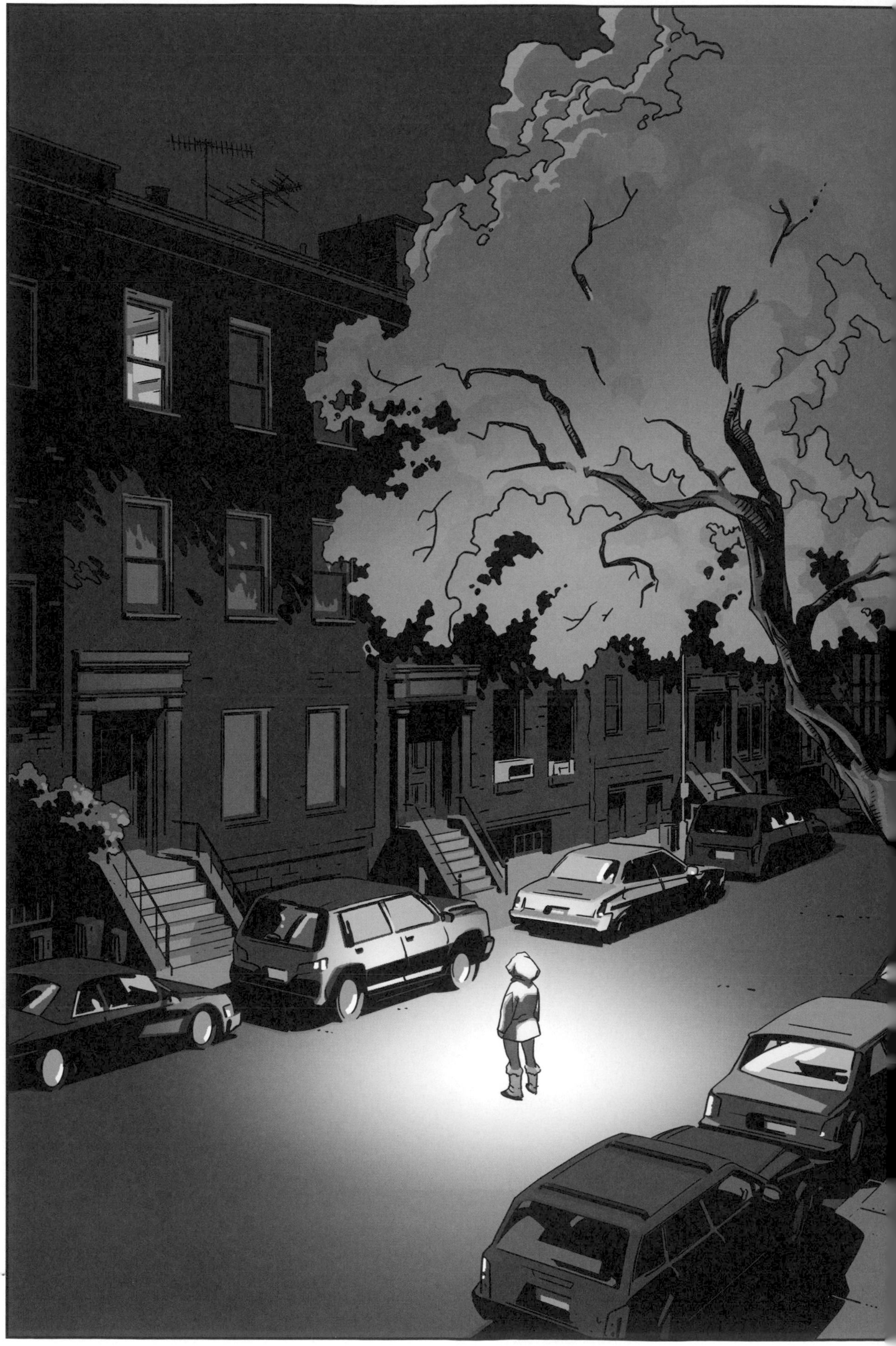

VII

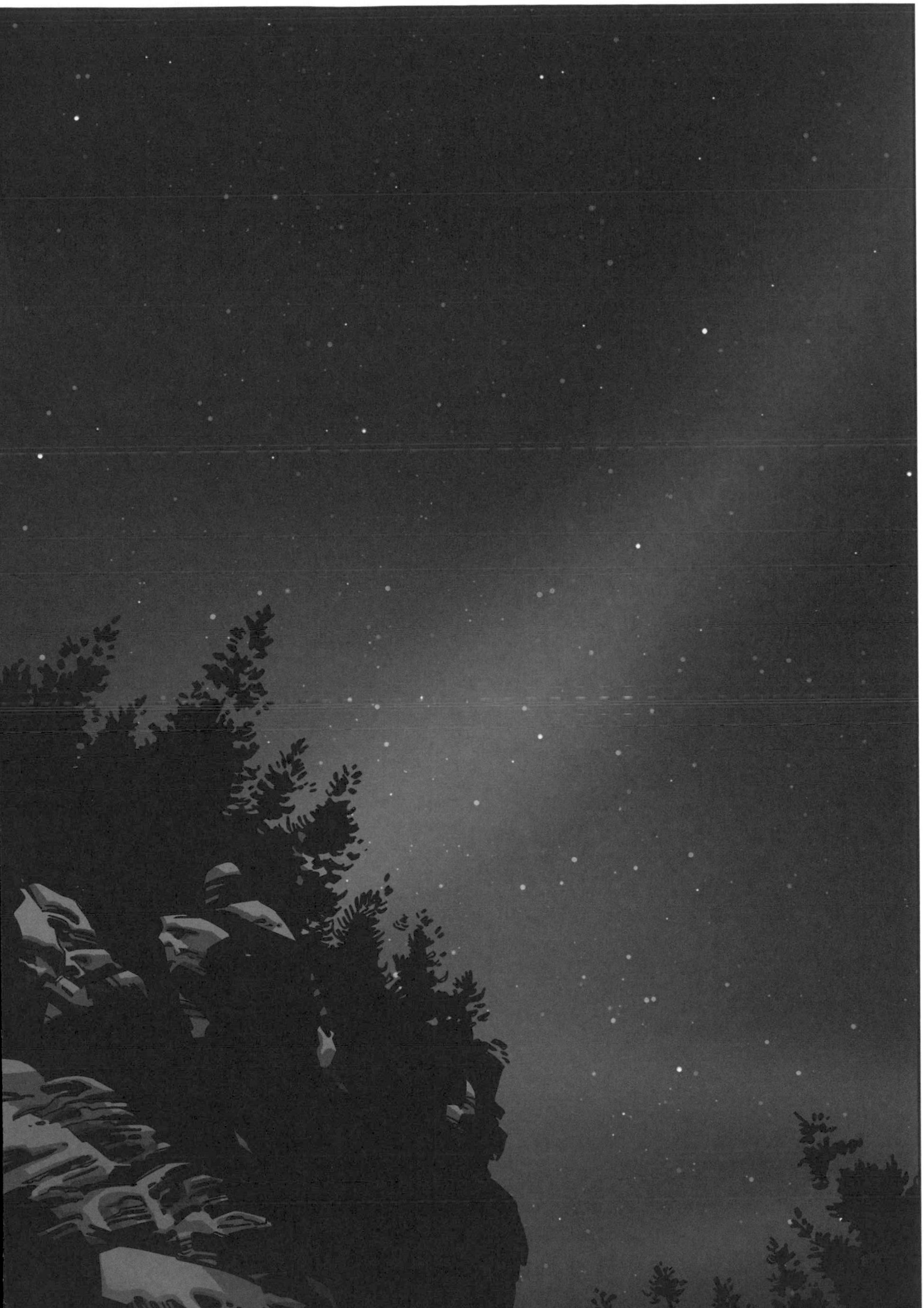

VIII

for Olive

I had an English teacher
who told me that
the truth is in the
metaphors. I failed to see
how describing a thing
in terms of something it
literally *cannot* be could
be considered, even on
the greyest of scales,
anything approaching the
truth. She tried to explain
it to me. I still don't really
understand it.

I think now that, in most
cases, an explanation is
the least we deserve but
the most you should
expect. And *that's*
the truth.

When Jumbo, that epic elephant, died, P.T. Barnum put it about that the Prince of Pachyderms had perished saving Tom Thumb, the clown elephant. I remember reading that you could have any kind of clown act... acrobat clowns, dog clowns, elephant clowns, but there is no such thing as a tiger clown act. Not if you want to live.

Anyway, that's not how Jumbo died in 1885 in St. Thomas. And, in 1985, in St. Thomas, that's not how my dad died, either.

There's so little left of my father now. It hardly bears repeating except that every time I look in a mirror there he is repeating himself over and over. Every time I walk by a downtown office window, he passes himself back to me in a way that's of no use to anyone.

There's some office girl rummaging on the other side of the glass. She doesn't look up through the Spanish moss of her hair. A girl that's starting to kink up in the humidity and it's not even lunch yet.

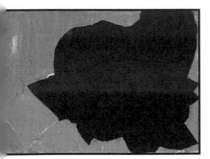  

I was watching this public
television program. I was
watching a bunch of old
men trying not to cry.
I could hear the radio from
the other room because I
couldn't be bothered to
go and turn it off. I don't
know why the alarm is set
for seven. I haven't slept
past six in years. And I was
listening to a man
describe how he'd buried
three of his men after
their tank had be blown to
smithereens. He may not
have said 'smithereens.'

But all three men fit in a
tin the size of a shoebox.

I only bring it up because that's about all that I've got left, too. Except mine's a biscuit tin. The kind that looks like it should be holding four generations of shirt buttons not a stack of time clock cards, a pair of cufflinks. A hard ball of cigarette papers. A key to the old garage. Two national park day passes. It's a pretty crappy inheritance, if that's what it was. But it's just what I salvaged before my mother donated everything to the Wednesday trash collection.

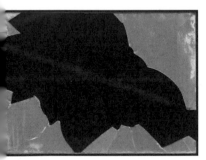  

The last time I saw my dad, he was in the basement soldering contacts on a switch for his model railroad. He went from cameras to telescopes to trains. I've met a lot of guys since who would be about his age and it seems to be a common career path. To be honest though, it wasn't the last time I saw him. It was the last time I *heard* him. The chattering of the trains in the basement. The clap of the screen door closing. Hours later, my mother asking if I'd seen my father.

Our house backed onto a
vacant lot that had a case
of terminal asphalt.
Cracked and heaving.
Divided into squares with
gutters of dandelions and
wild carrot. Practically
agricultural. If you were
after tar or broken glass.

I went out and stood in
the uncut grass, at the
border of ours and not
ours, and looked past the
darkness to the next
street over. Someone
struggled by on a bike
with one flat tire. Behind
me, I could hear my
mother on the telephone.

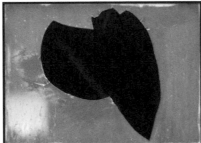

That night she talked to
her sister for a good long
while, which wasn't
unusual. And then she
called her mother, which
was. She called the Legion
Hall and the gas station.
I heard her talking to Bud
over at the curling club.

Bud ran the bar and
always sat me down with
free popcorn whenever I
was sent to organize my
dad. It took me a long
time to realize he wasn't
doing it for me. Took me
even longer to realize that
he wasn't doing it for my
dad neither.

I stood out there for a
long time, listening to her
calm voice. To the long
pauses while she sucked
on a cigarette. I stood out
there with the damp
creeping through my
shoes, crawling up my
pant legs. I wondered
about the northern lights.
I pulled on a hangnail until
it stung and bled and I
thought about spiders.
I worried vaguely about
my overdue books. And I
tried to make things seem
brighter by looking at
them out of the corner of
my eye. But it didn't
really work.

  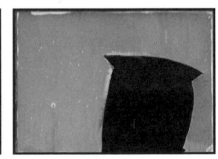

And then, when I got tired
of thinking about
baseball, of wondering
whether or not I was
responsible enough to
have a dog, which my
mother said I wasn't, of
worrying about looking
stupid with my shirt
tucked in, of trying to
figure out why
Stan at the corner store
didn't laugh at my Chinese
fire drill joke when
everybody else did, of
squishing my toes into my
wet insoles, I went inside,
past my mother,
and up to bed.

She was bent over the stove, lighting a cigarette on the burner. She turned and looked at me as I stopped in the kitchen doorway. I wanted to ask about him. About when he'd be back. But the way she leaned back against the stove and crossed her arms made me think that whatever came out of her mouth wouldn't make any sense to me at all. Like, literally not make any sense. Like she was going to open her mouth and Russian was going to come out of it.
Or Chinese.

  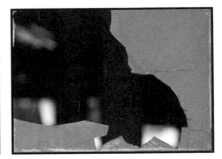

And I didn't think that I would be able to handle it. So I just said good night and she said mmhmm, which did nothing to allay my suspicions that she was some kind of sleeper agent, and I went to bed.

I heard her make one more phone call. I thought for sure she was going to call the police. But she didn't. She ordered a pizza and I tried to stay awake long enough to hear the knock on the front door. But I couldn't and I didn't.

And that was that.

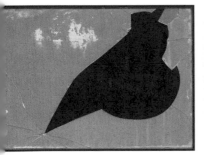 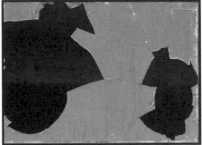 

Jumbo was twenty-one
years old when Barnum
bought him from the
London Zoo. I've always
thought that twenty-one
was kind of old. But I can't
think about it too much
though because then I
find myself wondering
what that elephant
thought its life was going
to be when it was
imported from the French
Sudan to Paris to London
and then to Planet P.T.

'Imported.' There's a
euphemism for you.

I mean... I'm no elephant but I don't think it's unreasonable to think that he might have had some expectations. A hundred thousand children wrote to Queen Victoria petitioning her not to sell the elephant. Clearly she didn't care or, more likely, the elephant wasn't hers to sell. I like the second way less, somehow. I wonder what happened to all those letters.

Anyway, I just think the elephant might have had his own ideas about where he wanted to finish up.

Because I think we all do,
that we all have some
idea of where we'd like to
end up. I can't really see
how it could be otherwise
because, I'm telling you,
there's no other
explanation for everyone,
and I mean *everyone*,
walking around with that
look on their face, that
look of not knowing
how they got there.
Then there're the other
folks who totally look like
they know where they're
going. But I think we're all
aware it's just a matter of
time before they end up
like the rest of us...

dead.

So, I'm twenty-one and
I'm standing in the kitchen
with my head in the fridge
and for the last couple of
months, I've woken up
every morning thinking
that I can't go on like this.
That if I have to haul
myself down to the Auto-8
motel lounge one more
time and tip out one more
congealed bar cherry,
rinse out one more beer
bottle, clean up one more
violated plastic plant, then
something is going to
snap. And while I'm
sorting out some cold
cuts, I think, maybe it
already has.

All I really want to do is sit
on the floor and eat
salami. But I don't have
salami, I've got this weird
turkey that I really don't
think is turkey at all. More
like something you'd
make a turkey out of
when you were in Grade
One. Strange construction
paper that disintegrated
when wet, modelling clay
that sucked every ounce
of moisture out of your
hands, gave you hang
nails and then coated
them with salt. I know
what I learned, regardless
of what they were trying
to teach us. That
materials, things, are
designed to let you down.

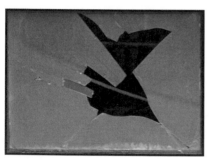
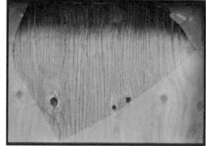

Of course, that object
lesson just becomes
something of a broader
issue with wider
applicability as you
become older. Your only
base hit all season will
take a wicked bounce and
break your best friend's
nose. The squirrel you're
trying to help get out of
your house will run under
the furnace and light itself
on fire. The car you saved
up for will drop its
transmission on the
highway one month later.
But maybe that's just me.
It's hard to tell when
you're blinded by despair.

But anyway. I have to get going, because if I'm not on the corner of Ward and Perth by a quarter to twelve, I'll miss my ride and then I'm looking at a half hour walk past where the bus short turns and it's all rusty tin cans and bent needles and no sidewalks. And single shoes. I don't understand that at all. Who loses a single shoe? Okay, high heeled shoes maybe because there's always some girl stumbling out of her pumps. But like a running shoe or a dress shoe? Or even a well fitted loafer. They don't just come off, you know?

I should just buy a bike. But, as I pointed out earlier, I can't really even afford salami. The salami that I'm still thinking about when Brewer pulls up in his burnt out Civic, spraying gravel and stinking of diesel. I'll probably find both of those things in my underpants when I finally get home tonight. I went to high school with a guy like him. Plastic drain board over the hole under the clutch, unusual lengths of rope in the trunk, esoteric knowledge of train schedules.

You know the type.

 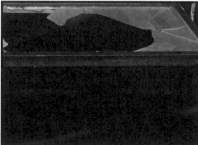 

The front seat is taken up
with a pile of dry cleaning
so I crawl into the back
and lie down. Somebody's
getting fancy up at the old
Auto-8 if they're sending
out their cleaning. The
back seat of Brewer's car
smells like old coffee and
dog, maybe. Chlorine. It's
been a hot summer, dry.
It helps. I drift in and out
on the ten minute drive
while Brewer talks about ...
chambermaids, Metallica,
who'll give you a better
price on dope if you pay
in US dollars, and the
difference between
butterflies and moths.

Already I'm
not listening.

Already I'm
somewhere else.

Already I'm preparing
for a solid ten hours
of broom-focused
bar cloth introspection.
I guess I'm just practicing
on Brewer. He's the warm
up act and believe me,
he's not as easy to ignore
as you might think. You
know how some people
just ramble on and it
starts to sound like water,
or Spanish, after a while?
For some reason, he's not
precisely like that. I think
it's because at any
moment he could give you
some intel that might save
your life one day.

So, you find yourself paying attention in spite of the danger that, if he notices, you run the risk of flipping from lecture to conversation and then I always find myself either saying something I don't believe or believing something I wouldn't have otherwise.

I decide to focus on the floor of the car. Checking for single shoes. Totalling up the loose change. Thirteen cents. They found coins, rivets and keys in Jumbo's stomach. Clearly he was financing and planning his escape.

The day I told my mother I was moving out, she said, "What difference do you think that's going to make?" I remember being in Grade One and asking the teacher, pretty much every morning, "Where are we going?" meaning, is today a gym day or a French day or a music day. And on the days that we didn't have anything scheduled, she seemed to take perverse delight in telling me, "Nowhere."
She did it with a smile, but I could tell, underneath, there was something she wasn't saying but she was sure thinking it.

When I get to work, Bob Legett is already sitting in his booth, reading his free paper that he picked up off of someone's doorstep. He'll nurse a pitcher of draft for the next six hours or so and then he'll retire to the pool out front until it's too dark to see. The pool hasn't had water in it for about ten years now but I remember coming out here with my dad when I was a kid. Back when he knew the guy that ran the place. A guy that really understood that sometimes you just need a place to cool off.

There's a note behind the bar for me. It's a girl's handwriting. Cute... in an uptight way. My mother called. Which might seem a little weird but I can't really afford a phone. She keeps bugging me to get on that action. That's actually what she says. What can I tell you, I blame the Bingo. But as far as I'm concerned things like phones are for my convenience, not for other people and I'm just not that fussed about it.

And it's not like I'm hard to find.

As she's just proved.

  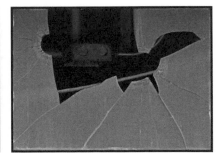

So you can imagine, I don't call her back right away. It's been years since we actually had anything to say to each other. If I'm being honest, I think it probably started the night my dad left and she didn't say a word to me about it. Not then, not since. So, really what is there to say? I'd like to ask her if she knows where he is. But I'm pretty sure I know the answer. But lately, I've been thinking about him more and more. Just wondering. Which is why I wish Bob Legett hadn't left yesterday's paper lying around.

 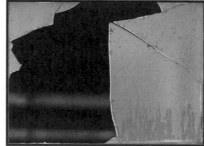 

These are the things I read the paper for: the horoscopes because it really helps with the small talk. Occasionally the rental listings just to make myself feel better about where I'm living. The dog ads at the Humane Society. The five dollar theatre movie listings. The four dollar plate special coupons at the Melrose. The long range forecast because Brewer is not as reliable as he likes to make himself out to be.

And the obituaries.

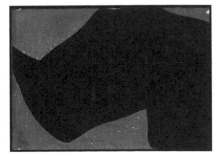

What can I say? I'm my
Gramma's boy. I probably
didn't mention that the
house I grew up in was
actually my
Grandmother's house.
I think now that the fact
that my mother owned
the house my father lived
in was maybe a problem
for him. Or maybe it was a
solution. He didn't *own*
anything. He didn't *owe*
anything. To *anyone*.

I remember my Gramma
reading me the obituaries
at breakfast. I remember
lying underneath her bed,
listening to her dying.
That's all, really, but it's
enough. You know?

But anyway. Bob Legett's paper.

"The body of the man found last Saturday in an upstairs room at the abandoned Food "N" Foam Drive-In Restaurant on Highway 4 is still unidentified as police continue their investigation. County road neighbours were shocked by the grisly discovery but not surprised. Local Carol Potts says, "I remember when blah blah blah blah blah blah blah blah blahblahblahblahblahblah ...

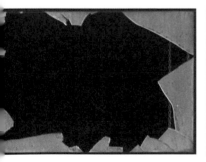  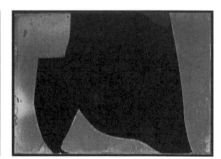

And I can't stop thinking
about it.

Is this the way things work?

Which is why, two days later, I find myself standing in front of the now seriously defunct Food "N" Foam. Floats. Sandwiches. French Fries. Hot Dogs. If you try to look the place up, you get a lot of information on people who are having disgusting problems with their pets. As it is, the big yellow sign out front says that it's 'or sale'. The grass is pushing up the pavement, the traffic is pushing past behind me. There are three windows on the second floor. One has curtains. I wonder if that was the room.

  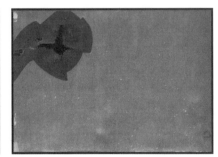

A car pulls into the house next door. It's a dog groomers with one of those clever names that could either be exactly what you think it is or something else entirely like a private lab for gene splicing ... or meth. As it is, it probably is just "Dog training and b rd g." A woman gets out of her car, glances at me and heads inside. I wave. Just to, you know, say that I see you seeing me please don't call the police. The door of the house closes, and then the car beeps as she locks it. I guess that's for my benefit.

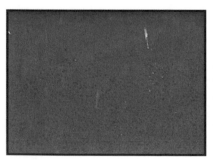

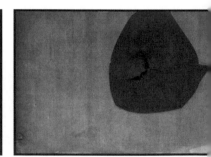

It's so hot. I spend most
of the year waiting for it,
so I'm not complaining
but the heat in August is
as much a fact as corn in
Kansas or Train in Vain.
It's as heavy on your head
as a bad haircut. I
remember reading that
Bob Barker had finally
convinced the zoo to
relocate the elephants. Go
Figure. Bob's spent over a
million dollars to transfer
other elephants to
warmer climes. He's in his
eighties. Time's running
out. For everybody.

What else is new.

The Food "N" Foam is a
strange building that looks
like the Wright Brothers'
less successful cousins
decided to get into foot
long hotdogs and hard ice
cream. The parts where
you drive in extend on
either side of the main
building like airplane
wings. The failing mansard
roof has this aerodynamic
prow sort of action going
on. Someone's idea of
modern. It's a piece of
crap that probably never
looked new. And now
looks like the worst kind
of place to pitch up dead.
I can't bring myself to get
any closer. I want to sit
down.

There are the remains of
tables and benches
penned up in front of the
boarded up order
windows that look like
they've been set on fire.
Repeatedly. I walk across
the parking lot and under
the rusted red beam of
French Fries Hot Dogs.
The cicadas have taken up
residence inside my head.
I make the mistake of
listening to them. And
then I'm no longer
hearing the metallic buzz
but instead am actually
listening to my ear drums
vibrating. Meta sound.
This was a mistake.

And I'm not talking about
the bugs.

I've got a confession to
make.

About five years ago, there was this little item in the paper. An unidentified man had been swept over Niagara Falls and the body never recovered. Up until that point, I had always assumed my dad was alive and well somewhere. Living on sardines and Colt 45... but still. When I read that article, for the first time, it occurred to me that this might not be the case. This is the confession: I began to hope that this wasn't the case. Because it seemed like it would increase my chances of finding him.

No. This is the confession.
I don't really want to find
him. I just want to see
where he ended up.

No.

This is the confession. I
wanted it to be
somewhere worse than
where he left us.

 Let's hear it for the Food
"N" Foam.

 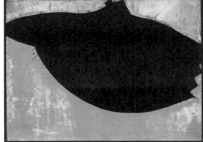 

I keep walking past the building. To the end of the pavement. I push past some shrubs, jump a ditch and then I'm standing beside a garbage heap in a farmer's field. There's a transmission tower plunked right in the middle. I always thought you could follow those towers to the ocean the way you could follow train tracks to the sea. Behind me, I hear a next door dog start barking. I'm eight again. I'm ten again. Wishing it was my dog. Again and again. Shit.

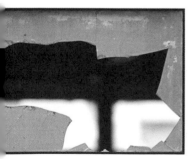

I'd like to turn around.
Sew my way back
between the sumac and
the phragmites. Stumble
across the edge of the
asphalt. Leave one shoe
behind on a lump of tar.
Lose the other one to a
piece of gum. I'd like to
slip one eye through the
lock on the back door.
Worm my way into that
building. Slide my spine
up the stairs to the
second floor. Casually
back stroke down the
hallway until I came face
to face with my old man.
In the room with the filthy
curtains. Upstairs at a
drive-in that's been left to
its own devices.

I feel like I could go to sleep in this heat the way drunks go to sleep in snow banks. Which is to say, permanently. A grasshopper ricochets off my pant leg. The sound it makes, a decisive lil lle thwack, is incredibly satisfying. I pick a glass jar with a rusty lid out of the pile of tin cans and broken lath and discarded clothing. Maybe I know. Maybe I know it's not my dad they found up there. Maybe. I need to talk to someone. I need some information.

I get as far as the New Elgin Motel. About a hundred steps down the highway back towards town. "Motel! It feels like coming home." I sure hope not. But I appreciate the exclamation point. Although I continue to hope that ironic punctuation abuse has reached a breaking point. Not that this qualifies exactly but their sign reads like a poster for a revisionist musical. A pornographic revisionist musical. There's a white plastic patio chair outside the office door. The moment I sit down I don't think I'll ever move again.

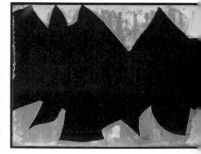

I've heard, more than once, that elephants sleep standing up but only for a few hours at a time. I've always thought that was kind of a hilarious distinction to make. I know it's few as opposed to many and not hours as opposed to days. It still sounds odd that sources seem so insistent. I've also heard that they're light sleepers. This kind of makes me like them more. I myself am not a light sleeper. It's gotten me into trouble... more than once.

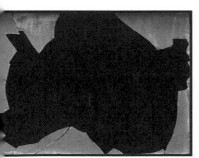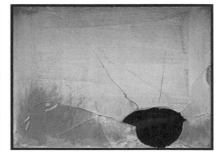

And then there was
someone saying my name.
I remember closing my
eyes and leaning my head
back against the brick
wall. Tiny fingers grab
and pull at the back of my
head. My dad used to tell
me I'd never go bald. It's
not in the genes. I could
smell burnt coffee and...
and... and barbecue
somewhere. I could hear
cars on the road. And the
tok tok as the grasshopper
popped up against the
metal lid of the jar that I
held in my lap. Doors
banging closed. Kids
yelling. They seemed
even further away from
me at that moment than
they do now.

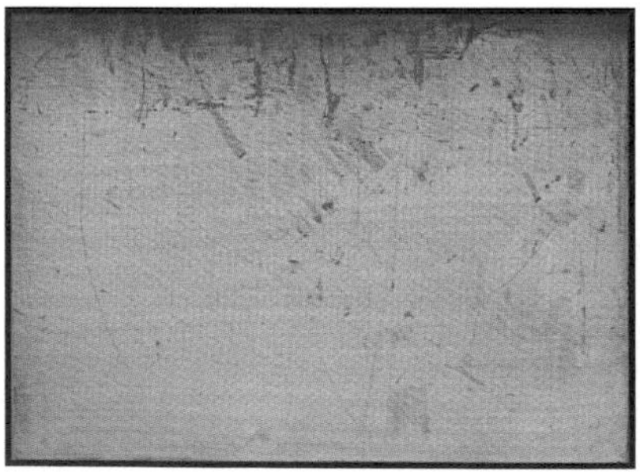

And then there was a
hand on my shoulder. I
opened my eyes and
there was some not so old
guy standing about six
feet away from me,
holding the screen door to
the office open, wanting
to know if I was looking
for a room. I was relieved
he was speaking directly
to me because I was
starting to feel like the
only things keeping the
molecules of my body
together were the clothes
I was wearing and the thin
layer of sweat that
veneered them to a
carcass that was starting
to feel like someone
else's. Evaporating.

  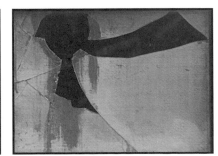

Closed. And he was still
there. Floating white on
black against the inside of
my eyelids.

Opened. And I told him
that I'd just been up at
the road looking at the old
drive-in. He squinted at
me and said it was still for
sale and he'd call the
agent if I was interested.
He said he could run me
into town to the office. I
think he was giving me
the hard sell, rural road
style. The chances that I'd
end up in a ditch were
good. That we'd stop for a
beer first were better.

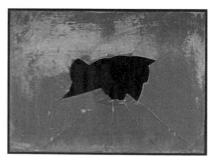

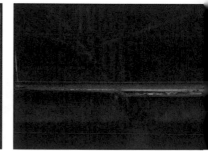

The grasshopper
thwacked up against the
jar lid again. I looked
down at it and, for the
first time, saw that what I
had in my lap was a
peanut butter jar of no
sure date. Rolled out but
you could still see the
words on the lid. Pretty
much, anyway. I looked at
the palm of my right hand
and the orange lines of
rust. I wanted to lick
them. A huge bee idly
detached itself from a
bunch of petunias and
casually bumped into my
knee before droning off in
another direction.
I wanted it to hang around
a little longer.

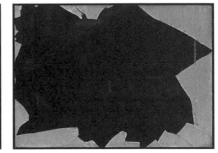

I asked him if the body
they'd found had been
identified and he told me
it had turned out to be a
kid, not much older than
me. Death by
misadventure. Which
sounds so old-fashioned.
As though he'd sailed over
the horizon in search of
mermaids. He could find
the paper for me. If I was
interested. So not an old
man, then. Just some kid.
Not much older than me.
I wanted to ask for a glass
of cold water but instead,
I asked if he could show
me where Jumbo had
gotten hit by the train.

  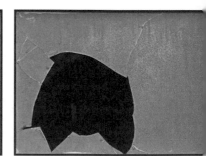

And then I started crying
like a crazy person.

Want to know what's left
of the greatest elephant
on earth? Not much.
His hide (stuffed by
Critchley and Akeley, who
sound like a Vaudeville
team) was destroyed in
a fire and his ashes are
in a Peter Pan Crunch
Peanut Butter jar in the
office of the athletic
director at Tufts
University. So that's
Massachusetts. His tail is
in their Digital Collection
and Archives. His
skeleton was donated to
the American Natural
History Museum. New
York. His heart was sold to
Cornell University. Also
New York.

It's obscene.

Don't ever let anyone tell you that people aren't generous. It's not true and I've been on the receiving end more times than I can count. He dropped me off in front of the plaque, just north of a bunch of small houses and then some light industrial buildings and the tracks. It was in front of a fence that had signs for 8 Person (h)ot tubs and Plasma TVs. That it told me only that he had died 'near this site' seemed unbearable. It also didn't say 'slowly' and 'far from home'...'at the age of 24'. About half a life. In every damn way.

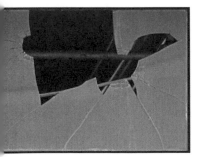  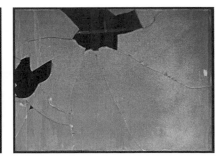

I turned back south to the tracks and left the sidewalk to follow them to the sea. Past towns like Paynes and Paynes Mills. Bairds. Middlemiss. Ekfrid. Bothwell. Northwood and Arkwood. Skirting the very southern edge of a shallow, still lake until I reached the Detroit River. Where I would attach a wire to the drainpipe of a bedroom corner sink. And, with a greasy ivory plastic snail in my ear, listen to music that was coming from another country. In my room in the house that didn't belong to my father.

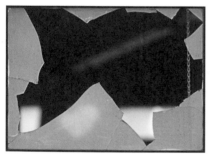  

But that was a long time
ago.

And as I sat on the bank
by the tracks and released
a grasshopper, that
suddenly didn't want to
go, into the weeds, and I
thought

about whether or not
what I had left of my dad
would fit into that jar

about how much a room
at the New Elgin motel
might be

and, for the first time in a
long time, about how
much I used to like to
draw.

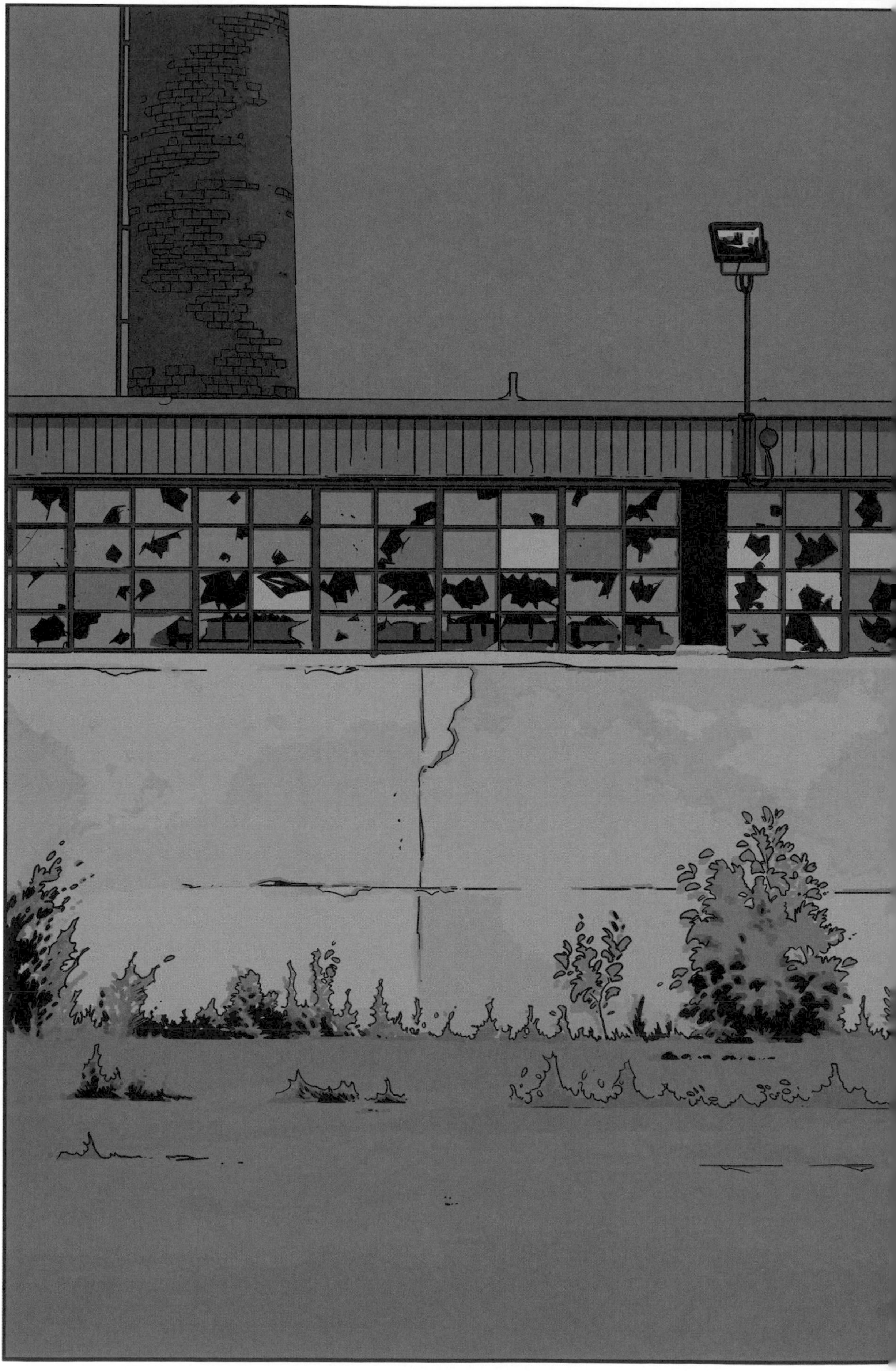

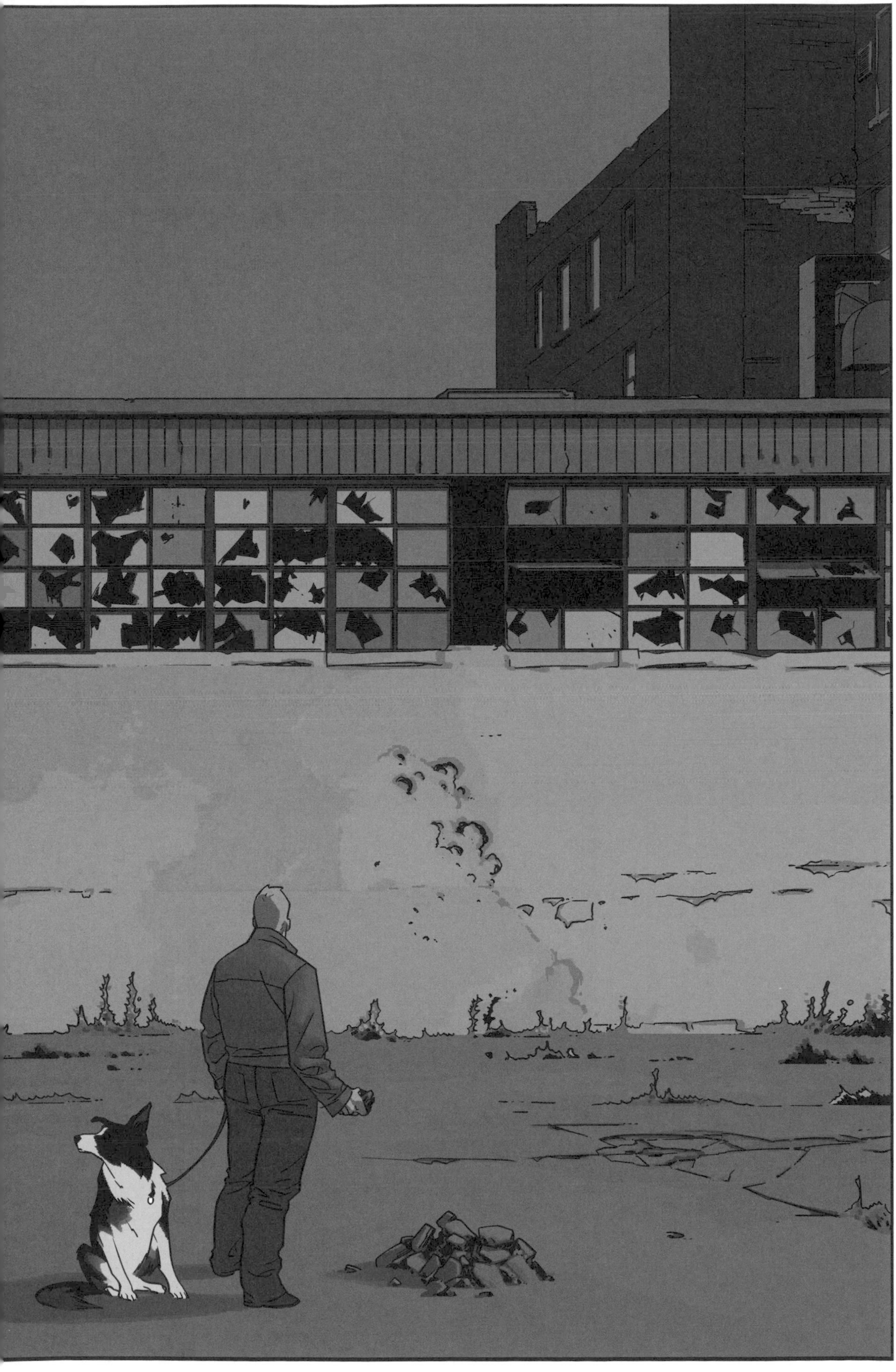

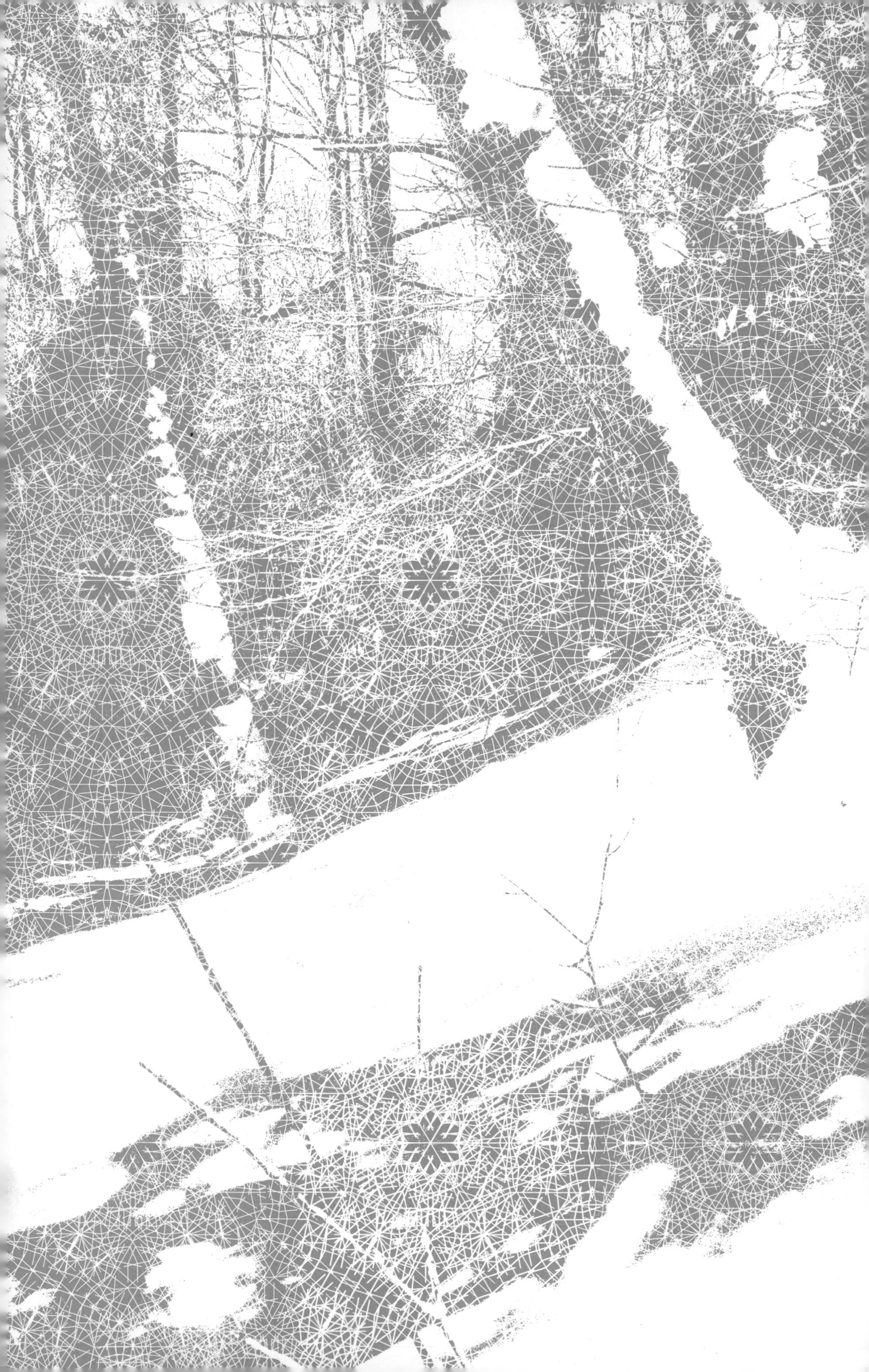